FICKLE MAN

FICKLE MAN

Robert Burns in the 21st Century

Edited by

JOHNNY RODGER
and
GERARD CARRUTHERS

SANDSTONEPRESS
HIGHLAND | SCOTLAND

First published in 2009 by
Sandstone Press Ltd,
PO Box 5725,
One High Street,
Dingwall,
Ross-shire,
IV15 9WJ,
Scotland,
United Kingdom.

www.sandstonepress.com

Note on the illustrations.

Fickle Man is a collaborative project by
The Drouth and Sandstone Press Ltd.

ISBN: 978-1-905207-27-5

Consultant Editor: Robert Davidson

Cover Design: Gravemaker + Scott, Edinburgh
Typeset by Iolaire Typesetting, Newtonmore
Printed and bound by Cromwell Press, Trowbridge, Wiltshire.

CONTENTS

∾

LIST OF ILLUSTRATIONS

જી

Special thanks for help in creating, finding, securing and preparing the images for this book are due to Pat Donald, David Buri, Vivien Carvalho, Craig Laurie, Andrew Lee, Pauline Anne Gray, John Onyango and The Glasgow School of Art.

Colour Plates

ACKNOWLEDGEMENTS

๛

The publisher acknowledges help towards the cost of publishing this volume from the Scottish Arts Council, The Glasgow School of Art, and the University of Glasgow.

Scottish
Arts Council

MACKINTOSH SCHOOL
OF ARCHITECTURE
THE GLASGOW
SCHOOL OF ART

University
of Glasgow

Centre for
Robert Burns
Studies

INTRODUCTION

❦

Robert Burns at 250: A Restless Ferment

JOHNNY RODGER and GERARD CARRUTHERS

Is it just a truism to assert that each age constructs not only its conceit of itself, but discovers in that self regard a conceit for every other age that passed before? For over two hundred years now the life and work of Robert Burns has presented a convenient peg upon which successive generations of Lowland Scots and others could hang their dearest and most current of such conceits. But why Robert Burns, we might say? Twentieth century poet Hugh MacDiarmid, in many ways the successor to Burns, commented on the phenomenon almost one hundred years ago, albeit in a more pessimistic and pejorative mode:

> A greater Christ, a greater Burns, may come
> The maist they'll dae is to gi'e bigger pegs
> To folly and conceit to hank their rubbish on.

The present age could thus hardly claim to be the first to understand something of relativity. But nonetheless we might not be so ready to dismiss out of hand certain aspects of *Burnomania* as of no value or interest. Given our current day penchant for questioning the notions of authenticity and truth, and for accepting and investigating the validity of appearances, truisms, superficiality, images, conceits, reputations, virtual reality – and in this book at any rate, follies, then the protean phenomenon of Burns presents itself as an almost irresistible paradigm for study.

Just so, Murray Pittock begins his essay below with the ostensibly solecistic interrogation 'What is Robert Burns?'. Yet as his subsequent list of alternatively cherished images of the poet shows, it would be not only a fruitful line of enquiry, but an unavoidable one in today's

intellectual climate. Tim Burke rightly and carefully preserves the
notion of Burns the peasant poet, but also alerts us to the idea that
determining [the poet's] 'class status is extremely difficult for both
theoretical and historical reasons'. Burke cautions us that reading
'plebeian' or labouring-class poetry remains an unfolding literary
critical and historical project, which until recently has been too little
understood. Burke suggests, as do other writers in this book, that
Burns's 'peasant' mantle is both self-mythology and, paradoxically, a
brilliant aesthetic project calculated to garner success in a literary
market-place were patronage otherwise remained crucial. If we should
beware the Bardolators, we should also beware the Bard. Not for
nothing might Burns be claimed to be the first of the 'Romantics',
operating from a platform of carefully inscribed primitive authenticity.

But Burns is not a phoney, he is a great artist and as true a writer as
any other. We celebrate here the 250th birth anniversary of the poet by
publishing a collection of essays on his life and work. Around half of
these essays were originally published in *The Drouth*, a current period-
ical which styles itself as 'Scotland's Only Literary/Arts Quarterly'.
What is perhaps most interesting and even astonishing about this work
published here, is the extent to which more than 200 years after his
death, discussions over the value and legacy of Robert Burns can still
be controversial. The legends, the images, and the reputations of his
life and work are still evidently so central to some person's and
peoples' conceit of themselves, that these essays have already pro-
voked some public outrage, and even expressions of warning – not to
say also, threats – about the danger of opening 'unorthodox' discus-
sions about Burns in the 21st century. While the *Sunday Herald* said of
one essay here, when it appeared in *The Drouth*, that it was 'an open,
mature, and vital reading', *The Independent* said of the same, 'We salute
the reckless courage of Gerard Carruthers . . .', before going on to
warn, 'editor Johnny Roger (sic) can expect a hostile reaction'.

Yet what is the current 'orthodoxy' – or indeed, what are the
'othodoxies', in the representations of Burns, over which the recklessly
transgressing critic might 'expect a hostile reaction'? It is argued time
and again in this collection, and not only by the editors, that it is the
very ambivalence and multiformity of the poet's work that allows for
him to be claimed by all 'factions', 'believers' and 'heretics', as one of
their own. And when Pittock asks 'What is Robert Burns?' it is not
simply the case that he himself is acting as some sort of high-priest of

the Marxian black Mass, transforming the spirit of Burns into an assortment of consumable and saleable commodities. Instead, what he does is draw our attention to the fact that since the day Burns walked out in public in his poetry, he was always already adaptable, and allowing himself to be adapted, as a symbol for the sort of myths and legends peoples use to celebrate the identities and values manifest in the social situations in which they find themselves. In that sense, the 'orthodoxies' may not only have little value as pure literary criticism, but to disprove their 'truth' by textual analysis might have little effect, as the real source of the myth or legend is likely to be located elsewhere in some powerful social reality. So as Pittock shows us, it is possible to have the coexistence of valid, if contradictory, images of Burns reputed as 'a Scottish nationalist with unfortunate British tendencies' and as 'a British nationalist with understandable Scottish tendencies'. For as Durkheim put it, social facts are things; that is to say that Burns or part of the Burns reality and/or his work has been in each case assimilated and exploited by an underlying structure of social or collective tendencies which latter cannot necessarily be reduced to a rationalistic or positivistic set of relationships.

This lack of rationalistic or positivistic basis of social myths might explain why the various 'factions' or social groupings claiming Burns might feel 'hostility' when their ownership of the symbol is challenged. But these multiple realities to which the Burns phenomenon lends itself also mean that a collection of essays like the present, by several authors and critics with their varied backgrounds, voices, interests, and specialisms, is an exceptionally efficacious model for getting at and exposing the many headed and polyphonic manifestations of the poet and his work. It is furthermore, the reason why a major part of this book is taken up with critique on the explicitly manufactured material images of the poet presented to us in various fields like visual arts, sculpture, architecture and film.

The discussion here would hardly constitute the first to examine the iconography of Burns as there is in existence a tradition of such writings with important contributions by D. W. Stevenson, Basil C. Skinner and James A. MacKay, and more recently by Murdo Mac-Donald. Indeed already in 1892 in the first annual edition of the *Burns Chronicle*, the sculptor D. W. Stevenson starts his discussion of 'The Portraits of Burns' with an apologia, declaring that 'the last word, historically speaking, has probably long ago been said, concerning the portraits of Burns.' Stevenson goes on to lay faith in 'Nasmyth's alone' as the 'best realisation'. His subsequent analysis of other images leans heavily – but not quite entirely – on the rather promiscuous notion of public acceptance, with his cute dismissal of Peter Taylor's painted portrait as 'It is impossible to believe that this hard featured man had charmed the "belles" of Edinburgh . . .'. Skinner, in his short book *Burns, Authentic Likenesses* (with an introduction and additional text by James A. MacKay) develops this type of critique into a more subtle, if less prurient, tool. He speaks of the 'tangled jungle of pseudo-Burns portraiture', and assigns grades of authenticity to individual portraits on grounds of whether the portrait was drawn from life, on whether the artist knew the poet, and on how successful a likeness the image was deemed by those who knew the poet well. Thus the Nasmyth (Plate 1) is an authentic likeness drawn from life, while on the other hand the chalk rendering of Nasmyth's painting by Skirving, who did also know the poet but did not draw from life, is considered the most pleasing image on 'aesthetic' grounds.

These writings push the discussion as to authenticity as far as it is possible to go given the historical evidence available. But this discussion of the visual artist serving the poet's, or at any rate literature's, ends is turned at least some way on its head when we come to the work of Murdo MacDonald. In his essay 'Envisioning Burns' in the book *A Shared Legacy*, we find an approach less concerned with assessing verisimilitude, and hence avoiding the placing of only a secondary or minor significance in the visual arts as a critical phenomenon. MacDonald cites David Wilkie, the painter and creator of *Cottar's Saturday Night* (1837), as advocating an 'intellectual art worthy of Scotland'. By examining responses to Burns's work in the visual arts MacDonald attempts to emphasise the importance of visual thinking as central to the Scottish Enlightenment, and approvingly speaks of a type of art where 'what the intellect is applied to in each case is the exploration of social and societal relations.'

This approach, with the visual art seen as critical and complementary, broadening and clarifying the scope and significance of Burns's life and work is recognisably similar to the approach taken in various essays here. If we may refer to such an artistic commentary upon Burns's poetic commentary as a meta-Burns then Sheila Szatkowski almost takes the absence of a Burns image to make greater comment than its existence. The artist John Kay (1742–1826) was a contemporary of Burns, who, based at this barber's shop in Parliament Square in the centre of the city, made etchings of all sorts of Edinburgh folk. Kay was at the height of his artistic activity when Burns visited in 1786–87, and his models were the very people who Burns knew and who populated his world. Indeed throughout this book we have placed illustrative etchings by Kay of people Burns had dealings with, people with whom he socialised and with whom he worked. Yet the intriguing point for Szatkowski, is that if in fact Kay did not make an image of Burns – this famous poet who cut such a dashing figure, rolled in to town and published a best-selling book of poetry – then why not? Szatkowski explores the 'social and societal' implications of this 'lack': Kay's politics are well known, was it on political grounds that he avoided Burns, refused to 'immortalise' him? What could those grounds be?

Interestingly, both the essay on Burns monuments, 'The Burnsian Constructs', and the one on Burns and Film, 'Missing Reels' seem to imply a similar conclusion: namely, that Burns is in some way so central to particular aspects of Scottish culture, that his absence from a specific discourse is sometimes more significant and telling than any positive representation could be. This silence that speaks volumes, as it were, makes us think too of MacDiarmid's apparently nihilistic claim that the finest line Burns wrote is 'Ye arena Mary Morison!' But the analysis of the social phenomenon of Burnsianism in Scotland through the solid stone architecture built in the poet's name, and a comparison of that architecture with the sort proposed in the name of the greatest vernacular poet of world fame, Dante, is an unexpected way, to say the least, of getting at those significant voids. Yet the simple question that essay both leaves us with and suggests an answer for, is that if five architectural monuments to Burns were built at regular intervals through the 19th century and two have already been built in the 21st century, then why were none at all built in the 20th century? Again in Alistair Braidwood's essay on film he draws attention to the fact that there was a 'cinematic absence' in terms of films about Burns between 1947 and 2004. This surely, is odd given that films were made throughout that period from the works of Walter Scott, Robert Louis Stevenson, Muriel Spark and Irvine Welsh among many others. Granted Burns's work itself is not so evidently readily adaptable to celluloid as is his legendary life story, but nonetheless there ought to be at least a sociological interest in why his life and work featured so strongly on domestic Scottish TV programmes every January, yet never managed to the big screen. Again, perhaps a comparison with Dante might be a useful one; for despite the flourishing and world renowned film culture in Italy there is, as it happens, no great and definitive treatment of the 'national' poet's life or work. Can we maintain then that the absence of Burns onscreen carries a specific cultural significance, or is there a more general phenomenon here, where the 'fundaments' of these nations' literary culture are not susceptible to visualisation?

David Hume wrote that the role of the essay writer could be considered as that of an ambassador from the dominions of learning to those of conversation. What a collection like the present one can demonstrate however, is that the essay can operate simultaneously in at least two such senses. Not only, that is to say, does this collection reaffirm that ambassadorial role in bringing learning from experts, academics, scholars and critics to the general reader, but this latter is furnished here with a vista of possible and as yet little explored territories, and encouraged, what is more, to loosen their intellectual and emotional loyalties and take their *own* researches and explorations further. We are drawn for example, by various essays on Burns and his engagement with his contemporary world, to examine again and from many different angles, that historical phenomenon of 'Enlightenment' as it is alleged to have unfolded in 18th and 19th century Scotland. Exemplary of this opening up of the field is the essay by Nigel Leask, who invites us to look once more at the controversial Currie biography of the 1800 edition and to speculate on the reach and influence of lesser known, and perhaps we may say decadent aspects of Enlightenment 18th century Edinburgh. We are aware of the breadth and range of characters around the capital in that era from the pictorial evidence of Kay's etchings, and also from the earlier, famous testimony of Amyat, when he asserted to Smellie that standing 'at the Cross of Edinburgh . . .' he could take 'fifty men of genius and learning by the hand'. But with Leask we start to understand something of the restless ferment of ideas, learning and scholarship which underlies the crust of famous personalities (Smith, Hume etc) who front our 'conversational' image of the Enlightenment.

We ought nonetheless to remember that Hume, in his disquisition on essay-writing deliberately writes for the 'elegant part of mankind' alone. This sort of social exclusion – the human species are explicitly divided into the elegant, and those 'immersed in the animal life' – was nothing new for its time. It's an elitism that has a long philosophical pedigree reaching all the way back to Plato, who considered in *The Republic*, that only the rulers of that perfect city could be 'just' because only they had full command of reason. But nor was this exclusivity – elegant or animal – particular to Hume in his time, for as Murray Pittock tells us, Adam Smith held views very similar to those described immediately above as Platonic. Yet if Smith held that only the 'rich and sophisticated' (Pittock) were capable of 'sympathy' as they were liberated from hand-to-mouth existence and the arguably selfish concerns of day-to-day survival, then Robert Burns, as an animal of what Ken Simpson calls the 'Vernacular Enlightenment' following in the tradition of Ramsay and Fergusson to challenge both literary and social hierarchies, had the necessary tools to 'interrogate', resist, and ultimately humanise Smith's theories. This intellectually humane value of Burns's work is nourished, as we see in Ralph McLean's essay, by the poet's ceaseless engagement with various levels and social strata of both enlightenment and moderate Presbyterian thinking. And as Pauline Anne Gray goes on to show by examining the 'reserved canon' of Burns's work, one of the most powerfully charged weapons he had in his vernacular armoury was a peculiar and defiant ability to exploit sexual subject matter in rejection of social hierarchies and in exposal of the absurd nature of class-based controls and limits placed on human relationships.

In the 'Burns Abroad' section there is a wide ranging examination of the poet's engagement with others: with peoples, places, politics and poetry. Essays from Thomas Keith, and from Rhona Brown and Kirsteen McCue, both inspect the sexual politics implicit in Burns's writings. But rather than make a direct critique of his explicit stances on international and state Politics, Religion, Morality and Ethics, as seen in Pauline Anne Gray's essay, we are given instead and analysis of a more private, intergenerational, intergender and interclass politics at a personal level. Who was the 'Lass o' Ballochmyle' and under what circumstances can the song's success as a 'sentimental' work be considered merely a posthumous construction, ask Brown and McCue? Keith reveals an evidently harder-nosed Burns attitude to sexual politics, but surprises us in our prejudices by revealing nonetheless that in over one fifth of the published songs the poet sings in the voice of a woman. If nothing else the manifold approaches to

Burns's politics in this collection make clear that it would be an unsustainable posture to remain true to the poet's texts yet insist on fixing his work in some categorical drawing-room cabinet.

This has however not stopped the man and his work from continually being placed abroad on one pedestal or another. If Burns in 'To a Louse' follows the morally sentimental Adam Smith in advocating we imagine ourselves sympathetically into another's point of view, then Irish views of the significance of Burns might be revelatory. Ireland is after all that near-abroad, which is both here and there, both very similar to and very different from Scotland for reasons historical and social, happy and otherwise. That Burns is esteemed and even revered on that island is evident in the essays from both Owen Dudley Edwards and Carol Baraniuk. But sometimes, as Edwards shows us, he is elevated as much as an example to struggle against as to struggle towards.

It is arguable that this very 'revering' of the poet has given house-room to the mythomanics of Burns lore. It often seems indeed that if there is a void or gap – as discussed above – in the verified history of the man and his work, then under implied encouragement from the widespread reverencing of the man and public acknowledgement of his genius, the myths, legends, and clichés have operated to create smoothened-out, consistent and one sided images, often for party purposes. Gerard Carruthers together with Norman Paton and then Jennifer Orr has worked to expose and deconstruct the manufacturing of some dubious aspects of the image of Burns. First of all the construction of the out and out revolutionary poet, who allegedly – according to some editions – wrote the 'Tree of Liberty'; and then of the adamant revolutionary activist, who allegedly was reckless and headstrong enough to send arms to the Jacobins in Paris. The detailing of the invention of these myths make for a fascinating and intriguing sociological vignette, but no more so than in Carruthers other 'what might have been' piece on 'Burns and Slavery'. The mythmakers are shown here to have been strangely reticent themselves when it came to Burns's silence on the Abolition movement and the scandal of 18th century slavery. On the face of it, as Carruthers shows us, it seems an incongruously inhumane note from the 'Poet of Humanity'; yet near completely silent Burns was. Further glimpses of the historical and political conditions of that silence are hinted at in the psychological portrait of Burns given us by Mitchell Miller in a long contrast with a contemporary of the same geographical background, but who none-theless inhabited a very different social world – namely James Boswell. Boswell, and of course his biographical alter ego, Johnson, both were Tories aspiring to a 'high' church, one an aristocrat, the other a self confessedly eager doffer of caps to such, yet both were at one time or another outspoken against slavery, and Boswell also tackled head on the notion of the noble savage in the person of its most celebrated theorist, Jean-Jacques Rousseau. Why then no poetic word on slavery from the author of 'A man's a man for a' that'? Is it because Whigs and radicals on this side of the Atlantic were reluctant to criticise or jeopardise the success of the American Revolution – a social experi-ment in class war led by free thinking republicans who counted nonetheless, slave owners among their number? More research could be done here: it may seem somewhat tenuous as an explanation, but there is surely a ring of truth to the pragmatic grounding of the pure political stance in pre-existent social and emotional loyalties.

Our title alludes to the fickleness, perhaps, of Robert Burns in love, livelihood (song-writer as much as poet; farmer and then excise man), mode of living (drawing room dandy; drinking den randy) and even in culture and politics (peasant poet, in large measure his own construc-tion; polished prose pusher as well as, at his best, near perfect prosodist; Presbyterian; philosophe; Jacobite; Jacobin, at least up to a point; patriot for Scotland, for Britain and against the dastardly French of the 1790s). No surprise, then, that history's estimation of Burns has been full of fickleness and often fecklessness. Socialist superhero, much read by Scottish communists in the twentieth century, the poet has also been a pin-up boy for the conservative Orange Order, both in Scotland and Ulster (for instance, one of his most prominent editors of the nineteenth century, William Mother-well, being also a demagogic rabble-rouser in the name of Orangeism and against working-class democracy). Monumental and malleably morphic, Burns is not so much an everyman as a delivery man peculiarly proffering back to many commentators their own politics, perspectives and prejudices. The cult, the iconography, was from the conception of Burns's literary career (as 'heaven-taught ploughman', according to Henry Mackenzie on reading his first published book of poems in 1786) a subject nearly as worthy of note as the writing itself. It is curious that so many academics have joined the queue of misty-eyed worshipers, both from supposedly right and left-wing political view-points, insisting that Burns is without ideological impediment, uncorrupted, that the body is not myth-eaten, as they refuse to chew on the sacred words of the Bard and instead swallow things whole that they should be interrogating. Fickleness and fecklessness have some-times been joined by fraudulence in 'Burns Studies', a removed piece of text here, a de-contextualised passage there, the ignoring of the full evidence everywhere, and we have the Burns that *I* want. Is Burns a national poet and if he is, is this because a whole nation of variegated views vigorously lays claim to him? Is this manifest hollowness, this fickleness, at the heart of Burns or at the centre of Scotland, of the world even? What does Burns's reception and reputation, indeed his own constructed writerly status, tell us about humankind, that it is fickle? If it does, his work was there long before as it essayed the uncertainty of human behaviour and society. More certain is the intellectual and emotional force across Burns's writing. Its enduring appeal for fickle, feckless and fraudulent people, is maybe a sign that Burns is, truly, the poet of common humanity.

THE IMAGE OF BURNS

❧

LABOUR, EDUCATION AND GENIUS

கூ

Robert Burns and the Plebeian Poetic Tradition

TIM BURKE

In the decades between the birth and death of Robert Burns, there was an explosion of interest in writing by, and about, members of the poorest classes of society. Servants, weavers, threshers, milkmaids, indeed members of most trades and occupations, experimented with the increasingly available and legitimate technology of writing. The mania for writing, and improving rates of literacy generally, owed much to the introduction of a system of Sunday schools, and opportunities for participation in the new liturgies of dissenting sects. The value of 'plebeian' writing, to use the adjective recently deployed by William J. Christmas, was also enhanced by the intellectual vogues for primitivism and antiquarianism, and the appearance of philosophical theories of 'natural genius'.[1] No less important was the significant demographic shift in the system of patronage, which by the century's end had, to a great extent, become a signature of middle-class sensibility, as ministerial and aristocratic patronage waned. By the end of the eighteenth century, the labouring-class poetic tradition in English writing, traceable back at least as far as Stephen Duck in the 1730s, had come of age, and its first international celebrity was Robert Burns.

With celebrity came mythology. Burns is still largely, in the popular imagination, the romantic and solitary figure depicted by William Wordsworth in his poem 'Resolution and Independence' (1802). After lamenting Thomas Chatterton, the boy-genius who had 'perished in his pride', Wordsworth's speaker's thoughts turn to 'him who walked in glory and joy / Behind his plough, upon the mountain side'. In its primitivist tableau of one subordinated by hard labour but consoled by the joy of creative activity, Wordsworth's romantic monody is typical of the innumerable poems about Burns written in the decade after his death. Verses of this kind shaped, and to an extent distorted, the cultural memory of Burns the man, Burns the poet, and the plebeian poetic tradition to which he believed he belonged. They also isolate him from the local communities and the national history which often lend his verses their characteristic energy. This essay attempts to redress some of these distortions by studying the often complex and sometimes contradictory relationships between Burns, the labour he performed, the working communities in which he lived, and contemporary understandings of creativity amongst the so-called 'uneducated' classes of society.

There is evidence both for and against the charge, made in 1797, by Robert Heron in the first biography of Burns, that 'he began early in life to regard with sullen disdain and aversion, all that was sordid in the pursuits and interests of the peasants among whom he was placed'.[2] Far outnumbering the poems which, like 'The Cottar's Saturday Night', paint pastoral-tinted scenes of lower-class respectability and discipline are those expressing affectionate tolerance and sometimes eager endorsements of rustic 'pursuits'. Poems like 'Halloween', and 'Tam o'Shanter' fulfil the claim made by Burns in an autobiographical sketch sent to Dr John Moore in August 1787, shortly after his first poetic success: 'my first ambition was, and still my strongest wish is, to please my Compeers, the rustic Inmates of the Hamlet, while ever-changing language and manners will allow me to be relished and understood'.[3] Surprisingly, then, his response to those 'Compeers' who followed his example in composing verse was, in most cases, to ignore, or even express contempt for their efforts. There is no question that most of the several labouring-class Scots producing poetry in the late 1780s and 1790s were heavily indebted to Burns, not just for the inspiration and courage that his example lent to them, but for their techniques, styles, and the creation of a market in which their works were (briefly) valued. Among the dozens of poets to prosper in the immediate aftermath of Burns's success were Gavin Campbell, Alexander Wilson, and John Learmont, but as early as 1789 Burns was describing the work of his imitators and admirers as mostly 'nonsense'.[4] The verses of Janet Little, a dairy worker, were posted to Ellisland by Little's patron Frances Dunlop, a friend of Burns, with infuriating regularity. Despite Dunlop's entreaties, Burns's reply was delayed and reticent, noting only that she had produced 'a very ingenious but modest composition.' On a visit to Dunlop House in December 1792, Burns seems to have been more forthcoming, though still less generous, for Dunlop's next letter to Burns expresses deep annoyance: she had 'felt' for Janet, and regretted having 'subjected one of mine [i.e. Little] to so haughty an imperious critic'.[5]

There were happier encounters with David Sillar, who was a year younger than Burns, and also the son of a tenant farmer. Sillar's Poems were published at Kilmarnock in 1789 by John Wilson, a recurrent champion of the plebeian poets of Scotland, both as a printer and as a subscriber. Burns and Sillar became firm friends in 1783, and the 'Epistle to Davie, a Brother Poet' is one of Burns's finest verse letters. John Lapraik, a poet of respectable birth fallen on hard times, prompted another. A young Scottish bard cannot be one who would 'think to climb Parnassus / By dint o' Greek' ('Epistle to J. L*****K, An Old Scotch Bard', ll. 71–2), and so, he tells Lapraik, he will not 'climb' but 'drudge' through the soil of lowland Scotland:

> Gie me ae spark o' Nature's fire,
> That's a' the learning I desire;
> Then tho' I drudge thro' dub an' mire
> At pleugh or cart,
> My Muse, tho' hamely in attire,
> May touch the heart.
>
> (ll. 73–8)

Burns's 'hamely' work is consistently downplayed in the poem as mere 'crambo-jingle', 'rude an' rough' though 'weel eneugh':

> I am nae Poet, in a sense,
> But just a Rhymer like by chance,
> An' hae to Learning nae pretence,
> Yet, what the matter?
> Whene'er my Muse does on me glance,
> I jingle at her.
>
> (ll. 49–54)

The 'Muse' and the vocation to which the Epistle to Lapraik refers is elaborated upon in 'The Vision', Burns's fullest account of his social and literary status as a rustic 'peasant' poet. 'Coila', the muse of Kyle (an ancient name for his native corner of lowland Scotland), appears before the poet and lends her blessing to his attempts to create an aesthetics rooted in the soil of Coila and founded on the values of communities living on it. For those in the 'lower Orders' of 'SCOTIA's race', she tells him, there are many vocations, each with its own protective spirit. The rustic bard is but one of these, and thus not above but part of the community into which he emerges. All that he has done and written has been watched and guided, she tells him, but he must not overreach himself or betray his destiny: 'Thou canst not learn, nor I can show, / To paint with Thomson's landscape-glow; Or wake with bosom-melting throe, / With Shenstone's art; / Or pour, with Gray, the moving flow, / warm on the heart' ('The Vision', ll. 247–52). Instead, she insists (in surprisingly refined and elevated English) that he must take inspiration from the Scottish landscape and language.

Burns's dialectal Scots in the first half of 'The Vision' confirms his election to the office of bard of the 'humble sphere' (l. 260), and poems like 'A Winter Night', 'To a Mouse', 'Man was Made to Mourn' and 'When Wild War's Deadly Blast was Blawn' testify to his detailed and sometimes personal knowledge of the sufferings of the humble. Such acuteness is rarely found in the remoter perspectives taken on these matters by his near-contemporaries Crabbe, Cowper, and Wordsworth. Moreover, unlike these poets, Burns also wrote extensively in celebration of the pleasures to be had within the rural community, and the carnivalesque energy of his fellow 'Inmates of the Hamlet'. The poem which most effectively reconciles these two tendencies in Burns's writings on the rural poor remained unpublished in his lifetime: The Jolly Beggars; or Tatterdemallions. A Cantata was first published at Edinburgh in 1802 to general scandal, but it is of great importance to an understanding of Burns's identity (sometimes disavowed, as well as enthusiastically embraced) as a writer in the labouring-class tradition. Its contents are largely summed up in the title by which the poem is now more often known 'Love and Liberty – A Cantata', since its music is made by a band of beggars liberated, in some senses, from social, economic and moral obligations. Yet as their songs develop, it becomes clear that this liberation is not to be unproblematically endorsed or celebrated; these men and women – injured soldiers, penniless bards, drunken robbers and prostitutes – are as much refugees as escapees from modern society and its codes. It is a poem which reveals the breadth of Burns's reading, drawing on sources as diverse as Elizabethan sonnets, early eighteenth-century operas of low-life, and contemporary song. The concluding chorus resembles Blake's Songs of Innocence and Experience in its rejection of arbitrary powers and mind-forg'd manacles: 'One and all cry out, Amen! / A fig for those by Law protected, / Liberty's a glorious feast! / Courts for Cowards were erected, / Churches built to please the Priest' (ll. 278–81).

Burns wrote with great respect and sympathy for the lower ranks of late eighteenth-century Scotland. Determining his own class status is extremely difficult, for both theoretical and historical reasons. It is ultimately, perhaps, even undesirable to attempt an answer, given the uses to which the 'truth' of his class status has been put in the last two hundred years, by commentators of all political hues, employing a variety of methodological perspectives. Judged by his economic fortunes and his access to education, two potential indicators of such status, the evidence is distinctly mixed, and even the conditions in which he was born cannot be readily relied upon as credible indicators of his status, for like so much else, the circumstances of the poet's birth have been subject to extensive mythologisation. For example, Burns described the house in which he was born as an 'auld clay biggin', and both this two-roomed thatched cottage built by the poet's father in 1757, and the storm which battered it in the days following his birth, were deployed by nineteenth-century advocates and scholars in attempts to align Burns's place in Scotland's history with the nativity of Christ in Israel's. As Nicholas Roe has shown, several nineteenth-century biographers interpreted the Alloway biggin as a scarcely modernised version of a Bethlehem stable, and read the storm as the portentous sign of a saviour's arrival.[6]

This saviour was ill-equipped to ensure his own financial salvation, however. Although the last seven years of his life were spent in non-manual labour, collecting taxes for the Excise, his pay was low (beginning at £50 a year with little advancement), the work was difficult, and its effects on his health were baleful. His earlier farming ventures, like those of his father, William Burnes, had met with at best equivocal success. The land he worked was often poor, demanding relentless and often unassisted labour, for uncertain returns. Much of Burns's childhood was spent at Mount Oliphant, a hilltop farm, and for much of the time the family could afford, according to Robert's brother Gilbert, 'no hired servant'; in 1774, Robert was the 'principal labourer'. Three years later, the family left to rent the more congenial Lochlea farm near Tarbolton, but Burns left for the expanding manufacturing town of Irvine in 1781 to train as a flax-dresser, until the shop (in which he had invested) burnt down the following year. These losses, Burns recalled, 'left me like a true Poet, not worth sixpence.'[7] Despite this claim, he was shortly afterwards able to afford, in conjunction with his brother Gilbert, a rent of £90 on Mossgiel farm, three miles from Lochlea, which was taken on after the death of their father. The Mossgiel years were characterised by a succession of difficulties. By the middle of the decade, Burns's financial, emotional and physical state had deteriorated to the extent that he could see no alternative to finding employment as book-keeper to a West-Indian plantation owner. His first volume, *Poems, Chiefly in the Scottish Dialect*, was issued at Kilmarnock in 1786 with the hope that its profits might defray his travelling expenses, and only its unexpected success prevented him from taking a role in the administration of Britain's commercial and colonial interests in the slave economy.

After the success of the Kilmarnock volume, and the expanded second edition of 1787, Burns was able to operate in the rarefied circles of the Edinburgh literati, but it was his fame, not his connections or his wealth, that gained him entry. A taste for drink and sexual scandal ensured that these doors were closed as quickly as opened. In 1788, the poet was again to be found farming in his native region. During his life, but especially after his death, supporters and critics took sharply different positions in identifying Burns's social rank and its significance for his writing. The obituaries by George Thomson and Maria Riddell were particularly influential in this regard.

Thomson, the editor of *A Select Collection of Original Scotish Airs* (1793–1818) in which several of Burns's songs were published, informed the English readership of the London Chronicle in July 1796 that 'Burns was literally a ploughman, but nether in that state of servile dependence or servile ignorance which the situation might bespeak in this country [i.e. England].'[8] Thomson emphasises the dignified simplicity of the Scottish peasantry, and Burns's subsequent excesses are implicitly attributed to his removal from a rural caste whose proximity to nature was responsible for his natural genius in the first place. 'Probably he was not qualified to fill a superior station to that which was assigned him', Thomson speculated on his employment by the Excise, though the poet's 'genius . . . would have distinguished itself in any situation.'[9] Thomson had never met Burns, but Maria Riddell, who knew him well, reacted to Thomson's clumsy portrait with carefully controlled anger when she insisted in the pages of the Dumfries Journal of August 1796, under the pseudonym 'Candidor', that Burns's lower-class origins had helped to shape, but had not determined, his subsequent career. Social rank was not a fixed 'situation', as Thomson had twice put it, but dynamic and changeable. She conceded that Burns's 'figure seemed to bear testimony to his earlier destination and employments', appearing 'rather moulded by nature for the rough exercises of agriculture, than the gentler cultivation of the Belles Lettres'.[10] But his nature and origins could be transcended, and because his abilities permitted a genuine social elevation, Riddell dismissed claims that the 'Ayrshire ploughboy was an ingenious fiction, fabricated for the purposes of obtaining the interests of the Great'. In her view, poems like 'The Cottar's Saturday Night' would seem more extraordinary had they been written by 'a hand more dignified in the ranks of society', rather than from one in 'the humbler shade of rustic inspiration' from which such poems had 'really sprung'.[11]

Riddell's claim to possess the authentic account of Burns here is apt from one taking 'Candidor' as her pseudonym, and she played a significant part in making the language of candour, testimony and sincerity the grammar of Burns criticism. Few of her successors were able to resist staking their own claim to the 'truth' of Burns and his life. In 1800, James Currie, Burns's first editor, argued that the poems were 'the transcript of his own musings on the real incidents of his humble life'; and because his characters and incidents 'have the impression of nature and truth', displaying minds 'under deep impressions of real sorrow', they offer 'surest proof' of his genius, and were thus 'truly interesting'.[12] Frances Jeffrey insisted in 1809 that Burns, unlike Wordsworth, was a poet of 'fidelity', but could never be 'rightly estimated' until 'that vulgar wonder be entirely repressed which was raised on his having been a ploughman'.[13] In the same year, Sir Walter Scott argued that Burns was 'in truth the very child of passion and feeling'.[14] In the 1810s, George Glieg saw Burns as a purveyor of more universal truths for 'readers of all classes', who 'shall be led to look into themselves for the truth of those pictures which he has painted'.[15] Others compared Burns's realism and sincerity with that attempted by his contemporaries: Professor John Wilson grouped Burns with James Hogg as a 'genuine child of nature'.[16]

Francis Jeffrey by John Kay

Was Burns the 'child of nature' that Wilson claimed? One might expect the education of a farmer's son in the 1760s and 70s to be severely circumscribed, limited to the rudiments sufficient for him to pursue his agricultural endeavours. There is however nothing unusual in the decision, taken in 1765 by the poet's father William Burnes and his Alloway neighbours, to establish a village school: there were many such schools in the lowlands of Scotland. It was Burns's good fortune that so skilled a schoolmaster as John Murdoch was hired. From Murdoch and other tutors, and also from their father directly, Robert and his brother Gilbert obtained introductions to studies in Latin, French, and mathematics, and were able to read a range of sophisticated works on natural history, astronomy and theology. Murdoch gave Burns a grounding in modern English poetry, introducing many of the authors who would become 'bosom-favourites': Pope, Sterne, Thomson, Shenstone and Henry Mackenzie, author of *The Man of Feeling* (1771). This broad and extended education equipped Burns with the confidence to tackle a work as demanding as Locke's Essay Concerning Human Understanding, no ordinary text for a farmer's son to be reading in 1779.

Burns knew the value of publicly disowning the education that he had received, however. In the 'Preface' to his debut volume, he claimed, with at best partial justification, that he was 'Unacquainted with the necessary requisites for commencing Poet by rule' and was thus only capable of singing of 'sentiments and manners', in other words, 'of that which he felt and saw in himself and his rustic compeers around him, in his and their native language'. Burns's Commonplace Book contains a number of rhetorical experiments in which he styles himself as a child of nature, and his use of the third person suggests an attention to the terms in which his work would be received: 'As he was but little indebted to scholastic education, and bred at a plough-tail, his performances must be strongly tinctured with his unpolished, rustic way of life'. Robert Anderson, recognising the adeptness of these 'performances', saw through these poses, and recalled in a 1799 letter to Currie that the poet had admitted to him that it was 'part of the machinery, as he called it, of his poetical character to pass for an illiterate ploughman who wrote from pure inspiration'.[17] Yet, the tenets of genius theory (derived from Addison and Akenside early in the eighteenth century and refined by Edward Young, William Duff and Alexander Gerard from their positions in

Scotland's finest universities during their enlightenment heyday) were
still regularly invoked as the best way to explain Burns's prodigious
talent.[18] 'Natural genius' is the theory informing Robert Nares's
detection of the 'truly wonderful' in 'the writings of this uninstructed
and unpolished genius' in 1800; Sir Egerton Brydges, in 1805, insisted
that schooling would have crushed Burns's fledgling talent: 'It seems
to me in vain and idle to speculate upon education and outward
circumstances as the causes or promoters of poetical genius. It is the
inspiring breath of Nature alone which gives the powers of the
genuine bard'.[19] Robert Heron's biography begins with an insistence
that Burns was not a natural or original but a 'studious' genius, who
thus produced the 'true effusions of genius, informed by reading and
observation'; later, however, Heron claims 'native ardour' as prior to
education in forming the poetic genius.[20] Plainly, the classical notion
of poeta nascitur non fit (the poet is born, not made) still held
considerable force in the early nineteenth century, but Henry Mac-
kenzie, in the earliest review of the Kilmarnock edition in *The Lounger*,
thought the poems so astonishing as to raise their author above the
vulgar, quotidian business of both nature and nurture: Burns, he
claimed, was the 'heav'n-taught ploughman'.[21] In a culture in which
Robert Bloomfield was destined to be known as 'The Farmer's Boy'
long after leaving his uncle's farm, it is unsurprising that Mackenzie's
memorable coinage should so easily capture the imagination of
Burns's audience, and remain attached to the poet for the rest of
his career, and for a considerable time afterwards.

Heaven-taught or not, it is clear that Burns's placing behind his
plough, in Wordsworth's 'Resolution and Independence', is inade-
quate to a full estimate of his poetic achievement and legacy. His life
and his poetry were in any case as frequently shaped by poverty and
depression as by 'glory' and 'joy'. But Wordsworth's lines on Burns are
apt in at least one regard, since it is true to say that he enjoyed more of
the limited supplies of the 'glory' available to plebeian poets than his
many contemporaries, men and women who just like Burns attempted
to record their lives, loves, fears, and faiths in poetic form. There was a
hunger for writing amongst the peasants, artisans, and servants of late
eighteenth-century Britain, and it seems safe to assume that those who
found their work published, in newspapers, or periodicals, or in books
funded by subscriptions, are only the visible tip of a vast cultural

iceberg. The example of Burns's poetic versatility and energy, a shrewd understanding of the ways in which he might be most effectively marketed, a complex nationalism, as well as his forceful charismatic personality, were of enormous consequence to many. He certainly found a receptive audience in Scotland, and prompted a massive expansion of the literary horizons of its labouring men and women. The nineteenth-century history of self-taught writing is marked by a breathtaking increase in poetic production by Scots, which was carried through the Scottish Diaspora to all parts of the British empire. These poets, like their predecessors in the 1780s and 90s, almost invariably dedicate some portion of their work to Scotland's 'Bard'. Of course, it was not just Scottish authors who benefited. The labouring-class or 'plebeian' tradition, hitherto dominated by the English voices of Stephen Duck, Mary Collier, Mary Leapor, James Woodhouse and Ann Yearsley, was reinvigorated by the cross- and counter-cultural force of Burns's bilingual poetics: Robert Bloomfield and John Clare are only the most notable of the many who openly acknowledged their debt by writing poems of tribute to, and in imitation of, him.

Carol McGuirk argued in 1985 that Burns was 'the only great poet ever to emerge from the British peasant class', but since then, a number of worker-poets, principally John Clare, have had their significance within British literary culture reassessed.[22] Burns's exclusive status as the only poet of consequence in the labouring-class tradition may no longer be secure, but there is no reason yet to doubt that Burns is responsible for its greatest aesthetic achievements and its most sustained period of impact upon the literary and social culture of Scotland, Britain and Europe.

(This essay is an edited version of Tim Burke's entry on Robert Burns in *Eighteenth-Century English Labouring-Class Poets*, 3 vols (London: Pickering and Chatto, 2003).)

NOTES

[1] William J. Christmas, *The Lab'ring Muses: Work, Writing and the Social Order in English Plebeian Poetry, 1730–1820* (Newark: University of Delaware Press, 2001).

[2] From Donald A. Low (ed.), *Robert Burns: The Critical Heritage* (London, Routledge, 1974), p. 119.

[3] J. De Lancey Ferguson and G. Ross Roy (eds), *The Letters of Robert Burns*, 3 vols (Oxford: Clarendon, 1985), I: 88.

[4] On Burns's relationship with fellow labouring poets, see John D. Ross, *Robert Burns and his Rhyming Friends* (Stirling, 1828); James Paterson, *The Contemporaries of Robert Burns and the More Recent Poets of Ayrshire* (Edinburgh, 1840); Henry Shanks, *The Peasant Poets of Scotland* (Bathgate, 1881); Donna Landry, *The Muses of Resistance: Laboring-Class Women's Poetry in England, 1730–1796* (Cambridge: Cambridge University Press, 1990); Valentina Bold, 'Janet Little, the "Scotch Milkmaid" and "Peasant Poetry"', *Scottish Literary Journal*, 20 (1993), pp. 21–30; Valentina Bold, 'Inmate of the Hamlet: Burns as Peasant Poet', *Love and Liberty. Robert Burns: A Bicentenary Celebration*, Kenneth Simpson (ed.) (East Linton: Tuckwell Press, 1997), pp. 43–52; Moira Ferguson, 'Janet Little and Robert Burns: The Politics of the Heart', *Romantic Women Writers: Voices and Countervoices*, Paula R. Feldman and Theresa M. Kelley (eds.) (Hanover: University Press of New England, 1995), pp. 207–19; Ann Janowitz, *Lyric and Labour in the Romantic Tradition* (Cambridge: Cambridge University Press, 1999); Tim Burke (ed.), *Eighteenth-Century English Labouring-Class Poets*, vol. 3 '1780–1800', (London: Pickering and Chatto, 2003).

[5] Frances Dunlop to Robert Burns, March 16 1793, in William Wallace (ed.), *Robert Burns and Mrs Dunlop: Correspondence Now Published in Full for the First Time*, 2 vols (New York: Dodd, Mead and Company, 1898), II: 242.

[6] Nicolas Roe, 'Authenticating Robert Burns', *Essays in Criticism* 46 (1996), pp. 195–218; Bold, 'Inmate of the Hamlet: Burns as Peasant Poet', p. 49.

[7] *Letters of Robert Burns*, I: 142.

[8] Reprinted in Donald A. Low. *Robert Burns: The Critical Heritage* (London: Routledge, 1974), p. 99.

[9] Ibid., pp. 99, 100.

[10] Ibid., p. 102.

[11] Ibid., p. 105.

[12] Ibid., pp. 132, 133, 141, 140. See also Carol McGuirk, 'James Currie and the Makings of the Burns Myth', *Selected Essays on Scottish Language and Literature*, Steven R. McKenna (ed.) (Lewiston: Mellen, 1992), pp. 149–61.

[13] Reprinted in Low, *Robert Burns: The Critical Heritage*, p. 178.

[14] Ibid., p. 199.

[15] Ibid., p. 251.

[16] Ibid., p. 317.

[17] Ibid., pp. 8–9.

[18] On genius theory, see Penelope Murray (ed.), *Genius: The History of an Idea* (Oxford: Blackwell, 1989); Christine Battersby, *Gender and Genius: Towards a Feminist Aesthetics* (London: The Women's Press, 1989).

[19] Reprinted in Low, *Robert Burns: The Critical Heritage*, pp. 157, 171

[20] Ibid., p. 119, 121, 124.

[21] Ibid., p. 4

[22] Carol McGuirk, *Robert Burns and the Sentimental Era* [1985] (East Linton: Tuckwell Press, 1997), p. xiii.

THE WORD ON BURNS

ᶜᴼ

GERARD CARRUTHERS

Deep in the heart of an often sectarian-minded Scotland, at the former townhouse of the Earl of Glencairn in Dumbarton, someone has scratched "mason" on a plaque commemorating a visit by Robert Burns in 1787. In recent years a poem has been recited in the "glee" spot at Burns Club meetings where the narrator, drunk and asleep on a bench beside Burns's statue in George Square, Glasgow, is vouchsafed a vision of the bard who has clambered down from his plinth. The apparition gives the following essential, bronze-nosing advice to the narrator, "Love your God and honour your Queen." All too often, Scotland has had a despairing or desperate relationship with its greatest poet as is attested, respectively, by the brutally metonymic reduction of Burns in the "Catholic" alienation from him or the iconolatry of the "Protestant" adoration of him just cited. One of the wittiest teases of Burns's significance for Scotland is to be found in Edwin Muir's proposition that the poet is a warped Christ-surrogate (or an ironically denuded Holy Willie), writing proudly upon the page of his sinfulness for the vicarious enjoyment of a Presbyterian confraternity too douce to be openly bad itself.[1] We might take the joke a stage further and identify in this transacted erection Burns as the flesh made word.

'Burnomania' (a term first coined in 1811), took Burns *at his word* from the beginning of his published career.[2] One of the poet's earliest efforts in Scots, "Poor Mailie's Elegy" (1786), enjoins "a' ye Bards on bonie Doon" (l.43) to take part in the melancholy chorus for the imagined demise of Burns's pet yowe.[3] The point is, of course (and this is part of the mock-heroic fabric of the poem), that there are no bards anywhere in the vicinity of South Ayrshire; there is only a fledgling "Bardie" (as Burns refers to himself several times in the poem). Inspired by Burns's success, however, there is no end to the number of Ayrshire and Scottish bards cluttering the countryside by the late 1780s. Burns's engendering of creative space for himself and for others is one of the most nicely ironic of phenomena in the history of Scottish poetry. In his verse-epistles to John Lapraik, David Sillar and William Simson he consciously encouraged the work of others with the result that the myth persists to this day among some bardolators that the verse-epistle form practised by Burns and these minor-versifiers arose naturally out of the couthy, earthy genius of Ayrshire rural life (over which the presiding poetic muse might be said to be "Soila"). For Burns, however, the origins of the form are to be found most specifically in the work of his great predecessor Allan Ramsay. Ramsay's verse-epistles, in an unapologetic (though not entirely unselfconscious) Scots "dialect," reveal him to be an accomplished Augustan craftsman taking his cue from Alexander Pope (the notion of sociable, urbanely modulated poetry marking intercourse between the most cultivated minds is the key to the eighteenth-century verse-epistle form).

Burns's debt to this earlier eighteenth-century context is perhaps best seen in "To William Simson, Ochiltree" (1786). This poem ranges in its perspective from Scotland to the Magellan Straits and offers a disquisition on history, logic and natural science. The piece is also, as part of an *urbane* rather than any specifically *"heaven-taught"* persona, an extended "modesty topos" and the extension here is not merely personal but national. Burns invokes his poetic predecessors, Ramsay, Robert Fergusson and William Hamilton of Gilbertfield (the most famous of Ramsay's verse-epistle correspondents, which highlights precisely the place from which Burns is consciously taking his lead, or his "leid"). Burns depicts these poets as figures purveying vivid landscape portraiture, vibrant communal fun and easy worldly-wisdom, and this identification might make them appear as rather limited poetic quantities as seen through Burns's eyes. However, the "modesty" of Burns's claim for himself and his national poetic forbears is not a disavowal of literary (perhaps English literary) complexity, but is rather a demonstration of, and a claim to, *literary facility*. Two things are crucial in this context. First of all, an important idea, emerging in reaction to seventeenth-century British sectarian turmoil, was that *the word* was not something entirely reified (as the rapidly proliferating religious denominations of that century asserted), but an instrument that could be employed through literature as part of a common, realistic cultural outlook unifying and communicating all men of goodwill, and of widely differing creeds and even none. This perspective is strongly associated with European rationalism in the later seventeenth century from which sprang the eighteenth century Enlightenment. Secondly, and partly as the result of both English and Scottish anti-Presbyterian prejudice, Scotland had been depicted as a peculiarly fanatical place, not amenable to the secularising effects of literature. There is a strong line, then, from Allan Ramsay to Robert Burns that seeks to show that poetry and "polite" letters can find an *easy* (as the early eighteenth century Edinburgh club to which Ramsay belonged was named) niche in Scotland. Critics sometimes conflate this assertion of cultural ease by Ramsay, Burns and others with the catchall notion of primitivism, and the result is an overemphasis upon eighteenth-century Scottish disavowal of conscious creative artistry and the failure to recognise as fully as ought to be the case the eighteenth-century *assertion* of *literary* Scotland by these writers.

From day one, Burns's position as a literary artist attempting to emphasise his continuity in a line of Scottish poetic creativity was misunderstood. One of his dreadful shoal of imitators, Janet Little, reveals exactly the misidentification of Burns's cultural location. She writes:

> Loved Thalia, that delightful muse,
> Seem'd lang shut up as a recluse,
> To all she did her aid refuse,
>   Since Allan's day,
> Till Burns arose, then did she choose
>   To grace his lay.[4]

Little is either ignorant of Robert Fergusson (so emphatically invoked by Burns in his early work), or perhaps even seeks to excise the problematically "urban" Fergusson from the line of Scots poetic succession. Most probably, Little, like so many Scots had a knowledge of eighteenth-century Scots poetry before Burns which was largely limited to Ramsay's "The Gentle Shepherd" (1725). This was a text that, somewhat paradoxically, was taken essentially to enshrine the robust and demotic folk traditions of the Scottish rural scene. While certainly re-popularising the set-piece folksongs it included, this pastoral-drama argued that "high" culture as well as folk culture needed to be restored as part of a composite hierarchy to engage with a Calvinist blighted Scotland. The very title of the piece (with its Gentle-*man*) points to this Tory and, indeed, Jacobite agenda. For various, perhaps very good, reasons of political and cultural identity, however, many in eighteenth-century Scotland tended to lay emphasis upon the primacy of the "primitive", less sophisticated (especially when compared to England) literary voice of the nation. It is in this emphasis, though, that the origins lay for much of the subsequent unfortunate inattentiveness to the literary amplitude of Burns and other Scots-language poets of the eighteenth century.

Little's idea of the randomly chosen, specially inspired and humbly-born Burns (we can see precisely why Edwin Muir was to satirise the messianic status of the bard) is flung exactly against the pretensions of English literature:

> Did Addison or Pope but hear,
> Or Sam, that critic most severe,
> A ploughboy sing with throat sae clear,
>   They in a rage
> Their words would a' in pieces tear
>   And curse your page.[5]

Here we have the nadir of Scottish literary nationalism in the eighteenth century. Previously in the hands of Ramsay, Fergusson and others the vaunting of Scottish literary prowess over England had been playful (though with the serious aim of making a claim of right for the Scots language and for Scottish literature). Little's crude dismissal of English literature is a harbinger of some of the worst excesses of popular anti-literary and anti-intellectual bardolatry in Scotland during much of the nineteenth century and still not without some expression in the opening years of the twenty first century.

One of the wittier contemporary engagements with Burns came in the poem, "The Deil's Reply to Robert Burns" by "James Ditchburn." In this poem Satan replies to Burns's "Address to the Deil" (1786) attempting to debunk some of the calumny which he has been made to suffer through the propaganda of the Bible:

Jenny.   And what would Roger say if he could speak!
             Am I oblig'd to guess what ye're to seek.

Gentle Shepherd

And Rab, gin ye'll just read your Bible
Instead o' blin' Jock Milton's fable,
I'll plank a croon on ony table
                Against a groat,
To fin' my name, you'll no' be able,
                In a' the plot.

Your mither, Eve, I kent her brawly;
A dainty quean she was and wally
But destitute of prudence wholly,
                The witless hizzie,
Aye bent on fun, and whiles on folly
                And mischief busy

As for the famous serpent story
To lee I'd baith be shamed and sorry,
It's just a clever allegory
                And weel writ doon
The wark o' an Egyptian Tory –
                I ken the loon.[6]

A possible candidate for authorship of the piece (on the basis simply of the initials of the pseudonym and of the fairly comprehensive irreverence in the poem) is James Dalrymple. Like Burns, Dalrymple was part of the milieu of the Ayrshire Enlightenment where culturally mobile men such as tenant-farmers, lawyers and shop-keepers met, often in a freemasonic context, to discuss the politics, religion, science, philosophy and literature of the day. According to Burns, Dalrymple socially had "a pulse too hot" and so he must really have been a wild man.[7] But, assuming him to be the author of "The Deil's Reply", he shows above a heated, problematising, enlightened intellect also. Ditchburn's Beelzebub warns Burns against the literary word, while Ditchburn crucially acknowledges Burns's reading in the *British* literary canon (indeed, appropriates "Jock" Milton to acknowledge the Scottish experience of this canon). Ditchburn also, however, teases the Bible (the early days of German "higher criticism" are clearly registering in Enlightenment Ayrshire). The word of the Bible too is literary, is allegorical and not so literal as the simplest of eighteenth-century Presbyterians and other Christians were prone to reading it. The devil speaks here as a "Whig" heavily reliant on the truth of the everyday word and castigating scripture as the work of a "Tory" ideological enemy. The whiggish Devil has a very clear-sighted, reductive view of "evil", or "fun", in that it all stems from sex (or human nature). Nicely, though, what is conflated – or collapsed – here is the doctrine of Original Sin and an important and cosmopolitan Enlightenment idea very present in Burns's work that human *nature* or the flesh should not be so despised as it had become in post-medieval Aristotelian Christian theology (of which Calvinist Puritanism represented only one branch). In a few deft strokes, then, Ditchburn incisively handles the supposed oppositions between "literature" and everyday "reality", between the "theological" and "scientific" (or "common sense") conceptions of humanity, leaving the matter demonically open as to which among all of these categories is to be trusted to deliver "the truth". As Ditchburn in effect also codifies so knowingly and neatly here the debate that the phenomenon of Robert Burns was beginning to present to the world over the relative merits of literature and nature, of tutelage and inspiration, one might be tempted almost to suggest that Burns himself was the author of "The Deil's Reply".

The nineteenth century, on the whole, was not a happy time in the estimation of Burns's life and work. An inauspicious start was made as James Currie failed to publish "Holy Willie's Prayer" as he deemed it to be too scandalous for the first collected works of Burns. Written in 1785, the poem did actually appear in a textually incomplete form during the same year as Currie's edition, 1801, in Thomas Stewart's *Poems Ascribed to Robert Burns*, but it was not until the 1890s that seriously printed versions of the poem routinely included all that Burns wrote for one of his greatest productions. The moral censoriousness of Burns's biographers such as "Honest" Allan Cunningham and John Gibson Lockhart directed a confederacy of Tory "men of letters" and a burgeoning, crass populist cult of Burns determined to separate the bad from the good in the poet's moral and political behaviour. The unspoken desire of this confederacy was that Burns might finally be held up as an exemplar of essentially good-hearted, morally sober and plain-talking Scoto-Britishness as this colonised the world (the transplantation of the Burns cult so widely and effectively overseas shows how successful this insidious process was).

At the same time, though, another channel of reception to Burns ran through the nineteenth century. This was politically mixed to begin

with but prepared the way for a Burns whose significance ran counter
to the emasculated, lobotomised oracle of saws which the poet was
being reduced to in Burns clubs at home and abroad. One of the first
responsible critical voices to counter the too discriminating approach
of Lockhart's biography (a book much read by generations of Burns
devotees between 1828 and down to the 1920s – its last major
reprinting in Britain was in 1914) was that of Thomas Carlyle. Often
politically reactionary, Carlyle was, nonetheless, well-versed in the
dialectically inclusive approach of German philosophy and deemed
that almost all of what Burns wrote – either morally good or bad –
could be subsumed under the defining rubric of "sincerity, [of Burns's]
indisputable air of Truth."[8] That great American cultural commenta-
tor, Ralph Waldo Emerson, also made a powerful statement in the
reorientation of Burns's reputation at the mid-point of the nineteenth
century when he declared that "[Burns was] not great, like Goethe, in
the stars, or like Byron, on the ocean, or Moore, in the luxurious East,
but in the homely landscape which the poor see around them – bleak
leagues of pasture and stubble, ice and sleet, and rain and snow-choked
brooks . . ."[9] This reclamation of Burns as part of the Romantic
movement was important. English Romantics such as Wordsworth
and Hazlitt had seen Burns in such a context, though this had been
very effectively denied in Scotland. Tories like Lockhart and William
Motherwell had been busy pronouncing Burns to be too morally
flawed and too lowborn to count as a really great creative artist of the
final decades of the eighteenth century. The Whig political grouping in
Scotland too, centred on the *Edinburgh Review*, saw Burns as lacking in
decorum, a failure that it read as a widespread failing amongst the
British Romantics. Francis Jeffrey saw Wordsworth's work as often
trivial and condemned Burns in the *Review* for having too much
"vehement familiarity."[10] Emerson began a re-canonisation of Burns
in the pantheon of Romanticism, which has been only partially
successful down to the present day. His emphasising of Burns as
the poet of a melancholy rural scene was a corrective to the masses of
illustrations of Burns's songs featuring a happy bard wooing the lasses
amongst scenes of agricultural plenty. By 1880, Robert Louis Steven-
son, was, very precisely, lauding Burns's "vehement sensibility" when
he wrote of Burns's "[sympathy] sometimes flowing out in byways
hitherto unused, upon mice, and flowers, and the devil himself;
sometimes speaking plainly between human hearts; sometimes ringing

out in exultation like a peal of bells!"[11] For Stevenson, then, Burns's poetic word is commendably riotous and unstable. We have here an acknowledgment of the immersion of Burns in the Scottish Enlightenment (where "sympathy" is one of the milieu's key concepts) and a recognition of the Romantic application of this idea by Burns to match a world rapidly fluctuating and reconfiguring itself under the pressures of American, Agrarian and French revolutions.

From the 1930s Burns studies saw the attempt to establish Burns's word in a hitherto unparalleled fashion. The chaotic textual history of Burns in terms of censorship, wrongly attributed works, bowdlerisation and even forgery made for a huge layer of muddied accretion around Robert Burns. The work of J. de Lancey Ferguson on Burns's letters from the 30s brought a rigorous textual empiricism to Burns studies that set a benchmark all subsequent critics have had to match (as we shall see, in the *Canongate Burns* there is a significant failure to do precisely that). In the same decade as de Lancey Ferguson was hard at work on Burns, Catherine Carswell produced her life of Burns which has become (and perhaps especially since its republication in 1990), what Lockhart's life was to the long nineteenth century. Carswell's book is really a brilliant novel; for historical reliability its score is pretty dismal. She herself acknowledged that her "researches" alarmed de Lancey Ferguson, the man who was part of a small group of American Burns scholarship which was very determined to scrape away a century plus of mythic grime. What Carswell did was to add to this grime. Her emphasis upon Burns's sexual proclivities, intended to counter nineteenth-century sanitised versions of Burns, went so far as to distort knowledge. Her biography is gripped by a Modernist sexual hysteria, of the kind that perhaps only a thoroughly bourgeois person could produce. So determined was Carswell to have her own version of *Lady Chatterley's Lover* that she claimed that Burns and "Clarinda" (Agnes M'Lehose, the middle class married woman with whom Burns so creatively flirted in letters) sexually consummated their relationship. There is no evidence for this, and the best surmising of modern Burns scholarship was that this did not happen. Again without warrant, and in as lurid a re-creation as almost anything thrown up by nineteenth century bardolatry, Carswell claims that "Highland Mary" died while pregnant with Burns's child.

Carswell's Burns repeated what is, in fact, a very old-fashioned phenomenon of trying to pinpoint an all too sullied Burns (or perhaps "solid" would be the preferred variant here). Her priapic Burns has tended to be the Burns of choice for many modern amateur enthusiasts alongside a Burns of nationalistic and leftist leanings. Though a nationalist myself, I was staggered to share a public platform with a leading light of the Burns Federation and to hear this otherwise very sensible man (highly knowledgeable about his favourite poet) make the claim that Burns would have been a modern Scottish nationalist. This kind of projection, given the entirely different national and political circumstances in which Burns lived, is simply untenable. I write this in Clydebank where many old, revered stalwarts of the labour movement keep Burns's words to hand for endorsement of their own humanitarian principles. This selectivity is entirely legitimate and I am personally, politically glad that Burns should work in this way, but we have to bear in mind that Burns in his life flirted with each of French revolutionary sentiment, more moderate Whiggism and a reactionary Toryism.

No-one since the 1920s has seriously doubted Burns's interest in radical politics, but the recent *Canongate Burns* (2001) edited by Andrew Noble and Patrick Scott Hogg attempts to be over-assertive on both the political and the sexual solidity of Burns (the ghost of Carswell is never very far away in this book). Two big examples are exemplary. The claim is made that Burns suffered from melancholia as an after-symptom of venereal disease. The claim is also made that the Crochallan Fencibles, famed as the context in which Burns produces *The Merry Muses of Caledonia*, was more or less a political cell rather than simply a glee club. Where is the evidence in either case? If the editors have found proof of Burns's sexual disease then they really ought to present it rather than simply asserting it. Is there evidence for the claim about the Fencibles other than the very thin case that the club-name was parodic of state-loyal militia groupings of the period? Perhaps the most ultimately absurd moments of the Canongate Burns occur in the treatment of "Address to A Haggis." Typical of the slipshod syntax throughout the commentary by the editors, we are served up with the following explanation: "A peasant dish compounded of meat left-overs, oatmeal, spices, offal, all packed in a sheep's stomach, Burns portrays the haggis as causative of the virility of the Scottish common people".[12] So Burns is a spicy peasant dish? The editors speak truer than they know. Worse, we are told that "To A Haggis" is "more subtly knowing and dissident than first appears."[13] "Knowing"? "Dissident"? So the poem implies sexual consciousness which equals political radicalism? Here, as in so many places in the *Canongate* Burns, we have a Burns of thesis-driven, literalism (though this literalism is derived from the bargain basement of 1960s psycho-babble).

There is another disturbing element with regard to *the word* in the *Canongate Burns*. This concerns the alleged recovery of "lost poems" in the book. One of the biggest mysteries (leaving aside the editors' secret knowledge of VD and politics) comes with regard to a poem that, in fact, does not appear in the book. What gave rise to the Canongate project was Patrick Scott Hogg's *Robert Burns: The Lost Poems* (1997) which lists as its "A1" poem a piece entitled, "On the Year 1793" which Hogg had retrieved from the radical press with the pseudonym, "Aratus" appended to it.[14] The poem is strangely absent from the Canongate Burns, though it is mentioned in the book, in the note to "Lines in a Lady's Pocket Book" with the claim that these four lines "are very close in sentiment and expression to the poem *On the Year 1793*, printed in the *Edinburgh Gazeteer* on 8th January, 1793 and if inserted at the end of that poem seamlessly complete it." Until I found this note I wondered if the editors had, in fact, discovered the poem to be by someone else. This seems not to be the case, however, since the introduction to the *Canongate Burns* states, "Only two of Scott Hogg's discoveries have been found not to be by Burns."[15] I should confess here to my particular interest and, indeed, suspicion, since these two poems mentioned by the editors were discovered by me to be the work of the radical poet and priest, Alexander Geddes.[16] In the case of "On the Year 1793," has this been mistakenly dropped from the Canongate Burns? I do not know, but, having been alerted, I decided to try an experiment and see if I could find any reason why the poem should not be included in the Canongate book. Intriguingly, I discovered another "Aratus" writing in 1793. This "Aratus", like Hogg's was a radical and produced the pamphlet, *Voyage to the Moon Recommended to all Lovers of Real Freedom*. This prose-fantasy sees a man ascend in a balloon and observe a world of eight million snakes ruled over by a Great Snake (the population and system, clearly, make for a very thin allegory of Great Britain in the 1790s). At one point we find a poem addressed to the deity and appealing for greater worldly justice. It's first four lines run as follows:

> Him *who could* space unlimited define,
> Who *bade th'*obedient sun on us to shine!
> At *whose command* the spiral vortex rise
> In *tow'ring* columns, to the vaulted *skies*[17]

Now compare this to the first four lines of Hogg's "On the Year 1793"

> Thou*, who couldst* man create,
> And *bade th'immortal* soul his being animate!
> At *whose command* sub-marine mountains rise,
> And *towering* Aetna's smoke obscures the *skies*![18]

I do not know who wrote *A Voyage to the Moon* (curiously the pamphlet has a little fame among science fiction buffs, but I've yet to find any theory of authorship from within that community). It seems fairly clear though, that this Aratus and Hogg's Aratus are almost certainly one and the same. It seems fairly clear that another "lost poem" has fallen down. There is no good reason why someone would adopt the same name and much of the same template as happens between the two poetic cases. What we see in this case, I believe, is an example of the diffuse nature of radical writing in Britain of the 1790s. Radicals spray their work all over the place and to conclude so readily as Hogg and Noble, especially as they do where a Scottish provenance is concerned, that they are mining a secret vein of Burns represents yet another (and modern and also sentimental) version of "Burnomania." Burns continues to struggle from under a weight of words which, as so often in the past, have nothing to do with the poet himself.

NOTES

[1] See both Edwin Muir, 'Robert Burns' in *Freeman* vol. VII (9th May 1923), pp. 202–4, & 'Burns & Holy Willie' in *Left Review* II (November 1936), pp. 762–4.

[2] See William Peebles, *Burnomania: The Celebrity of Robert Burns Considered* (Edinburgh, 1811) especially the poem, "Burns Renowned", which is reprinted in Donald Low (ed.), *Robert Burns: The Critical Heritage*. London and Boston: Routledge & Kegan Paul, 1974, pp. 249–51.

[3] James Kinsley (ed.), *Burns: Complete Poems & Songs* (Oxford: Oxford University Press, 1969), p. 27.

[4] See *The Contemporaries of Burns* (Edinburgh: Hugh Paton, Carver & Gilder, 1840), p. 80.

[5] *The Contemporaries of Burns*, p. 81.

[6] See John D. Ross, *Robert Burns and his Rhyming Friends* (Stirling: Eneas Mackay, 1928), pp. 21–22 [pp. 20–25].

[7] See Robert Burns, "The Vision" [additional stanzas from the Stair Manuscript] in Kinsley (ed.), *Burns: Complete Poems and Songs*, p. 85 [l.27].

[8] Thomas Carlyle, *Essay on Burns* Andrew J. George (ed.) (Boston: D.C. Heath, 1901), p. 13.

[9] See Ralph Waldo Emerson, 'Essay on Burns' introduced by G. Ross Roy (Printed by the University of South Carolina), p. 3.

[10] Francis Jeffrey Review of R. H. Cromek, *Reliques of Robert Burns* (1808) in the *Edinburgh Review* (January 1809) reprinted in *Robert Burns: The Critical Heritage* p. 182 [pp. 178–195].

[11] Robert Louis Stevenson, 'Some Aspects of Robert Burns' (1879) republished in Jeremy Treglown (ed.), Robert Louis Stevenson, *The Lantern-Bearers and Other Essays* (New York: Farrar Straus Giroux, 1988), p. 124 [pp. 100–125].

[12] Andrew Noble and Patrick Scott Hogg, *The Canongate Burns* (Edinburgh: Canongate, 2001), p. 214

[13] Ibid., pp. 213–14.

[14] Patrick Scott Hogg, *Robert Burns: The Lost Poems* (Glasgow: Privately printed, 1997), pp. 78–91.

[15] Andrew Noble and Patrick Scott Hogg, *The Canongate Burns* (Edinburgh: Canongate, 2001), p. xcvii.

[16] Gerard Carruthers, 'Alexander Geddes and the "Lost Poems" Controversy' in *Studies in Scottish Literature*, XXXI (1999).

[17] *A Voyage to the Moon Strongly Recommended to all Lovers of Real Freedom* (London: 1793), p. 13.

[18] Hogg, *Robert Burns: The Lost Poems*, p. 78; see Gerard Carruthers, '*The Canongate Burns*: Misreading Robert Burns and the Periodical Press of the 1790s' in *Review of Scottish Culture* Number 18 (2006), pp. 41–50, for the unravelling of Noble's and Hogg's extremely poor textual practice.

THE PAPARAZZO, THE PUBLISHER
AND THE POET

స౬

SHEILA SZATKOWSKI

"In London, Paris, and all other great cities of Europe, though they contain many literary men, the access to them is difficult: and even after that is obtained, the conversation, for some time it is shy and constrained. In Edinburgh, the access to men of parts is not only easy, but their conversation and the communication of their knowledge are at once imparted to intelligent strangers with the utmost liberality. The philosophers of Scotland have no nostrums. They tell what they know, and they deliver their sentiments without disguise or reserve."[1]

At the start of a cold winter in November 1786 one such intelligent stranger, Robert Burns, made his first visit to the capital. He was soon enjoying the warmer hospitality of many of the great Scottish intellectuals and "the constant collision with good company" in the taverns and homes of former friends from Ayrshire together with the stimulus of fresh acquaintances in the Old and New Towns. Edinburgh at the end of the eighteenth century was a city in transition. A rapidly increasing populace and a desire to expand beyond the city's medieval confines had led to the building of the New Town and a new urban order. The city's good fortune was to have its own eighteenth-century 'paparazzo', John Kay (1742–1826), the barber turned miniature painter, who recorded a unique and perceptive visual chronicle of an old order that was passing away. Kay's likenesses of the Edinburgh citizenry also provide the best social document of the capital that feted and caressed the ploughman-poet.[2]

This essay sets out first to examine Kay's record of the Edinburgh characters whom Burns knew and then to discuss the reasons why Burns, the great social satirist of eighteenth-century Scotland, might have been ignored by Kay, the great social caricaturist of the same period.

Cushioned by an annuity from his former patron William Nisbet of Dirleton, the self-taught John Kay forsook barbering for art in 1785 and set up shop, first in the High Street of the Old Town then later in the Parliament Close. Kay's print offerings at one guinea for a first impression and half a guinea for a second were a far cry from the studio portraits of his contemporary Sir Henry Raeburn (1756–1823), Scotland's greatest Enlightenment portrait painter which could command a fee of 50 guineas or more.

Amongst Burns's legal and academic acquaintances were William Robertson, Lord Monboddo, Lord Braxfield, Lord Newton, James Hutton, Joseph Black, Andrew Duncan, Alexander Wood, Hugh Blair, Alexander 'Jupiter' Carlyle, Sir William Forbes, Henry Erskine and Sir Walter Scott, all of whom sat for Raeburn. However, John Kay produced remarkable likenesses of the very same Edinburgh elite but without sittings, preferring to observe them in the street, at the pulpit or in the courtroom. Others who worked and associated with Burns in Edinburgh and who were etched by Kay include William Smellie, Andrew Bell, Sir John Whitefoord, Stabilini, the violinist, Sir James Hunter Blair, James Gregory, John and Alexander Campbell, Louis Cauvin, his French teacher, and John Dowie, the unctuous proprietor of one of the bard's favourite howffs in Liberton Wynd.

Various biographies and newspaper advertisements claim that Kay produced etchings of 900 characters in his long career spanning thirty years.[3] To date less than 400 of these have been identified or published and the search for the missing ones, if they exist at all, remains an ongoing quest for historians and collectors.

Raeburn never had Burns sit for a formal portrait. Kay, however, prided himself on creating a likeness from as little as a passing glance, and had ample opportunity to make the bard who was a familiar sight on the streets of Edinburgh during much of 1787 and 1788, a subject for his burin. Given the range of subjects known to have been drawn by Kay, images of Robert Burns and the eminent William Creech, publisher of his Edinburgh edition of *Poems, chiefly in the Scottish Dialect*, are all the more conspicuous by their absence.

A recent examination of an album of works by John Kay in the archives of the Royal Scottish Academy has revealed several unidentified portraits, some of which are unsigned and undated. Two of these, pasted in close proximity to each other within the album, appear to be of more than passing interest. The limited documentation for these portraits makes the process of identification and attribution difficult but a comparison with other likenesses of Burns and Creech permits some simple observations to be made while at the same time it raises some new questions.

Plate 2 is a pen and ink drawing of a seated male in profile, left-facing, holding up a small book in his right hand and wearing a wig and dress coat. Comparing Plate 2 with a portrait of William Creech by Raeburn (page 41 *after Raeburn*) and another authenticated pencil drawing of Creech by John Brown (page 42), one may assert with a degree of confidence that in Plate 2 Kay had indeed committed the great publisher and man of letters to paper. Despite the obvious years between the sittings, there are several points of agreement between Kay's drawing (Plate 2), the engraving after Raeburn (page 41) and the pencil drawing by Brown (page 42), notably the eyebrows, the corners of the sealed lips and the lively eyes. There is no known published print of Creech by Kay but he must have seen the "upright, pert, tart, tripping wight" on a daily basis given the proximity of their premises in the Old Town. One can only speculate that Kay was unwilling to make public a caricature of Creech and thus risk the loss of an engraving commission from the capital's leading publisher. It is interesting to note that Kay in his eightieth year executed a fine etching of another great Edinburgh publisher, Archibald Constable (1774–1827), which appeared in 1822.[4]

Plate 3 is a pen and ink and wash full-figure miniature depicting a male in profile in a rural setting, leaning on the stump of a tree in a relaxed pose, and wearing the attire of a country gentleman. He wears a wide-brimmed hat, shows a slight paunchiness and a hint of a double chin. Some of these details prompted a review of the best-known likenesses of Burns executed in his lifetime. There has been much scholarly contention about which, if any, is the most "authentic" contemporary representation of the poet. Those cited are the ubiquitous idealised and much graven Nasmyth portrait (1787, Plate 1), the Miers silhouette (1787), the Peter Taylor oil (1786), or the Alexander Reid miniature (1795).[5] However, none of these were the work of a recognised professional portrait painter, but variously that of the acknowledged "father of Scottish landscape painting" (Nasmyth), a silhouettist of some note (Miers), an obscure miniature painter in Dumfries (Reid) and an Edinburgh house- and coach-painter (Taylor)!

William Creech after Raeburn in James Grant's Old and New Edinburgh

William Creech by John Brown (from a private collection)

Burns, and his contemporary 'beholders', differed in their opinions of these portraits. Nasmyth was satisfied neither with his own incomplete rendition of the head of Burns nor with Beugo's engraving. Burns on the other hand was flattered by the Beugo engraving which, interestingly, required several sittings.[6] He sent copies to his friends but he later described the Reid work as "the best likeness of me ever taken." In the summer of 1788 he remarked in a letter that his sitting for Miers "did not exceed two minutes." Clarinda, Mrs McElhose, directed James Paterson, who penned the biographies of Kay's Portraits, to look at her picture of Burns by Horsburgh (after Taylor) and remarked, "You will know who that is – it was presented to me by Constable and Co. for having simply declared, what I knew to be true, that the likeness was good."[7]

Returning to Kay's pen and ink and wash (Plate 3), the subject is clearly wearing a wig and although Burns was often seen with his hair tied back, there is no record of him ever wearing such an accessory. Although the fashion for wigs was waning at the end of the eighteenth century, Burns, whether in the literary salon of Adam Ferguson, at the Canongate-Kilwinning Lodge or at Monboddo's learned suppers, might even then have been perceived by these gentlemen as a *sans-perruque*. The subject in Plate 3 is also wearing shoes but the only full-length authenticated portrait done by Nasmyth in 1828 from a 40-year old pencil sketch shows Burns in knee-high boots. Accounts vary of the physical appearance of Burns: Allan Cunningham described the poet thus: "tall and sinewy . . . his form was vigorous, his limbs shapely, his knees firmly knit, his arms muscular and round, his hands large, his fingers long and he stood five feet ten inches high".[8] Sir Walter Scott recalled, "I would have taken the poet, had I not known what he was, for a very sagacious country farmer of the old Scotch school . . . the douce gudeman who held his own plough." The debate on authentic likenesses has been given new fodder at a recent auction with the appearance of a gold-framed miniature with the inscription, *Robert Burns* on the back. Despite confirmation of its provenance from the poet's family, the likeness was quite different to all the other authenticated portraits of Burns. It showed a striking figure with dark hair tied back, a fronde of hair on the forehead (somewhat similar to the Reid miniature) and long curls to either side of the face, wearing a ruffled shirt, maroon jacket and pale blue waistcoat.[9]

The number of discrepancies in portraits and contemporary ac-

counts of Burns raises the question of why Creech gave a young
Nasmyth the commission over David Allan or Henry Raeburn who
were older, established artists with a well-deserved reputation for
portraiture. Why was the young, talented but relatively unknown
Beugo asked to prepare the engraving when John Kay had already
produced admirable portraits such as that of Lord Provost Sir James
Hunter Blair, commissioned in 1785.

Another painting may offer some further insight. *The Inauguration of
Robert Burns as Poet-Laureate of the Lodge* by William Stewart Watson
(1846),[10] though depicting an event that may not have happened, does
provide a record of the many friends and associates of Burns who were
fellow masons at Lodge Canongate-Kilwinning. The figures repre-
sented include William Creech, Alexander Nasmyth, the Earl of
Glencairn, Henry Mackenzie, William Nicol, William Cruikshank,
Robert Ainslie, Louis Cauvin, Dugald Stewart, James Johnson, Alex-
ander Wood and Francis Grose. Nasmyth is the only limner shown
and being of an age with Burns (Nasmyth was born in 1758) perhaps
the commission from Creech came as a favour to a young fellow
mason. Likewise Beugo was just beginning his career, he was the same
age as Burns and they both attended French classes with another
fellow mason, Louis Cauvin. Whether out of gratitude to Creech or
friendship for Burns, Nasmyth and Beugo made no charge for the
portraits of their new companion and friend, a gesture unlikely to have
been made by the astute Sir Henry Raeburn.

John Kay was of a different generation, belonged to a different
Masonic lodge (Lodge St. David No 36) and social snobbishness may
well have kept the urbane Creech from approaching a barber turned
miniature painter to provide the frontispiece for such a prestigious
work as Burns's Edinburgh Poems. Kay was one of the independent
and self-taught engravers sitting at the lower end of the print market
serving a local audience who wanted portraits and miniatures of the
local characters along with a record of notable curiosities and events.

On the other hand, in view of Kay's choice of subjects, perhaps
Burns was not the type of character to be selected for his pencil. An
analysis of known works by John Kay shows that by the end of 1787,
nearly three years after setting up his print shop, Kay had produced
almost 100 plates. The range of subjects may be categorised thus: legal
and philosophical luminaries; street traders, eccentrics and beggars;
town council worthies; soldiers, medics and clerics. Also pertinent to

THE *British Antiquarian*   18

Francis Grose by John Kay

this discussion are the visitors who came to the city. Kay clearly had a penchant for public spectacle as demonstrated in his 1785 engraving of Lunardi and his balloon about to ascend in front of a wide-eyed audience of some 80,000 at Heriot's Green in Edinburgh. Lunardi, Byrne the Irish Giant, the miniature Count Borolawski and Mrs Siddons were the kind of transient celebrities favoured by Kay. If Burns had given a public recital at the The Cross,[11] in the new Assembly Rooms or Theatre Royal, then Kay might well have recorded the event for posterity and bequeathed another contemporary and, perhaps more authentic likeness to add to those portraits of Burns already mentioned.

To the list of celebrities may be added criminals and political reformers. William Creech was on the jury that convicted Deacon Brodie in 1788 and he did use two of Kay's etchings (*Mr Brodie* and *Smith at the Bar*) as illustrations for *An Account of The Trial of William Brodie and George Smith*, published in 1788 after the execution of the defendants. In the introduction to the second edition Creech desribes Kay's work as "not highly finished in point of engraving" but in the absence of any other contemporary likenesses, Creech knew the commercial value of including these illustrations. Kay also produced frontispieces for published accounts of other trials including those of Thomas Muir and Joseph Gerrald, commissions probably not sought after by other engravers in the city who mostly produced small-scale work for the local book trade.

Even if Burns did not read Creech's account of the Brodie trial with the Kay illustrations he would most certainly have passed Kay's window in the Old Town. He may well have stood behind the quidnuncs of the day and smiled at caricatures such as *Four Bucks* which included his friend Stabilini, or *A Sleepy Congregation* with the Reverend Webster and his friend John Campbell the precentor, or *Courtship* featuring a couple with grotesque looks but still enamoured of each other. With his own predilection for satirical verse, Burns was no doubt approving of caricature and refers to "Hogarth's magic Pow'r" in his *Lines on an Interview with Lord Daer*.

Kay and Burns were both lifelong students of the human comedy. Like a true satirist, Kay drew attention in his caricatures to the human frailties such as vanity, pomposity and greed, themes often alluded to by Burns in his poetry, and with a similar degree of subtle wit and sympathy for humanity. However, while Burns secured easy access to men of parts in the capital and had immediate success with the Edinburgh edition of his Poems, Kay tried and failed to have his work commercially published in his home town. Although he enjoyed modest success throughout a long career, a lack of title or connections ensured Kay's sojourn in an artistic backwater.

An advertisement in the Edinburgh and Leith Post Office Directory of 1838–9 for *Kay's Portraits*, a work published by Hugh Paton in Edinburgh, states that "hardly a citizen of any consideration or in short any individual whatever, conspicuous for public spirit, eccentricity, or personal peculiarity of any kind, escaped the penetrating eye of honest John Kay." Burns's encounters with the literary colossi are well documented but it is Kay's published etchings along with James Paterson's biographies in *Kay's Portraits* which provide a primary source of information on the wider social and literary circles in which the poet moved during his visits to Edinburgh. As a result we know about John Campbell, Precentor at the Canongate Church who facilitated an introduction for Burns to the local bailies to secure a memorial for Robert Fergusson; we know about Louis Cauvin who taught Burns French alongside Beugo and we have a first-hand account of Clarinda's remarks on her favourite portrait of 'Sylvander'.

In a letter of 30 December 1786 from Edinburgh, Mrs Alison Cockburn wrote that "the town is at present agog with the ploughman poet" but perhaps Burns did not satisfy Kay's requirement for visitors to be eccentric, whimsical or comical. Burns was no flamboyant aeronaut or gentle eight foot giant. Just as he exploited local interest in Thomas Paine by producing prints which sold in huge numbers at fifteen shillings each,[12] Kay may have been tempted to make a posthumous likeness after the poet's premature departure to that "bourne whence no traveller returns" in 1796. Nor is it unlikely that Kay, wandering that academic grove known as The Meadows in Edinburgh's south side, had observed Burns resting his elbow on a tree stump while savouring the open space and fresh air.[13] However, with no firm evidence unidentified works like Plate 3 must remain in identity limbo.

John Campbell by John Kay

NOTES

[1] See Kerr, Robert, *Memoirs of the Life, Writings and Correspondence of William Smellie* (1811), Vol 2 p 252

[2] See *A series of original portraits and caricature etchings by the late John Kay, with biographical sketches and illustrative anecdotes* (Edin., 2 vols. 4to, 1838; 8vo ed., 4 vols., 1842; new 4to ed., with additional plates, 2 vols., 1877) The work is often referred to as *Kay's Portraits*.

[3] An output of 900 etchings would be considerable but not an impossible task given that Kay was in business for 30 years.

[4] Archibald Constable appears in the 1877 edition of *Kay's Portraits*. See Plate CCCXXIX p. 473

[5] The portraits of Burns listed here are held by the National Galleries of Scotland.

[6] For further commentary on authentic likenesses of Burns see Skinner, Basil C, *Burns: Authentic Likenesses* (Edinburgh & London, 1963)

[7] James Paterson visited Mrs M'Lehose in February 1837. See footnote on p. 304 of the 1877 edition Kay's Portraits.

[8] Cunningham, Allan, *The Life and Works of Robert Burns* (1840) p. 130

[9] See *The Scotsman*, 24 May 2007, p. 18

[10] The painting is held by the National Galleries of Scotland.

[11] The Cross was located to the south east side of the Royal Mile in Edinburgh and was a popular meeting place in the capital.

[12] Thomas Paine never visited Edinburgh. Kay had relatives in America and this likeness was made from a miniature sent to him around 1794.

[13] Burns spent a lot of time on the south side of the city. His father had lived in Edinburgh from 1749 to 1750 and had assisted Thomas Hope in laying out The Meadows.

THE BURNSIAN CONSTRUCTS

 confused

JOHNNY RODGER

In his monograph *Robert Burns*, Carruthers[1] draws our attention to the significance of the 'poetic technology', the forms and the 'stanza vehicles' that the poet inherits, adopts or adapts in his work. The Christ Kirk stanza and Standard Habbie (latterly, and ahistorically misnamed the 'Burns Stanza') had been forms favoured by earlier poets of Jacobite, Tory, and Episcopalian, if not Catholic, sympathies. That Burns chose precisely those poetic frameworks to reupholster with the 'hodden grey' material of his native Whiggish Presbyterian culture demonstrates his adeptness at exploiting the tensions and complexities inherent in the question of historical identity. But this lesson holds just as readily for architectural technology as it does for the poetic: the point being surely that there is no such thing as a meaningless structure.

The purpose of this essay is to look across the landscape emboldened with this lesson, and to examine the physical structures which were raised in honour of, or in some way to memorialise, Robert Burns. The poet died at the close of the 18th century, and since that time – and especially through the 19th century – monuments and memorials have been raised not only throughout Scotland, but across all those countries significantly influenced by a Scottish diaspora – Northern Ireland, Canada, USA, Australia, New Zealand etc. This work abroad provided many commissions for 19th century Scots sculptors like Steell and the Stevenson brothers. Most of their work was based on an original sculpture by the English neo-classical artist Flaxman, which was initially housed in Hamilton's Edinburgh monument, and was modelled in its turn on Nasmyth's portrait (Plate 1). What interests us here however, are the purely architectural works which were erected either alongside those sculptures or in their own right as memorials. Although it's true that facsimile versions of the Burns birth cottage, complete with thackit roof, were constructed using plans and drawings of the original in Atlanta Georgia in 1910, and in St Louis (later moved to Portland, Oregon), and some sculptures like the Boston of 1911 are complemented by an architectural element, it is fair to say that the main architectural memorials are all sited within Scotland. Those include the Dumfries Mausoleum, and the Alloway, Edinburgh, Kilmarnock and Mauchline monuments (all examined here below). Goodwillie in his book *The World's Memorials of Robert Burns*[2] provides an extensive and often witty catalogue to most monuments, sculptural and architectural, built to the poet by that date. In the 1989 *Burns Chronicle* there is also a more complete list of monuments compiled by James A. MacKay.[3] There is however no real critical engagement or placing of the work in the historical context of an architectural, literary or plastic arts tradition either in Goodwillie or elsewhere. While the sculptures may communicate fairly clear discourses of meaning in terms of their physical and bodily representation of the poet's person (after Flaxman after Nasmyth) accompanied by various symbolic accoutrements like the pen, the plaid, the daisy, and (in Dumfries for example) one of the twa dogs, an analysis of the significance of the purely architectural monuments, of their meaning for Burns himself, for his work, for his readership – for his homeland and his compatriots at large – remains to be essayed.

Perhaps we should start by asking what can be the scope for a monument to a poet? Is the monument figured as an architectonic representation of the poet himself, of his literary work, or of the readership and their relationship to that work? In Burns's case there is perhaps no simple answer to that question, but there are nonetheless some models with which we can make comparison and attempt to clarify the architectural intentions here. Among the most well-known monumental spatial and architectural works created *by* poets in the 20th century, are the gardens by Ian Hamilton Finlay and Gabriele D'Annunzio, respectively Little Sparta in SW Scotland and *Il Vittoriale degli Italiani* in north Italy. Leaving to one side the question of the 'success' of these works (and the dubious taste of D'Annunzio's work, described by one commentator, Fred Licht, as a 'Fascist Lunapark'[4]) the point is that they are presented as poetry itself, they are not merely architectural representations of literary work that exists in written form elsewhere. Finlay indeed described himself in his work in laying out the garden, and arranging sculptural and architectural pieces, as a poet, and appeared to see that work as merely a continuation of his earlier written work. Clearly Burns did not design any of the monuments built in his name in the 19th century, and nor, apparently were they built as poetry to rival the Burns literary canon. But were they intended in some way to complement our understanding of Burns the man, or Burns's work? Or could we push the question even further and look not only for concrete correspondences between the monuments and the written poetry, but see the monuments built as strict architectonic representations of the literary work?

This last possibility may seem on the face of it extreme or fanciful, or even too plainly 'literal' an architectural undertaking to be worthy of the consideration of a serious architect. It may sound immediately like the sort of pastiche fantasy we see in the architectural (I use the word loosely here) representations of fairy tales in the various Disneylands. There is however, in the work of Giuseppe Terragni, the Italian modernist architect of the 1920s and 30s, an example of just such an undertaking, and one carried out in all seriousness and with evident intellectual rigour.

In 1938 Terragni submitted plans to Mussolini to build a monument – the Danteum – in Rome. The building on a rectangular plan was to be constructed half way along the then named *Via dell'Impero*, a principal road which Mussolini had had driven through the ancient Roman Fora between Piazza Venezia and the Coliseum. The symbolic value of this site, half way between the fascist headquarters (on Piazza Venezia) and the largest structure left to us by classical antiquity, is further heightened by the fact that it lies at the foot of *Via Cavour*, a street named after one of the heroes of the 19th century Italian Reunification.

Terragni's view of and relationship to the fascist regime may, like that of many of his compatriots up until the 1938 rapprochement with Hitler, have been at best a naïve one. There is however no doubting that Dante's vision of the interdependency of Church and Empire, with the Emperor receiving his sovereignty over the secular world directly from God, and the Church's power over the spirit being secured to posterity by the secular power of Empire, constituted largely the statement of the fascist regime's world view, and as such the poet and his work were accorded central importance and symbolic value by Mussolini for the Italian nation.

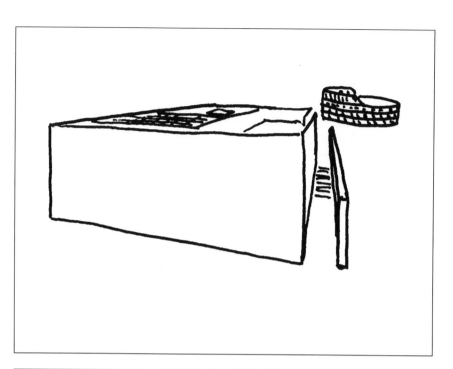

Sketch perspectives of Danteum by J Rodger

Terragni's attempt to map the literary work out in an architectural work is complex and profound, and the design is imbued with innumerable levels of symbolism and meaning, of which we can only sketch out a few details here. As the Danteum was never actually built, much of what we know is taken from study of the plans and watercolour drawings (which were used in a presentation to Mussolini), and also from the remains of a document detailing the significance of the Danteum which Terragni had presented to Il Duce (found in Terragni's office after the war) called *Relazione sul Danteum*. In that document we find, for example, this passage

> The architectural monument and the literary work can adhere to a singular scheme without losing, in this union, any of each works' essential qualities only if both possesses a structure and a harmonic rule that can allow each to confront each other, so that they may be read in a geometric or mathematical relation of parallelism or subordination.

If we take initially just the basic form of the plan of the Danteum, we can follow in the *Relazione* a discussion of the motives for its dimensions and its rectangular shape. In the first place Terragni notes that the perhaps more obvious choice of a circular plan would enclose an area too modest for it purpose, and that it would be inappropriate because of the 'immediacy of the confrontation which would be derived from its vicinity to the perfect and imposing ellipse of the Coliseum.' He also dismisses employing a conical form to represent the decreasing circles of hell as 'too literal'. On the other hand the vicinity of the curved walls of the Coliseum to the straight walled rectangular plan of the Danteum (which can be further broken down into two equal intersecting squares) is precisely proposed to evoke the medieval geometric symbolism of man as a square and God as a circle. The attempt to work out a relation in space between these two primary shapes here, symbolically connects not only religion, art and empire, but Vitruvius, Dante and Leonardo, or three stages of Italian history – ancient, medieval and modern.

The dimensions of the rectangular plan are furthermore, those of a golden section rectangle. This is of vital significance to the whole project. On a purely technical level this means that the ratio of the length of the short side to the long side is equal to the ratio of the length of the long side to the sum of lengths of the short and long

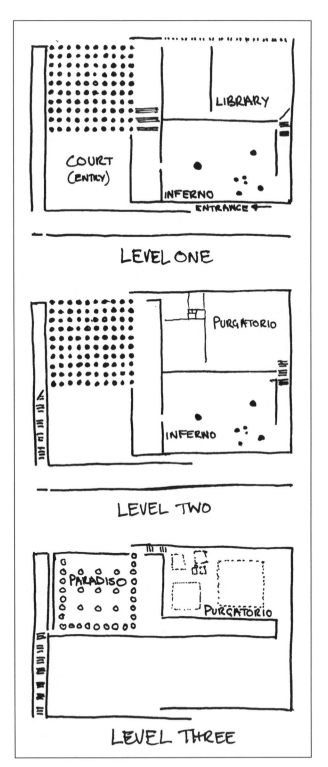

Sketch plans of Danteum by J Rodger

sides. This regulatory proportional system has for Terragni not only
(the fascistic advantage of) an ancient and established pedigree; it was
he says, 'frequently adopted by the ancient Assyrians, Egyptians,
Greeks and Romans'; but with its ordering by three variables (short,
long, short plus long sides) it further expresses physically a law of unity
in trinity, giving it a clear Christian significance while reproducing
Dante's poetical ordering – terzina verses, 3 canticles in one long
poem etc – in a spatial format. The final point about the exterior form
is that the long side of the Danteum is exactly the same length as the
short side of the Basilica of Maxentius, a Roman ruin on the opposite
side of Mussolini's new road, and also planned on a golden rectangle.

Once inside the building the ordering and layers of meaning and
symbolism certainly become no less complex, and again here it is
possible here only to take a brief overview of their significance. On a
very basic level of the symbolic, one enters into an enclosed courtyard
(interpreted by some as representing the 'lost' life of Dante up until the
age of 35), beyond that is a hypostyle hall with 100 columns close
together representing the 'dark forest' (*selva oscura*) where Dante finds
himself. Beyond this again are three golden rectangular 'rooms' in an
ascending spiral of levels representing Inferno, Purgatorio and Para-
diso. Terragni attempts to reproduce the poetic atmosphere of each
canticle: the descent into murky oppression in Inferno, the slow weighty
ascent to the peak in Purgatorio, and the exposure to clear brilliant light
in Paradiso, all by purely architectonic means. The Paradiso as the
highest room has, one might say, the most straightforward representa-
tion of that poetic atmosphere in terms of its glass ceiling and 33 glass
columns (at once contrasting with the 100 dense, and opaque columns
in the *selva oscura* below, and symbolising the 33 *canti* of Dante's
Paradiso). The promenade through the two previous rooms, Inferno
and Purgatorio, is however given a strict spatial representation again
through means of the order of the golden rectangle. One notable
technical aspect of the golden rectangle is that its area has the property
of further geometrical decomposition into a square and a smaller golden
rectangle. The smaller golden rectangle can thus then be decomposed
further into another square and an even smaller golden rectangle . . .
and so on. Terragni uses this feature of decomposition in order to
dispose single heavy columns across the space below the low dark
ceiling in Inferno. In this way, by potentially infinite regression, the dark
oppressive atmosphere of Hell is recreated through a 'parallel harmonic'

rule between the architectonics and the poesy, both of which reveal an infinite order manifested through laws related to the special number 3. This material manifestation of an infinite order is repeated in the opposite direction in the room representing Purgatorio, where the move is across successively raised platforms, again ordered by golden rectangle , under openings to the sky (again golden rectangles) and up towards the entrance into Paradiso.

It would not be true to say that Terragni's scheme for the Danteum has met with universal approbation. It has suffered naturally and especially from its association with the fascist regime. In 1968 for example, Giulio Carlo Argan, the Dean of the Italian Architectural Historians society, said of the Danteum

> . . . an enormous mistake: the idea of making a correspondence between the plan distribution of a building and the structure of a poem is almost comical, but not more than the intention of architecturally expressing victory, patriotism or the longevity of Empire.[5]

The backlash against a shameful period in the nation's history and everything connected with it is understandable, it does nonetheless not obscure the fact that just as literature can, as seen in Dante, be a codification of memory, so equally, through history buildings have been used to codify other specially significant cultural determinations. There may indeed be something 'comical' about medieval cathedrals, Renaissance Gardens, Hadrian's Villa and Burns Monuments, but are not all of these precisely structures whose meanings express and celebrate such abstracts as dismissed in Argan's final clause?

It's also valid to object that the 'user' of Terragni's building would have no immediate perception of the proportions, mathematical relationships, and, say, the relationship to the Basilica of Maxentius over the way. The meanings are thus obscure and arguably inaccessible. The user would indeed have to invest a good deal of imaginative effort to unravel the experience of the structure's meanings. Yet surely this difficulty is encountered in Dante's poem too: its structure and the relationship of its parts (the terzina plus three canticles to the infinite whole) only become revealed after the literary promenade through the whole and subsequent to some prolonged and serious intellectual meditation thereon.

This question of the relationship between the structure and the poetry in Dante's poem is not a straightforward one and has been problematised and argued over throughout the 20th century. The critic Croce separates the two,

> . . . only by making a sharp distinction between structure and poetry, placing them to be sure in strict philosophical and ethical relationship and thereby considering them necessary elements of Dante's spirit, but being careful to avoid any idea of a poetical relationship between them. Only in this way is it possible to enjoy all of the poetry of the *Commedia* profoundly and at the same time accept its structure, with some indifference, perhaps, but without aversion, and, above all without derision.[6]

Pirandello however disagrees with Croce, saying

> If he (Dante) wrote the *Commedia*, this indicates that he did not want to write a treatise or a work composed of poetical and non-poetical parts; but a poem . . .[7]

Terragni clearly agreed largely with Croce's ideas of the distinction between structure and poetry, indeed he was probably influenced by Croce in his belief that,

> The architectural Monument and the literary work can adhere in a single scheme . . . as long as each of these spiritual facts possess a structure and a harmonic rule . . .[8]

Terragni and Croce could whatsmore claim that the poet himself theorised a similar distinction in his poetic manifesto, *Vita Nouva*, where he says,

> . . . there would be great shame on him who (whose verses) lie(s) under figurative form or rhetorical colour, but who then, when asked, could not divest them of such dress, such that the truth be understood.[9]

At any rate the Danteum was never built, for Italy had entered into the war seriously in 1939 and the opportunity never arose again for Mussolini. Terragni himself died on the Eastern Front in 1943. The scheme remains as a fact however: an attempt to totally translate the literary oeuvre into one architectural work, and as such may be useful as a measure or paradigm (even if only an extreme one) in the study of other literary monuments.

Robert Burns was of course a very different poet from Dante. Both are claimed in some way as 'national poet' of their respective nation. Just so Burns may be said to write, comment and theorise on an equally wide a range of aspects of his 'national' culture as did Dante, in terms of religion, politics, society, morals, history, literature, music, agriculture, science, family, nature, priesthood, land and city-scape, and even mathematics. Yet unlike Dante, Burns could not claim to speak out from the power centre of a whole European civilisation, and a unified Christian one at that. Burns's commentary on all those varying issues of the day appear here and there through hundreds of short lyrics, epistles, letters and songs in numerous styles, rather than being combined to form one coherent and all-embracing work of great length, as in Dante's Divine Comedy. That's not to say of course, that we can make some simple judgement on the relative 'merits' of these men as poets; among other attributes that title, – poet – if true, surely denotes 'incommensurability'. The difference in the form of work produced however does mean that Terragni's type of project – disregarding for the moment the contentiousness inherent in his aims to map a whole literary work out by purely architectonic means into a built work – seems immediately inappropriate to the size, spread, context and tone of Burns's poetic works.

Nonetheless, architects – several of them – have constructed built works inspired by Robert Burns. Over the 19th and again in the early 21st century there have been numerous attempts – in many different styles, by architects some more successful and well-known than others – to represent something of the significance of Robert Burns and/or his works. But can we be enlightened in any way by comparison of these buildings with the type of project embarked upon by Terragni in the Danteum? Perhaps these Burns monuments say more about the significance of Burns for Scotland, or for his readers rather than anything directly about the poetry and its structures. Or is it possible, if these monuments each present a different aspect of Robert Burns as was particularly stressed or meaningful for the date in which it was built, then in a collective sense these structures unfold across time and space as comprehensive and meaningful an architectural mapping of the literary work as was carried out in one time and space in the project by Terragni?

It is in an attempt to move towards an understanding of the meaning of these structures, that I undertake a survey of the principal monuments in chronological order. The monuments studied here will include the Dumfries Mausoleum of 1818, the Alloway monument of 1820, the Edinburgh monument of 1830, the Kilmarnock monument of 1877, and the Mauchline monument of 1898, plus two recent works, one at the Kilmarnock monument of 2008, and finally the Birthplace Monument in Alloway completion due in 2009. There are obviously a number of different architects involved, and the monuments are completed in a variety of different styles: neo-classical, choragic monument, Scottish Baronial and post-modern. Why, we might ask, such a heteronymous range of styles of architectural memorialising? Is it simply because of the pluralistic heritage bequeathed us by this poet full of contradictions? Or is it perhaps something to do with that and the different emphases given to the reading of his work by different historical periods? The question might also arise as to whether some monuments are 'good architecture' – but how would this affect the 'meaning' of that structure?

The earliest architectural monument of importance to Burns was built in Dumfries(Plate 4). It was felt by some of the townspeople that the plain stone slab on the poet's grave in St Michael's church was an inadequate memorial, and in 1813 an appeal was launched to build a mausoleum. (One of the subscribers was the Prince Regent, later George IV) After a public advertisement 50 designs were received and the plans of the well-known London architect T. F. Hunt were approved. Hunt was a learned architect who had written several publications, so it ought not to be surprising that the domed neo-classical mausoleum he designed with ionic columns bears a striking resemblance to Dante's tomb in Ravenna, designed some thirty odd years earlier by Camillo Morigia to hold the Italian poet's remains. The Burns building was completed in 1818 and the marble sculpture of the 'heaven-taught ploughman' in the field receiving an airborne mantle cast by Coila, the goddess of Kyle (and Burns's muse in the poem 'The Vision'), is by Peter Turnerelli, a London sculptor born in Belfast of Italian parents. Burns's body was exhumed on the 19th September 1815 (he died in 1796) to be placed in the mausoleum, and legend has it that that 'immortal' poet was indeed discovered by the workmen in an undecayed form, still with perfect hair and teeth intact. When she died in 1834, Burns's wife, and subsequently the remains of his three sons were also placed in the vault.

The first real public monument to Burns was the one completed in Alloway (Plate 5) in 1820 near the poet's birthplace cottage. Unlike Dumfries, it had no specific purpose apart from memorialising, and as such was referred to in the first edition of the *Burns Chronicle* as a 'cenotaph'. The subscription to build the monument was set up by Alexander Boswell, local aristocrat and son of the great biographer. Alexander Boswell was also the last man in Scotland to die in a duel, only two years after the completion of the monument.

The design competition was won by Thomas Hamilton. This was Hamilton's first successful public project and he subsequently went on to become one of the most celebrated of 19th century Edinburgh architects. Hamilton refused the £20 premium for his successful design – a form of Choragic monument – but Rob Close sees a 'shrewd move' on Hamilton's part rather than simple altruism, alleging that this gesture would ensure 'he would be regarded with favour when further commissions arose in the county.'[10] Hamilton did in fact go on to win the commission for Ayr Town Buildings in 1827.

The Choragic monument was a circular planned temple on a high square podium, which was first erected by Lysicrates around 330 BC to celebrate a victory on the theatre competitions. The *choregos* was the sponsor who paid for and supervised the training of the dance chorus. This type of monument became a standard commemoration of victory in the drama competitions in ancient Athens.

Hamilton had never been to Greece and probably knew the Choragic monument from its description and depiction in James Stuart and Nicholas Revett's *Antiquities of Athens*, published in 1762.[11] Hamilton's adaptation of the choragic model here however is a free and judicious one. He used the Corinthian order from the temple of Castor and Pollux (with nine columns symbolising the muses), and removed the wall from between the columns. Inside the base of the monument is a domed room with two Doric columns in antis providing a niche for a bust of the poet.

The idea to use such a circular temple for this monument may have been inspired in some part by St Bernard's Well (Plate 6) by the

Choragic Monument by Stuart/Revett

Water of Leith in Edinburgh. This latter is a circular planned Roman temple set in woodland, which Hamilton would have known to have been designed by the engineer and artist Alexander Nasmyth. Nasmyth had received the commission in 1788, only one year after he painted the famous portrait from life of his friend Robert Burns. But whatever the specific inspirations behind Hamilton's design, the fact is that the circular temple (like say, Hawksmoor's at Castle Howard (1729)) had come to be associated with poetry, and in the romantic sensibility with eternity. And Hamilton's decision to remove the walls between the columns, leaving the natural Ayrshire countryside to be viewed through the perfect eternity of a geometric framework, is a delicate encapsulation of the late 18th century symbiotic relationship between Enlightenment rationality and romantic sensibility.

Thus far then, the appropriateness of the symbolism to represent something of Burns, his Romantic/Enlightenment outlook and the intellectual tensions to the background in which he flourished, is evident. But when it comes to the massive rusticated base of the monument perhaps the symbolism is a bit crude not to say 'comical'. The three corners of this monument out of ancient Athenian and Roman influence, point solemnly, so we are told, to the three 'great' (Close) divisions of Ayrshire: Carrick, Kyle and Cunninghame.

The Edinburgh monument (Plate 7) to the poet was proposed as early as 1812, but it wasn't till around 1831 that it was completed, again to a design by Thomas Hamilton. Goodwillie comments (in 1911) that as the Duke of Atholl chaired the subscription launch in the Freemason's Tavern in London, that it was the 'classes' rather than the 'masses' that erected this monument. Once again Hamilton chose the choragic model, but in many ways both his styling of the monument and the context in which it is sited, make it a very different building from the one in Ayrshire.

Among the many distinct features of this Edinburgh monument are : the base of the monument is on a chamfered square of ashlar stone (with the 4 chamfered corners, we presume, pointing bluntly at no 'symbolic' quarter); the combination of the Lysicrates model with the Temple of the Sibyls at Tivoli, and the Corinthian order of 12 columns reproduced from the Olympaeon at Athens; and the cylindrical stone cella set back within the colonnade with its walls decorated by carved lyres. The cella rises up through and beyond the colonnade to form an attic, again decorated by carved wreaths, and the tripod above is supported by carved gryphons, rather than by dolphins as at Alloway.

It's interesting that despite the proximity and indeed clear panorama of Arthur's Seat and the Salisbury Crags from its site, this monument turns its solid stone back, as it were, on the rustic element and on the open views of nature that we see in the Alloway monument. The monument may thus be understood to be playing down the romantic sensibility of Burns and claiming him directly as an Enlightenment poet. In that sense it is a very urban Edinburgh monument, celebrating specifically Burns's time in the Enlightenment city 1787–88. Indeed the solid ashlar stone walls of the cylindrical cella not only make it an extended but integral part of Thomson's Royal High School composition across the road, but claims Burns for a tradition starting with Robert Adam's Hume Memorial (Plate 6) of 1777, a cylindrical stone tomb modelled on that of Theodoric at Ravenna, and sited only several hundred yards to west of the Burns Monument.

The 24 ft high domed ceiling in the interior, supported by a 14m diameter ring of Doric columns originally housed the statue by Flaxman (mentioned above, unfinished on his death in 1826). Good-willie cites an East Linton wag on this installation:

> Puir Burns amang the Calton Rocks
> Sits lanely in his pepper box.[12]

Since 1936 however, Flaxman's Burns is 'lanely' no more; the statue having been removed to the Scottish National Portrait Gallery with various reasons cited: dampness, soot from the gasworks, and insufficient room in the interior.

It is notable that both the Hamilton monuments lay emphasis on accurate and correct measurement (in the tradition of Stuart's *Antiquities*) and on classical geometry – that latter especially prominent in Edinburgh's platonic forms of cylinder, circle and square. Through this architectonic language of forms Hamilton clearly intends to assert something about the mood of Burns's work. There may be an allusion here to Burns's prominence as a Freemason, and the calculation and abstruse formulae associated with that society (it is indeed possible that Hamilton himself was a freemason). But beyond those occult allusions there is surely in this work a more straightforward acknowledgement and clear representation of the important role for geometry and mathematics in general for the Scottish Enlightenment (again as seen in the Hume Monument). Mathematics and the Euclid[13] especially had always played a central role in Scottish education, and Hume in his *Enquiry* uses geometry as an example of a type of truth discoverable merely by 'operation of thought'. Burns was himself trained in this tradition, and as Murdo MacDonald in his essay 'Envisioning Burns'[14] points out, Burns in an account of his earlier life (letter to Dr Moore 2nd August 1787) describes a love affair which distracted him from his study of trigonometry. MacDonald then goes on to quote Burns writing (under the pseudonym of legendary gipsy, Johnny Faa) to a correspondent Charles Sharpe in 1791, saying

> Whenever I feel inclined to rest myself on my way I take my seat under a hedge, laying my poetic wallet on the one side, and my fiddle case on the other, and placing my hat between my legs I can , by means of its brim, or rather its brims, go through the whole doctrine of conic sections.[15]

Of course, as MacDonald implies, Burns is not only being 'conical' here but also 'comical'. The fictitious personage of the letter writer tells us that he was 'a kind of fac-totum to a country clergyman, where [he] picked up a good many scraps of learning, particularly – in some branches of the mathematics'. But is not Burns's self-mocking and his parody of purely speculative learning in this letter precisely an acknowledgement of the bastardised educational conditions in which he himself was learned in that pure intellectual and mathematical tradition?[16] For Burns was of the tenant farmer class, he employed labourers and worked at the same tasks alongside them out of both inclination and necessity. He could not be said however, to belong simply and in a straightforward way to the 'labouring class' himself, and had a piecemeal education organised privately by his father not just or purely as an intellectual exercise, but as one intended to train him for the necessary calculations to be made by a tenant farmer (and even, if his luck had run another way, as a plantation manager in Jamaica).[17]

Although largely built to the same programme as the Alloway and Edinburgh monuments – namely to memorialise Burns and to house statues, relics and collections of his books – the Kilmarnock monument (Plate 8) completed in 1879 is a very different building in a very

different style. In the intervening 40 year period there had been
something of a revival of a Scottish 'national' spirit, with a strong
ethnic tinge, and a notion of pride at the heart of a successful Empire.
In architectural terms this development was manifested by a revived
interest in historical and vernacular styles, and in medieval and
indigenous baronial architecture by the influential 1850s publication
of Billings's *Baronial and Ecclesiastical Antiquities of Scotland*. To some
extent the 'antiquarian' spirit of this nationalism can be said to have
been provoked by the worldwide success of the historical novels and
poetry of Sir Walter Scott (– and his own 'antiquarian' style house he
had built at Abbotsford in the 1820s could be described if not as the
first neo-baronial architecture, then at least as proto-neo-baronial)
Indeed the Walter Scott monument (Edinburgh completed 1846,
Plate 9) sets the tone for a series of mid-19th century monuments
to national heroes. Although it is interesting to note that in 1838 on
seeing the plans for the Scott monument , the *Gentleman's Magazine*
describes its format, in terms of its marble statue by a well known
sculptor (John Steell) housed in a fine piece of architecture (George
Meikle Kemp), as following in the tradition of the design of the
Dumfries Burns Mausoleum.

    For some historians and writers, such as George Davie[18] and
Marinell Ash,[19] this mid-nineteenth century hero-worship in main-
stream Scotland was part of a 'failure of intellectual nerve'[20] amongst
the Scots. If the successful indigenous bourgeoisie running Scottish
industry in that period saw the Reformation, the Union and the 1843
Disruption as progressive forms of 'freedom' to help them engage in
building the great British Empire and do business globally, then the
'death of Scottish history' as Ash calls it, was likewise a freedom from
the political complexities of Scotland's past. The past, however, was
'inescapable', so '(i)nstead, monuments were raised to meaningless or
highly selective images of Scotland's past; images which did not
endanger the new-found freedom from the past of which many
imperial Scots were proud.'[21] Thus we have the presentation of
Scottish 'history' as embodied in a selective series of emotional and
sectarian heroes like Robert the Bruce, Mary Queen of Scots, John
Knox, William Wallace, Charles Edward Stuart, Robert Burns, and of
course, Walter Scott himself. MacDonald claims that this 'period of
intense advocacy of Scottish heroes'[22] found its logical culmination in
the establishment of the Scottish National Portrait Gallery in 1889.

If the building of the medieval gothic Scott monument preceded the real mid 19th century Scottish baronial revival in architecture however (as provoked by Billings), then perhaps the next most notable landmark in the series of national hero valhallas is the Wallace Monument (Plate 9) of 1869 in Stirling. The model had been refined further for patriotic use here with the design of a neo-Scottish Baronial stone tower (by J T Rochhead), decorated by a bronze statue of the warrior William Wallace, by D W Stevenson. (Interestingly Italian national hero, Garibaldi, was one of the subscribers to the fund to raise this monument.)

The Kilmarnock monument sits easily in this mid century tradition of the heroic monument, and like the Wallace monument is a neo-baronial building , housing a statue to the hero. The subscription to fund this building was started by a civic process by Provost Sturrock of Kilmarnock and a local architect Robert Ingram (who had served his apprenticeship with Charles Barry, and designed widely in the county, including the Dick Institute, and Kilmarnock Academy) was appointed to design. The Sicilian marble statue of the poet was carved by W G Stevenson, brother of the sculptor at the Wallace Monument.

The building is constructed of local red Ballochmyle sandstone and basically consists of a two story pavilion fronted by a split baroque staircase leading up to the 8ft statue housed in a roofed alcove, and the whole surmounted by a tower reaching to 80ft tall. The building sits atop the hill in Kay Park and gives a panoramic view over the town of Kilmarnock.

In many ways a typical example of the mid 19th century neo-baronial style, the monument draws on an eclectic mixture of struc-tural and decorative features; vernacular, gothic, renaissance and baroque, but perhaps the most striking is the fact, that again like the Wallace monument, it displays an extravagant concoction of both secular and ecclesiastical elements. The building may have crowsteps beside battlements and gunloops, but nonetheless the tower imme-diately calls to mind a church bell tower, and furthermore, in their 19th century advert for the monument, the *Burns Chronicle* promotes it as 'a shrine to the Immortal Bard'. Votaries to the Burns Cult are thus invited to pay their respects here, and the spirit of Burns is invoked by this conflation of warlike and ecclesiastical elements, and inducted into that abovementioned pantheon of heroes – alongside Scott and Wallace – by means of which the 'nation' assumes a factitious and mystical personality.

In the light of such an analysis it might be enlightening to question
to what extent the Kilmarnock monument's relatively secluded situa-
tion in a park in the centre of an industrial town can alone explain the
sustained attacks of vandalism it suffered, especially through the latter
half of the 20th century. From the mid 1950s there was a colourful, not
to say violent reaction to the monument which seems to increase in
intensity as the period of post-war austerity fades. MacKay[23] describes
how in 1958 the walls were covered in graffiti and someone had taken
red lipstick and smeared the words 'I love Tommy Steele' across a
portrait of Burns. (Can we assume they were confusing the sculptor
with the pop-star?) But the authorities themselves were not entirely
innocent of such *desecration*. For a number of years a coin – operated
mechanical monkey was kept in the museum. Perhaps the holy willies
of Burns's Mauchline days would have considered this hidden inner
beast an appropriate juxtaposition to the whiter-than-thou giant
sculpture out front. But did the custodians of the monument really
pose this beastly companion to the true poetic relics as comment on
the mean spirited crowd that surrounded and fed off the famous poet?
Of one such 'friend', his 'sly',[24] money-grubbing publisher William
Creech, Burns wrote,

> So travell'd monkeys their grimace improve
> Polish their grin – nay, sigh for ladies' love!

The mind boggles at the possible meanings of the monkey in the
museum, but the 'official explanation', says MacKay, for this alter-
native display of sculptural mimesis framed in architectural delight,
was that it encouraged children to visit. The attacks on the monument
continued nonetheless, and in 1987 the balustrades were toppled from
the front staircase by vandals. The district council then decided to
protect the monument by bricking up the ground floor windows and
erecting a galvanised iron security fence all around it. This may have
diminished the neo-baronial éclat of the monument but it is unlikely
that it was as a result of some type of architectural protest that on 19th
November 2004 the Fire Service were called to the monument in the
early hours of the morning. At 5.20 am part of the tower collapsed as a
result of intense heat from a fire, and the rest of the tower had to be
subsequently demolished. Two firemen were seriously injured and had
to attend hospital, but the Stevenson statue was not damaged. The

East Ayrshire council minutes from a meeting discussing the disaster assert that 'Strathclyde Police have now advised that three males aged 16, 18 and 22 have been apprehended . . .'

By the time the last major architectural monument to Burns of the 19th century was built at Mauchline (Plate 10), Scotland and Scottish society were much changed. On the one hand the major population centres of Scotland like Glasgow were now an industrial powerhouse at the centre of the largest Empire the world had ever seen, while on the other hand Scottish society was evolving to become an integral part of the modern British state. In 1874 the Education Act ensured that the responsibility for universal education was taken out of the hands of the Church and other bodies and put into control of government local and central: in 1886 a Secretary of State for Scotland was established in the cabinet at the head of British government: and in 1897 the Scottish Trades Union Council was formed. The growth in importance of such civic and political authorities entailed a corresponding decline in the relative importance of more traditional post-Union authorities in Scotland like the church and aristocracy. (see above, Goodwillie the Burnsian, sneering at the aristocrats in 1911)

Running concurrently to the above, there was also what Hobsbawm[25] has described as the 'Beginnings of Decline' in British industrial world leadership sometime in the years between 1860–90. If the original phase of industrialism (previous to 1860) had involved more basic and elemental forces and materials – coal, water, iron etc – whose manipulation leant itself to a crude iconography of sheer strength and brute heroism, then a next phase was more technocratic. America and Germany were rising to the forefront of world industry through investment in technological and scientific advances and through more refined methods like major university educational opportunities in engineering and so on. Not only was Britain failing at this new refined stage of the industrial revolution, but there was a gradually increasing awareness of the terrible human costs of 19th century laissez-faire economics and of the sudden and almost total industrialisation of the country. Thus the cult of personality and the hero, as promoted mid-century by Thomas Carlyle and others, became less prominent. There was accordingly an attempt to start to deal with the dreadful overcrowded and unsanitary conditions in which millions of workers in Britain had been forced to live, and in 1890, for example, the Housing of the Working classes Act had given local authorities power to build housing for working people, which subsequently became known as 'council houses'.

Much of this change in Scottish and British society is reflected in the building of the Burns Memorial in Mauchline in 1898. The main part of the building work here is, like the monument at Kilmarnock, a red sandstone neo-Baronial tower. Both monuments appear to be modelled on the original (now refurbished) 16th century Baronial gatehouse to the medieval monastery at Crossraguel just south of Maybole, Ayrshire. But if the Crossraguel tower inspires a gothicised and ecclesiastical extravaganza in Kilmarnock, then it is a more direct formal ancestor of the Burns monument in Mauchline. Unlike the Kilmarnock building, Mauchline is at once a more sober and bold work, with a predominance of heavy baroque and castellated decoration and scarcely any of the ecclesiastical features. It is, that is to say, definitely not a 'shrine'. The geometry of the square plan tower and cylindrical stairtower – directly borrowed from Crossraguel – give quite a severe aspect to its castellated features. It seems to stand at the sharp end of the site almost like a declaration of war. But war on what? Is it poverty? There is no statue of the poet framed or displayed by the architecture, and it is perhaps not insignificant that respect for the cult of personality and the hero has diminished to such an extent here that the design chosen was one by a relatively unknown architect, William Fraser, who after designing this monument 'does not', as the *Dictionary of Scottish Architects*[26] puts it, 'seem to have prospered'.

Prospering in another sense does seem, however, to have been a major concern in the design of this monument. For the monument includes as an integral part of the design twenty red sandstone Cottage Homes set out as the base and sides of the triangular site which has the tower at its apex. These cottages are described by Goodwillie as being provided 'rent free with money allowance to the deserving portion of the community . . .'. The annual publication of the *Burns Chronicle,* which began in 1891, followed closely and reported on the promotion, subscription and finally, opening ceremony of the Mauchline Burns Memorial and Cottage Homes. While it is true that the patrons for the project were 'classes', including such prominent nobles as the Duke of Hamilton, Marquis of Bute and Lord Rosebery, it is notable that the proposition published in Glasgow in 1895 stresses Burns's charitable nature, quoting such lines as 'The best o chiels are whiles in want', and

Crossraguel Monastery Gatehouse by Billings

emphasising that the estimated cost quoted (up to £3000) is 'exclusive of the cost of any statue of Burns'. Again in the *Burns Chronicle,* in its report on the speeches given after a grand procession to the laying of the foundation stone, we note that beside the references to Burns's freemasonry in the speeches, the stress is again and again on the role of Burns as 'Poet of Humanity', on the 'virtues of charity and brotherly love', and 'a monument which will aid in a practical and permanent way.'

Doubtless the image of Burns as the 'Poet of Humanity' becomes stronger and more influential with the rise of civic Scotland, and indeed welfare Britain in the 20th century. The Burns Federation becomes less dominated by aristocrats, more usually led by people of the 'middling sort', and in fact, throughout the century not one single architectural monument to Burns of importance is raised. It may fairly be said too, that the First World War had made a definitive change in the notion of monumental memorialisation. At its most simple level we can say that all monumental efforts in the decades immediately after the war were spent in commemorating those who took part and fell in that struggle, and there would necessarily have been few resources – not to mention little will – to create any other kind of monument. At another and more profound level, the mass slaughter and also ineptitude of some military leaders in the face of the new industrialised warfare, meant that the whole notion of heroism was changed drastically by the experience of that war.

Just so, modern poets and commentators – especially those of left-wing sympathies – had started to pour scorn on the perceived sentimental excesses of the 19th century Burnsians. MacDiarmid, for example, begins an essay in 1934 with 'The Burns cult must be killed stone dead . . .' before going on to decry 'the worthless, mouldy, pitiable relics that antiquarian Burnsians have accumulated at Mauchline, Dumfries and elsewhere.'[27] MacKay in his description of the Kilmarnock monument characterises the change in the typical mid 20th century Burnsian attitude to the monuments and remembering the poet:

In more recent times the Monument has been perceived as something of a white elephant. Not for nothing did the late and much lamented J F T 'Jock' Thomson, secretary of the Burns Federation (1968–81) hold very firm views against perpetuating the memory of Burns by monuments. He felt strongly that the best method of promoting the 'immortal memory' of the bard was by charitable works, of which the National Memorial Homes and the Jean Armour Homes at Mauchline were the best examples.[28]

And perhaps it would not be too far fetched to suggest that with the 20th century mood swing to a political climate of welfare, works, charity and humanity, then it is no coincidence that the least austere, indeed the most extravagantly heroic of the 19th century monuments, is the one, the only one, to have suffered a decades long sustained level of vandalism and aggression.

With the turning of the 21st century there is activity again in Burns monument construction after a hiatus of over 100 years. Two projects, one at Kilmarnock and the other in Alloway were planned to be complete in time for the 250th anniversary celebration of the poet's birth in 2009. It is perhaps no surprise given the debates over Burns's legacy in the 20th century, and the resurgent nationalist politics of the early 21st century that these projects have become embroiled in political controversy.

In Kilmarnock, East Ayrshire Council is building the 'Burns Monument Centre', which is a single story building faced in Balloch-myle stone encircling the remnants of the Kilmarnock monument of 1877. Basically these post-fire remnants consist of the front stairway, and the roofed alcove above containing the Stevenson statue. The low copper-roofed building which wraps the remnants into an internal courtyard is a council centre bringing together Archive and Registration Services and providing facilities for research into family history and also a civil ceremony suite where weddings and other functions can take place. The council describe it as a 'sustainable visitor attraction which will enhance and revitalise the Kay Park', and 'a unique facility for ancestral tourists'. The remains of the original monument are still a prominent – if drastically lower – landmark rising above the low copper roofs containing them.

It seems that the administrators, bureaucrats and civic authorities just can't wait to get wrapped around some authentic 'culture' here – albeit a burnt-out rump of the real and original thing. But what is surprising, or even most bizarre about this project however, is that it may well have once been a 'shrine', but no-one appears to have

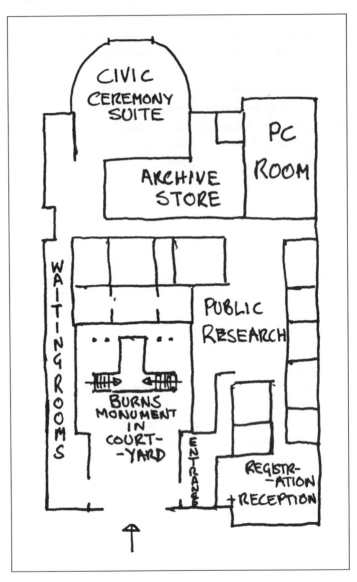

CIVIC
CEREMONY
SUITE

PC
ROOM

ARCHIVE
STORE

WAITING ROOMS

PUBLIC
RESEARCH

BURNS
MONUMENT
IN
COURT-
-YARD

ENTRANCE

REGISTR-
-ATION
+ RECEPTION

Sketch plan new Kilmarnock monument by J Rodger

considered the desirability of the symbolism of a nuptial ceremony taking place under the aegis of Scotland's notorious national Bard. What will it augur for the sealing of a til-death-do-us-part deal and the honest maintaining of its strictures that a man who continually operated on, and as R L Stevenson said, 'profited' from his 'random affections';[29] who fathered at least 12 children out of wedlock himself, and wrote the poem 'Welcome to a Bastart Wean' looks down on the ceremony with those eyes which 'literally glowed' (Scott)? What woman would risk it? What woman would want it?

The physical construction of this new facility was also somewhat controversial, with some local groups and voices being strongly of the opinion that the original monument burnt down in 2004 should be rebuilt as was. When the project was conceived and planned, East Ayrshire Council was run by a Labour administration. The largest opposition party at that time, the Scottish National Party, campaigned on the promise that if ever they came to power they would abandon this new build, and rebuild the original monument instead. The first turf on site was cut for the new project at a ceremony in March 20th 2007 with the declaration that the Stevenson statue would thus be 'protected for future generations'. At local elections in May 2007 the Scottish National Party took control of East Ayrshire Council from the Labour Party. They subsequently found that they were unable to live up to their promise to rebuild the original monument, and under their control the new Burns Monument Centre was completed in 2008.

A competition to design a new Robert Burns Birthplace Museum in Alloway was won by Edinburgh architects Simpson and Brown in 2007. Not only does their £6M design contain a new museum (with a main gallery, café, education room, stores and a retail space) but it is the intention of a holistic site design to tie together the various parts of Burns heritage that are scattered to the different ends of Alloway village. Thus we have at the north end of Alloway the Burns birth cottage, while at the extreme south is the Hamilton monument and the Brig O'Doon. The new museum then sets up a new axis cutting this N/S one by its situation due East of the Old Kirk of Alloway. The intention of the placement of the new museum, clad in part in dry stane walling, and with its rolling curved green sedum roofs (representing the 'pride of Coila's plains'?) is to tie together all these various

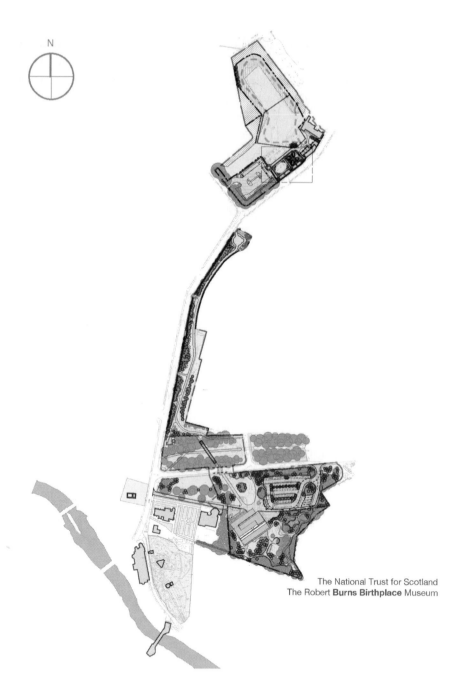

N

The National Trust for Scotland
The Robert **Burns Birthplace** Museum

Landscape/site plan, Alloway, thanks to Peter McGowan Associates Landscape Architects, Simpson & Brown Architects, and The National Trust for Scotland

elements listed across the landscape by design of various pathways, and to create a unified experience of Burns in Alloway. There are various promenades designed around these features delineating a narrative of Burns's life and his poetry: these are named 'Burns in love', 'Meet the Farmer Poet', 'A Walk with Burns', and so on.

Unfortunately the scheme suffered delays and was not finished in time for its originally scheduled opening to celebrate the Burns 250th anniversary in January 2009. On a more serious note, the national design advisory body Architecture + Design Scotland (A+DS) has made several criticisms of the new Museum building. They believe that the angled positioning of the building does not orientate to the advantage of the existing built environment at the site, and creates views which are 'forced and minimal'. And while the architects may claim that the design of the building and its surroundings are 'content led', and hence 'designed from the inside out', A+DS maintained the architectural ambition to be expected of an important international museum is thus compromised: it leaves in particular a 'blank face' to the SW garden aspect, and an inflexible interior which 'could very quickly become redundant'.[30]

Clearly then, no one single architectural monument manages to incorporate in a rigorously full and harmonious manner all the essential qualities of Burn's poetry in the way that Terragni aimed for with his monument to Dante. Burns may well have demonstrated a range of interests and concerns in his work comparable to those of Dante, but he does not bring them to bear in a single unified poetic work.

Equally, as Carruthers says,

> Despite the best efforts of critics to harmonize Burns's attitudes into a single cogent and coherent outlook however, it is perhaps time to recognise that the man and his work do, indeed, represent contradictions that remain irresolvable.[31]

That's not to say that there are not contradictions inherent in Dante's work, or indeed that architecture is unable to represent the idea of 'contradiction'. But nor have Scottish architects yet had the dubious advantage of a monomaniac fascist regime for a client which would probably provide for a considerable focussing of the mind.

Nonetheless, if the pluralistic heritage of Burns as a poet, and the scattered and multiform evidences of his poetic significance, are the telling factors here, then could we not argue equally that a similarly rigorous architectonic representation as we see in Terragni's one plan for one building in one city, the Danteum in Rome in 1938, is delineated across a range of times and spaces in the various Burns Monuments. Different aspects of Burns's poetic significance have been given differing emphases appropriate to differing locations and different historical periods. So if in one place, Edinburgh, a formal exposition in sandstone of relationships between platonic solids represents a mood of his poetry; then in another place, Kilmarnock, the mystic poet of the 'nation' looks down on that nation from his housing in a 'shrine'; and in the latest place in Alloway, the ordering of a promenade through various spaces and objects is inspired and controlled by the narrative content of one specific poem, Tam o' Shanter. On the other hand if we read these monuments as a representation of historic sensibility, and as facilities for the reader's induction into a meaningful relationship with the poet, we find in 1820 + 30 temples for the Burnsian as philosopher of the ideal, and contemplator of nature; in 1877 a 'shrine' for the Burnsian as votary of the national Burns cult; in 1898, a tower of strength for the Burnsian as social activist; in 2008 a suite of offices for the Burnsian as 'ancestral tourist' to the dead history of Scotland, or alternatively, as adventurer in risqué betrothal; and finally, in 2009 a gallery, café and shop for the Burnsian as consumer of Burns.

NOTES

[1] Gerard Carruthers, *Robert Burns* (Northcote House, 2006).

[2] Goodwillie, *The World's Memorials of Robert Burns* (Waverley Publishing, 1911).

[3] James A MacKay, 'The World Memorials to Robert Burns', in *Burns Chronicle*, 1989.

[4] Fred Licht, The Vittoriale degli Italiani, in *Journal of the Society of Architectural Historians*, vol. 41, no. 4, p. 318.

[5] Argan, 'Relazione', *Architettura* 163, 7. cited in Schumacher, *The Danteum* (Princeton Architectural Press, 1985).

[6] Croce, *La Poesia di Dante*, Laterza 1921, cited in Schumacher.

[7] Cited in Shumacher from Freccero, *Dante, a Collection*, 20.

[8] Terragni, *Relazione sul Danteum*.

[9] Dante Alighieri, *Vita Nuova e Rime*, Mondadori, 1985 (see *Capitolo* 25, *Vita Nuova*)

[10] Rob Close, *Ayrshire and Arran* (Rutland Press, 1993).

[11] In this highly influential book Stuart compared modern Edinburgh to Athens, and this is allegedly one source in initiating the tradition of referring to the 'Athens of the North'.

[12] In Goodwillie.

[13] In a letter to the Rev. Archibald Allison (14/2/1791) Burns says of Archibald's book '. . . except Euclid's *Elements of Geometry*, which I made a shift to unravel by my father's fireside, in the winter evening of the first season I held the plough, I never read a book which gave me such a quantum of information, and added so much to my stock of ideas, as your . . .' In G. Ross Roy and J. DeLancey Ferguson (eds), *The Letters of Robert Burns* (Oxford, 1985).

[14] Murdo MacDonald, Envisioning Burns, in Cullen and Morrison (eds), *A Shared Legacy: Essays on Irish and Scottish Art and Visual Culture* (Ashgate Publishing Ltd, 2005).

[15] G. Ross Roy and J. DeLancey Ferguson.

[16] In a letter to 'Clarinda' (18/2/1788)a similar parody of learned speculation is made: Burns opens the love letter with the sentence 'The attraction of love, I find, is in an inverse proportion to the attraction of the Newtonian philosophy.' In G. Ross Roy and J. DeLancey Ferguson.

[17] MacKay also claims that the study of mathematics was 'a prerequisite of his Excise calling' in James A. MacKay, *Robert Burns, the Complete Poetical Works* (Alloway Publishing, 1993).

[18] G. E. Davie, *The Democratic Intellect* (Edinburgh, 1961).

[19] Marinell Ash, *The Strange Death of Scottish History* (Ramsay Head Press, 1989).

[20] Davie.

[21] Ash.

[22] Murdo MacDonald, *Scottish Art* (Thames & Hudson, 2000).

[23] James A. MacKay, *Kilmarnock* (Alloway Publishing, 1992).

[24] Carruthers.

[25] E. J. Hobsbawm, *Industry and Empire* (Penguin, 1969).

[26] www.codexgeo.co.uk/dsa.

[27] Hugh MacDiarmid, The Burns Cult, in *At the Sign of the Thistle*, 1934, reproduced in *Hugh MacDiarmid Selected Prose* (Carcanet 1992).

[28] MacKay.

[29] R. L. Stevenson, Some Aspects of Robert Burns, in *Familiar Studies of Men and Books* (Nelson & Sons).

[30] Architecture + Design Scotland Report, 23rd April 2007, Planning Ref.: 07/0004/FUL.

[31] Carruthers.

MISSING REELS

An Investigation into Robert Burns's Absence from Cinema in the Second Half of the Twentieth Century

ALISTAIR BRAIDWOOD

What image is foremost when you think of Robert Burns? For most people it is highly likely to be the Alexander Nasmyth 1787 portrait (Plate 1) or at least an approximation of it (if you want an example of its prominence then go to Google Image and search 'robert burns portrait'). This single image is interesting as it has endured as well as Burns poetry has, arguably better. A picture, after all, can paint a thousand words; the problem is when it obscures them. It is a romantic depiction, a kiss curled Burns with a smile at the edge of his lips, which has come not only to symbolise the poet, but his poetry as well. Is it surprising that there has been no other image that has come close to rivalling it? Considering the continuing popularity of the man and his work I find it odd that this is the case. There have been performers who have personified Burns, and more of them later, but it is curious to me that there has been no big screen depiction that has captured the imagination. No screen performance we can point to and say, 'that was the definitive Burns'. Robert Burns is the most famous Scottish Literary name, both at home and abroad. His only real rivals to this title would be Sir Walter Scott and Robert Louis Stevenson. If we are to consider current literary figures then perhaps only JK Rowling or, at a push, Irvine Welsh, could come close to his fame, although I harbour doubts that we will be celebrating their life and work in 250 years time. All of these writers have had their names and works advanced by the relationship between their literature and cinema. But we cannot say this about Burns, at least in the last sixty years. This was the period when film cemented its place as the most successful global art form, certainly in terms of profile and capital.

Cinema is an unashamedly popular and populist art form. It sets out to entertain an audience, often attempting to inform as it does so, (admittedly on a sliding scale of intent and success). It is often at its finest when dealing with literary adaptations or subjects. Robert Burns, as I have suggested, is a popular and populist figure, yet his life and work have been absent from multiplexes and art house cinemas alike. We have had big screen depictions of Scott's novels; *Ivanhoe* and *Rob Roy* to name but two. There have been numerous film versions of Stevenson's writing, and then there is the phenomenal success of the cinematic Rowling or Welsh. (Indeed it can be argued that Welsh's fame in particular owes more to the film versions of his work than to his writing). Where is Robert Burns? Allowing for the fact that the others are novelists while Burns is a poet, (and I don't dismiss the importance of this fact) it seems strange to me that such a famous, well loved figure, whose life is ripe for film adaptation, would be completely absent from such a list for over three generations. Surely in purely monetary terms films about or related to Burns would make some sense, so why had none made it onto screen? These were the questions that I had in the back of my mind when I began compiling a filmography of Robert Burns related material.

It is here that I should confess that my credentials in embarking on such an endeavour arise from my interest in film, and Scottish film in particular. I am not a Burns scholar, my interaction with his life and work up to the point I started to compile the filmography was little more than that of the average person who came through the Glasgow comprehensive school system in the early 1980's; some poetry, (the big hits, with a splash of iconography to accompany it), once a year. This was a time when Scottish literature was notable by its absence in the Scottish School's curriculum, so any Scot being taught was unusual in itself. What was even more unusual was the fact that the poetry was secondary to the symbolism that accompanied it. It was more drama than literature. This focus on the symbolic nature of Burns Night is at the crux of many attitudes to Burns across the cultural board. People are always influenced by the way art is presented to them. Context is vital to understanding, and it is the presentation of Burns that has, for many of us, defined him. It was the iconography and the accompanying pomp and ceremony that were to the fore, not the poetry. It seems that it was more important to have the Burns experience than to actually deal with his work. Something for the nation to view, but not actually engage.

The other place to find Burns was on television, and the overriding focus on the iconography that I experienced in the classroom was repeated on the small screen. Televised Burns Night memories are of programmes featuring men (always men) in kilts toasting Haggis and drinking whisky in what appeared to be private clubs, reading the poems and singing the songs with such seriousness that any idea such occasions could actually be fun were ludicrous. The viewing public weren't invited to such parties, although we were allowed to keek in the windows. Here Burns was portrayed as the laureate for twentieth-century Tartanry, and it was something that the majority of the country couldn't relate to. As a result we turned away, and a long overdue rethink on how Burns was televisually presented occurred, with some genuinely innovative programming screened in the late 1980's continuing through to the present day.

So it is with this background that I came to approach my work on Burns, and as I began to research material one thing struck me more than anything else. In 1947 *Comin' Thro the Rye* was released into picture houses. This was the eighth Burns related film since Universal Studios released the silent feature *Tam o' Shanter* in 1915. Eight films in thirty-two years. In 2004 *Red Rose* was released, although you may have missed it, and it is a film I will return to later. It was, however, the first Burns related feature length film since *Comin' Thro the Rye*. The more I considered this timeline the stranger I found the situation. Cinema is the dominant art form of the twentieth century, and as such film companies are always looking for new stories to tell, or old ones to retell, yet Burns is absent. What happened after 1947 to keep him off the world's screens until the twenty first century? Art and culture always effect, and are affected by, ideas and fashions of their time. What was there in post-war cultural ideology in Scotland that had banished Burns to the cultural wasteland? The answer to this can be exemplified, if hardly crystallized, by the attitude to Burns of another Scottish literary giant; Hugh MacDiarmid.

As Alan Riach writes of MacDiarmid; 'His attacks on the Burns cult became notorious; his attacks on Burns's legacy to Scottish literature became infamous; and his attacks on Burns himself became scandalous.'[1] One of MacDiarmid's most famous proclamations was 'Not

Burns – Dunbar!' but it is too simplistic to read this as an attack on Burns, or a call to dismiss him. As usual with MacDiarmid the truth is more complex than it first appears. MacDiarmid himself explains:

> My attitude to Burns in particular has been sorely misunderstood, because of the necessity I have been under in attacking the *bourgeois* Burns Cult, a monstrous misappropriation of Burns, whitewashed and respectablized and made, like statistics, to prove anything and everything except the inadmissible things for which he essentially stood.[2]

This attitude seems to predate and confirm my own feelings formed in the 1980's, and confirms my suspicions that many of those who claimed to love Burns, to represent him, were more interested in what they believed he stood for, what he could do for them, rather than in the poetry itself. The problem with any idol is that the followers are often intransigent in their views. Theirs is the one true way. It seems that MacDiarmid knew he was facing a losing battle by engaging in discussion with such fundamentalism, so chose to attack it instead. Academic battles raged over the coming decades as it seemed that the intellectual couldn't, and had little wish to, accommodate the popular. There was a justified belief that the '*bourgeois* Burns Cult' that MacDiarmid attacked had no literary worth in the slightest, and their championing of Burns resulted in a 'dumming down' of his work. A casualty of this war was the poetry and song, sidelined as cultural arbiters sought to claim and disclaim Burns and what they believed he stood for, sometimes in the same breath. It was a struggle for intellectual copyright, the right to be able to use Burns image to promote their own particular cause. But this situation itself doesn't fully explain why Burns was absent from the big screen. He was still popularly seen as a romantic figure, and regularly made appearances on both BBC Scotland and STV. Despite intellectual opposition, Burns was very much in the public eye at this time, and if there was to be a big screen Burns it seems that only one man could have made it.

There has been a screen version of Burns that many people will remember; a man who came to be the definitive representation of Burns during the iconoclastic years of the late twentieth century. That man is John Cairney. While there was no cinematic version of Burns to capture our imagination, Cairney's performance and personality were strong enough to convince the viewing public that here indeed stood

Robert Burns. As Donny O'Rourke wrote in the 1994 collection of essays *Burns Now*:

> Many Scots believe John Cairney to be Robert Burns . . . *There Was a Man* (a solo play screened in 1965) established Cairney as Rabbie's representative here on Earth, eradicating the Nasmith and other portraits with a single toss of his pony-tailed head.[3]

John Cairney's name looms large in the story of Burns on screen. Dr Cairney himself told me that he had been approached by Screen Gems and World Pictures in the 1960's to make Burns films with him writing, producing and also starring in the lead role. His own hunch why these didn't happen were; financial problems, a recurring theme in this particular story, and a worry, I assume from the film studios, that a poet could not be seen as a heroic figure. He also wondered if they were unsure about using Scots dialect. This may seem an odd concern these days, but we should consider that at the time, outside of Scotland, broad Scottish accents were rarely heard, especially on the big screen. It is interesting to note his thoughts on how such a film could be made today. Cairney reckons we need an unknown as Burns, and a group of Scots to make it, but more importantly there needs to be a 'vibrant, self-confident Scottish Film Industry with money to spend'.[4] What is interesting about such assertions is that there has been a recent film that fits the first two of Cairney's criteria, and whose director has a lot to say about the third.

Robbie Moffat is the director of *Red Rose* (Plate 11), the aforementioned 2004 film made by Palm Tree Productions, and the perfect man to ask about how to solve a problem like Rabbie.[5] Starring relative unknown Michael Rodgers as Robert Burns, and written and produced by Mairi Sutherland, *Red Rose* portrays Burns as a political figure, a proto-socialist who is denounced by the authorities as a Republican sympathiser and persecuted as a result. All those involved with the film were aware of the Burns story, and the history of the iconography that accompanies it. Indeed, apropos of nothing, Moffat offered the suggestion that if there was to have been a film made in the second half of the twentieth century about Burns then John Cairney would have had to be involved, showing not only the strength of Cairney's presence, but also that Moffat is aware of what has come before. The

Portrait of Burns by Alexander Nasmyth By permission of the National Gallery of Scotland.

Etching of unidentified subject by John Kay By permission of the Royal Scottish Academy.

Etching of unidentified subject by John Kay By permission of the Royal Scottish Academy.

Dumfries Monument by Pat Donald

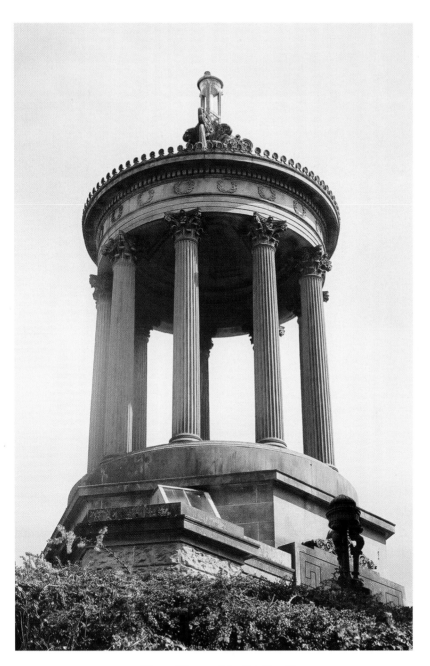

Alloway Monument by Pat Donald

*St Bernard's Well and
Hume Monument
by J Rodger*

Edinburgh Monument by J Rodger

Kilmarnock Monument. Images by Permission of East Ayrshire Council

Scott and Wallace Monument
by J Rodger and Morag Ramsay

Mauchline Monument by Pat Donald

Red Rose: *Michael Rodgers as Burns plus action still.*
By permission of Robbie Moffat

Burns Live *DVD, Christopher Tait. By permission of Christopher Tait.*

Dear bought Bess manuscript. By permission of the National Library of Scotland.

Holy Willie's Prayer

Argument

Holy Willie was a rather oldish bachelor Elder, in the parish of Mauchline, & much & justly famed for that polemical chattering which ends in tippling Orthodoxy, & for that spiritualized bawdry which refines to Liquorish Devotion.— In a Sessional process with a gentleman in Mauchline, a Mr Gavin Hamilton, Holy Willie & his priest, father Auld, after full hearing in the Presbytery of Ayr, came off but second best; owing partly to the oratorical powers of Mr Robt Aiken, Mr Hamilton's Counsel; but chiefly to Mr Hamilton's being one of the most irreproachable & truly respectable characters in the country.— On losing his Process, the Muse overheard him at his devotions as follows—

O Thou that in the heavens does dwell!
Wha, as it pleases best thysel,
Sends ane to heaven & ten to h—ll,
A' for thy glory!
And no for ony gude or ill
They've done before thee.—

22

I bless & praise thy matchless might,
When thousands thou hast left in night,
That I am here before thy sight,
For gifts & grace,
A burning & a shining light
To a' this place.—

What was I, or my generation,
That I should get such exaltation?
I, wha deserv'd most just damnation,
For broken laws
Sax thousand years ere my creation,
Thro' Adam's cause.—

When from my mother's womb I fell,
Thou might hae plunged me deep in hell,
To gnash my gooms, & weep, & wail,
In burning lakes,
Whare damned devils roar & yell,
Chain'd to their stakes.—

Yet I am here, a chosen sample,
To shew thy grace is great & ample:
I'm here, a pillar o' thy temple
Strong as a rock,
A guide, a ruler & example
To a' thy flock.—

Holy Willie's Prayer manuscript. By permission of the National Library of Scotland.

Lass o Ballochmyle portrait by Robert Hope.

'TWAS EVEN;—OR, THE LASS OF BALLOCHMYLE.

WRITTEN

BY BURNS.

AIR—JOHNY'S GREY BREEKS.

'Twas even—the dewy fields were green,
 On every blade the pearls hung;
The zephyr wanton'd round the bean,
 And bore its fragrant sweets along;
In ev'ry glen the mavis sang,
 All nature list'ning seem'd the while,
Except where green-wood echoes rang
 Among the braes o' Ballochmyle.

With careless step I onward stray'd,
 My heart rejoic'd in nature's joy,
When musing in a lonely glade,
 A maiden fair I chanc'd to spy;
Her look was like the morning's eye,
 Her air like nature's vernal smile;
The lily's hue and rose's dye
 Bespoke the lass o' Ballochmyle *.

Fair is the morn in flow'ry May,
 And sweet is night in autumn mild,
When roving through the garden gay,
 Or wand'ring in the lonely wild:

But woman, nature's darling child!
 There all her charms she does compile;
Even there her other works are foil'd
 By the bonny lass o' Ballochmyle.

O had she been a country maid,
 And I the happy country swain,
Tho' shelter'd in the lowest shed
 That ever rose on Scotland's plain!
Thro' weary winter's wind and rain
 With joy, with rapture, I would toil;
And nightly to my bosom strain
 The bonny lass o' Ballochmyle.

Then pride might climb the slipp'ry steep,
 Where fame and honours lofty shine;
And thirst of gold might tempt the deep,
 Or downward seek the Indian mine;
Give me the cot below the pine,
 To tend the flocks or till the soil,
And ev'ry day has joys divine
 With the bonny lass o' Ballochmyle.

* *Variation.* Perfection whisper'd, passing by,
  Behold the lass o' Ballochmyle!

'Twas Ev'n' manuscript, Thomson's version.

script was seven years in the writing as the production team wanted to make sure they knew as much about Burns as they possibly could before the cameras began rolling. It seems that authenticity was important to the making of *Red Rose*, and that included location. Moffat is keen to emphasise that those working at the coal face of the Burns industry, the people running the museums and collections and maintaining the physical Burns legacy, were extremely helpful in terms of allowing filming at key locations such as Tarbolton, Alloway, Ellisland Farm and the Dumfries museum amongst others. There were no precious attitudes to the Burns story, and those involved became consultants on the project, available to answer specific questions when problems or queries arose.

The major problems arose in trying to fund the film, and Moffat is scathing of Scottish Screen in particular, whom he accuses of running a closed shop, dealing only with those they already knew, and holding grudges from previous dealings with Palm Tree. He blames a campaign of negative press, which he believes was directed towards the film, for bias against it before it had even been released. One example of this was the film being dropped from that year's Glasgow Film Festival for reasons never fully explained. Moffat admits that this is as likely to have down to attitudes to Palm Tree Productions rather than any problem with the topic of Burns, but he does admit that in choosing to overtly politicise Burns he risked alienating many for whom the poet is a romantic figure and national icon and who don't want this ideal complicated with claims of Republican sympathies or apparent compulsive womanising, another aspect of the Burns legend explicitly depicted in the film.

Red Rose had a small release, almost no publicity, and disappeared from screens as quickly as it arrived with a mixed and muted reception. I first became aware of its existence when it was given away as a free DVD with *The Sun* newspaper to mark Burns Night. The film is obviously low budget; with the best known name involved being Isla St Clair, once a regular on prime-time Saturday Night TV as side-kick to Larry Grayson on the Generation game. Many may not know, but Isla is also a beautiful singer and her renditions of some of Burns most well known songs are highlights in the film. But for all its difficulties with funding and distribution at least *Red Rose* made it onto screens, and for that we should be both astonished and grateful, because it proves it can be done. Robbie Moffat, a man who was under no illusions about how his film would do in the box office, or how it would be received, still believes that other Burns films can be made despite the monetary problems, if the team is right, the script is right and the will is there. Other, higher profile, attempts, with corporate backing and Hollywood names attached, seem stuck in development hell, and rumours of money squandered accompany most enquiries into other prospective ventures.

The enduring interest in Robert Burns is a rare phenomenon, always with us despite fluctuations, and it seems that there is a spike in that interest after the turn of the 21st century. Perhaps it can be attributed to the dawning of a devolved Scotland, with a new found cultural and political confidence, perhaps it was the approach of a major anniversary, or perhaps it was just time. Whatever the reasons, there is hard evidence that the interest is there. As well as at least two other films in preproduction as this is written, there is renewed interest in Burns Night TV shows, and there is the annual 'Burn's an a' that' Festival which is now in it's seventh year and has featured as diverse performers as Eddi Reader, Pete Doherty and Patti Smith. On stage Christopher Tait's 'Live' show travels the world, where he performs Burns poetry and gives insight into the life of the man through various monologues. The successor to John Cairney's legacy as much as to Burns, Tait has performed all over the world, and his Live DVD (Plate 12) is one of the few examples of Burns work to be found performed in a modern format.

If Robert Burns is to move into the new century with relevance he must be looked at anew, be reconfigured while always remembering what went before. In the twentieth century he became another Scottish stereotype, one to be placed by many alongside tartan, haggis, whisky, heather and so on; imagery that had come not so much to define Scotland, but overshadow it. It can even be argued that he became the embodiment of all of these aspects of Scots mythology, an iconic representation. While such a list of stereotypes became shorthand for identifying Scotland, they were recognised as limiting and constraining. But it is a mistake to deny that those aspects of Scotland exist. They are powerful images that can be re-appropriated. For such imagery is as much part of the national language as any dialect or spoken word and must be included as part of any cultural conversation. It seems inconceivable that there will not be a big screen version of Burns in the coming years that will reflect such ideas and renewed interest. Inconceivable, but from far certain.

And perhaps we should not be surprised that this apparently perfect subject for cinematic adaptation has been absent from our screens for so long. Accessible to all, yet portrayed as the property of clubs and cliques; famed world-wide, his story is still only known to the few; out of favour and fashion with some, but with continuing popularity elsewhere. This story has many more twists and turns to take and the reasons for Burns cinematic absence in the late twentieth century are as complex as the man himself.

NOTES

[1] Alan Riach, *MacDiarmid's Burns, Robert Burns and Cultural Authority*, Robert Crawford (ed.) (Edinburgh University Press, 1997), p. 204.

[2] Hugh MacDiarmid, *Lucky Poet: A Self-Study in Literature and Political Ideas, being the Autobiography of Hugh MacDiarmid* (Methuen & Co. Ltd, 1943), p. 191

[3] Donny O'Rourke, *Supperman: Televising Burns, Burns Now*, Kenneth Simpson (ed.) (Canongate Academic 1994), p. 210.

[4] Dr John Cairney, e-mail correspondence with A. Braidwood.

[5] Interview with Robbie Moffat, Palm Tree Productions, 20/8/08

BURNS AND ENLIGHTENMENT

☙

THE VERNACULAR ENLIGHTENMENT

✧

KEN SIMPSON

'Vernacular' and 'enlightenment': in the same breath? How could these possibly be linked?

The first step in an attempt at an answer involved a visit to the dictionary. 'To enlighten': 'to shed light on/ give light to/ impart knowledge of/to'.

Of what does Scottish vernacular poetry of the eighteenth century give knowledge? – Scotland and Scottish culture. To whom? – Not just to their English partners in union, but also to the Scots themselves. 'O wad some Pow'r the giftie gie us/To see oursels as others see us' wrote Burns, evoking Adam Smith. But the crucial preliminary was that Scots see themselves. National self-identification in the early decades of the eighteenth century was a necessary prelude to the Scottish philosophers' subsequent investigation of personal identity.

'Now there's ane end of ane old song': Lord Seafield's words as Chancellor when, according to Lockhart of Carnwath, he signed before the Scottish Parliament the exemplification of the Act of Union. But the song endured (albeit sometimes in a more polite version). Paradoxically, when Scots became Britons they became more aware of what it was to be a Scot. Political union presented a threat to cultural identity; hence the need to preserve or revitalize the modes, forms, and language of the native tradition. There followed three decades of collecting and innovating, practices continued later in the century by Burns, Scott, and Hogg.

In the vanguard was James Watson who, as the prospect of political union loomed, initiated the work of conservation with his *Choice Collection of Comic and Serious Scots Poems*, vol.1 (1706). Watson shows a keen sense of the significance of the collection (both the activity and the outcome): he alludes to 'the frequency of Publishing Collections of Miscellaneous Poems in our Neighbouring Kingdoms and States' and notes that this is 'the first of its nature which has been published in our own Native Scots Dialect' . He is doing the nation a service, and he knows it.

Watson is determined to establish textual authority: 'as a Test of the Undertaker's Care to please his reader as much as he can, this first Essay is chiefly composed of such Poems as have been formerly printed most Uncorrectly, in all respects, but are now copied from the most correct Manuscripts that could be procured of them'. This represents a key stage in the transition from oral to written culture: collecting and publishing establishes the definitive text, a process that would enrage traditionalists such as James Hogg's mother.

The range of Scottish voices is remarkable. Watson's achievement was to present the nation's literary culture in a way that was socially and linguistically inclusive. William Drummond is represented by both 'Polemo-Middinia' and 'Forth Feasting'; 'The Flyting betwixt Polwart and Montgomery' and Hamilton of Gilbertfield's 'The Last Dying Words of Bonny Heck, A Famous Grey-Hound in the Shire of Fife' cohabit with 'The Discription of the Queens Majesties Maist Honorable Entry into the Toun of Edinburgh' by John Burel and 'Epithalamium Upon the Marriage of Mary Queen of Scots, to the Dauphin of France . . . Done from the Latin of Buchanan'. Watson has identified, preserved, and showcased Scotland's finest in all its diversity.

With access to the sixteenth-century Bannatyne Manuscript, Allan Ramsay continued the process of conservation with *The Ever Green* (1724). But here, alongside stalwarts like 'Christ's Kirk on the Grene', 'The Thistle and the Rose', and 'Auld Kyndnes quite foryet', we find imitations of the work of the Makars by Ramsay (e.g. 'The Vision') and his contemporaries. In the same year Ramsay produced *The Tea-Table Miscellany* which ran through 14 editions. Again the range is remarkable in terms of both language and subject-matter: contents include 'Come, Florinda, lovely charmer'; 'Gi'e me a lass with a lump of land'; 'How happy is the rural clown'; 'Jocky fou, Jenny fain'; 'Lassie, lend me your braw hemp heckle'. Ramsay's commentary is as much a medley as the contents. 'What further adds to the esteem we have for them, is their antiquity, and their being universally known', he asserts, then adds, 'my being well assured how acceptable new words to known tunes would prove, engaged me to the making verses for above sixty of them . . . about thirty more were done by some ingenious young gentlemen, who were so well pleased with my undertakings that they generously lent me their assistance'. There is an ambivalence in Ramsay's attitude: he will innovate and sanction innovation, but at the same time, like Watson, he wishes to authorise: 'The rest are such old verses as have been done time out of mind, and only wanted to be cleared from the dross of blundering transcribers and printers, such as 'The gaberlunzie Man', 'Muirland Willie' & c., that claim their place in our collection for their merry images of the low character'. Yet he also claims, 'I have kept out all smut and ribaldry, that the modest voice and ear of the fair singer might meet with no affront'. In *The Paradox of Scottish Culture* David Daiches emphasised the cultural dichotomy in eighteenth-century Scotland. A qualification was sounded by Thomas Crawford in *Society and the Lyric* with his suggestion that there was cultural interplay: the street/bothy song would find its way to the tea-table if it was any good. Yet there are here in Ramsay early indications of a civilising process that would lead to the situation later in the century where the custodians of naive art were 'people of taste'. By the time of Burns and George Thomson Scottish literary culture is hosting uneasy bedfellows: in particular, the zealous Scottish antiquarianism and the vanguard Scottish role in the vogue of primitivism do not always sit happily with the modernising and civilising impetus of Scottish Enlightenment thought.

In his Dedication to *The Tea-Table Miscellany* Ramsay exhorts 'British Lasses' to sing while the tea is brewing, then at the start of his Preface he says the songs are so infectious we're likely to dance to them. Ramsay upholds his right, as partner, to address a British audience, to contribute to the new British cultural identity. His Scottish contribution is distinctive. 'Elegy on Patie Birnie' ends,

> Sae I've lamented Patie's end,
> But least your Grief o'er far extend,
> Come dight your Cheeks, ye'r Brows unbend,
>   And lift ye'r Head,
> For to a' Britain be it kend
>   He is not deid.

For Ramsay, Scots have equal linguistic, as well as political, rights. In 'Richy and Sandy, A Pastoral on the Death of Joseph Addison', Sandy says of Addison, 'His Fame shall last; last shall his Sang of Weirs/ While British Bairns brag of their bauld Forbears'. For Ramsay, 'British bairns' is no oxymoron; he writes as a Scot, in Britain, to Britain. In the Preface to his *Poems* (1721) he refers to 'the Scots and English tongue' (singular) and to 'beautiful thoughts dress'd in British'; and he sees the linguistic range available to the Scot as a positive advantage:

> . . . of [English] . . . we are Masters, by being taught it in our Schools, and daily reading it; which being added to all our own native Words of eminent Significancy, makes our Tongue by far the completest.

Ramsay and his contemporaries established the momentum that would lead to Edinburgh's being acclaimed the Athens of the North by mid-century. Ramsay exudes sociability. Some of his activities were modelled on those of the English Augustans, with whom he corresponded: founding the Academy of St. Luke's; opening a theatre; helping to form the Easy Club (12 May 1712); and setting up a lending library in his shop in the Luckenbooths. The wig-maker who doubled as poet-librarian congratulates himself in 'An Epistle to James Arbuckle' (Jan. 1719): 'I theck [thatch] the out, and line the inside/ Of mony a douce and witty pash [head]'.

Soon the Scottish stamp was put upon these cultural establishments. Within eighteen months of its founding, the members of the Easy Club renounce their English pseudonyms and 'resolve to have Scots patrons'. No longer Isaac Bickerstaff, from Steele's *Tatler*, Ramsay becomes Gavin Douglas. This alias is significant. In identifying himself with the Bishop of Dunkeld who translated Virgil's *Aeneid* into Scots (1513) Ramsay is aligning himself with a master innovator, for Douglas had added prologues to each book of Virgil's epic. It is noteworthy that Ramsay, Fergusson, and Burns (e.g. in the epigraph to 'Tam o' Shanter') are intent on locating themselves within a Scottish tradition; in so doing they both celebrate their predecessors' achievements and legitimise their own.

Ramsay had little knowledge of Latin but, reliant on French cribs and familiar with English translations, he produced vernacular Scots versions of Horace's *Odes*. Ramsay's 'To the Phiz An Ode', inspired by Horace, *Odes* I, ix, contrasts favorably with English translations (e.g. by Edward Sherburne (1651); John Dryden (1685)). Ramsay's version is characterised by specificity and an essential humanity. This is the real Edinburgh – for Soracte, substitute the Pentlands; it's midwinter, so golf-course and bowling green are deserted:

> Driving their baws frae whins or tee,
> There's no ae gowfer to be seen
> Nor dousser folk wysing a jee
> The byas bouls on Tamson's green.

Human conviviality offsets nature's chill, and Ramsay conjures up a wonderful metaphor for the effects of wine:

> Good claret best keeps out the cauld
> And drives away the winter soon,
> It makes a man baith gash and bauld,
> And heaves his saul beyond the moon.

Dryden's version of this pales into insignificance: 'Produce the Wine, that makes us bold,/ And sprightly Wit and Love inspires'. With the very human particularity that vernacular Scots endows, Ramsay breathes new life into the representation of the rituals of courtship:

> Watch the saft minutes of delyte,
> When Jenny speaks beneath her breath,
> And kisses, laying a' the wyte
> On you if she kepp ony skaith.
>
> Haith ye're ill bred, she'll smiling say,
> Ye'll worry me ye greedy rook;
> Syne frae your arms she'll rin away,
> And hide her sell in some dark nook:
>
> Her laugh will lead you to the place
> Where lies the happiness ye want,
> And plainly tells you to your face
> Nineteen nay-says are haff a grant.

Scottish literature's fondness for the bizarre particular finds striking exemplification here: the suitor is advised to persevere; if he asks 38 times he'll ultimately have his way.

What particularly characterises the Scottish Enlightenment is the social and realistic basis of its activities across a broad range; the common factor is humanism. David Hume famously writes, 'Indulge your passion for science, says [Nature}, but let your science be human, and such as may have a direct reference to action and society . . . Be a philosopher; but amidst all your philosophy, be still a man'.[1] To secularise in this way, to place man at the centre of investigation of the human condition (rather than seeing him as an expression of God's will) was plainly to stir up a ferment in a country as theologically driven as Scotland. The vernacular poets are comparably radical: their challenge is to the authority of literary rules. Ramsay, Fergusson, and Burns challenge the traditional correspondence between literary hierarchies and social hierarchies (that is, there is high art peopled by the eminent, and low art inhabited by the commoners). The Scottish vernacular poets subvert this convention, using the props of high art to render the experiences of traditionally 'low' characters. They make a major contribution to the democratisation of literature but, unlike English poets who use mock-classical forms, such as Pope and Gray, they are not concerned merely to display their expertise in the mode: the distinctive dimension to the Scottish writing is the celebration of human experience. For Ramsay, Fergusson, and Burns, the expressive needs of the poet dictate the choice of form, mode, and language; not vice versa. To paraphrase Hume, 'Be a poet; but amidst all your poetry, be still a man'.

'People poetry': this is, for Maurice Lindsay, 'the outstanding characteristic of Scottish poetry'. The work of Ramsay, Fergusson, and Burns bears witness. Their's are particular people, particularly rendered. In 'Lucky Spence's Last Advice' the dying Edinburgh brothel-keeper offers practical advice to her lasses. It is more specific, and for that reason more useful, than the contents of any classical valediction, but the poem also enables Ramsay to highlight the double standards prevalent in polite society: the good citizens enjoy the services of the prostitutes but, to maintain the appearance of respectability, they ensure the girls are beaten monthly by the hangman to remind them of the vileness of their trade. In 'Elegy on Maggy Johnston' Ramsay's elegist is a customer of the deceased publican

David Hume

who laments her death not for her sake but for the fact that she takes with her to the grave the secret of her powerful brew. Ramsay puts his own signature on the conventions of classical elegy. Here is his take on the tradition whereby the elegist personalises universal grief by reference to his own experience:

> Ae simmer night I was sae fou,
> Amang the riggs I geed to spew;
> Syne down on a green bawk, I trow
> > I took a nap,
> And soucht a' night balillilow
> > As sound's a tap.

> And whan the dawn begoud to glow,
> I hirsled up my dizzy pow,
> Frae 'mang the corn like wirricow,
> > Wi' bains sae sair,
> And ken' nae mair than if a ew
> > How I came there.

What is Maggie's legacy to Ramsay's speaker? How is she immortalised? – Through the account of the hangover to end all hangovers.

What does 'music' mean to the ordinary citizen of Edinburgh?, asks Ramsay in 'Elegy on Patie Birnie'. Is it the classical myth of its invention by Apollo? No, it is the ubiquitousness of the devious and highly successful street busker, Patie, accompanied by the midget dancer, Johnny Stocks. In 'To Robert Yarde of Devonshire', Ramsay, mimicking the manner of the Augustans, offers a long essay on the virtues of moderation – 'Yet ae extreme should never make/ A man the gowden mean forsake' – and he applies it in particular to love. But then he totally undermines his thesis when it comes to specific advice to his friend:

> Then wale a Virgin worthy you,
> Worthy your love and nuptial Vow;
> Syne frankly range o'er a' her Charms,
> Drink deep of Joy within her Arms
> Be still delighted with her Breast,
> And on her Love with rapture feast.

Rules are abstractions, meaningless generalities; real human beings are individuals, a point further underlined by the poet's own practice within the poem: feigning adherence to classical formula, he then stamps his mark upon it.

Half a century on, Fergusson is equally inventive in personalising the standard poetic baggage. His poems, like Ramsay's, seem like a manifesto for Scottish poetry, a manifesto on which they deliver by example. In 'The Daft Days' the trappings of classical pastoral are identified only to be rejected as irrelevant to the reality of Edinburgh at New Year:

> From naked groves nae birdie sings;
> To shepherd's pipe nae hillock rings;
> The breeze nae od'rous flavour brings
> From Borean cave;
> And dwyning Nature droops her wings,
> Wi' visage grave.

The classical apostrophe to the presiding deity is now given contemporary relevance; and the reality is that if you have too good a time you will fall foul of the officers of the law:

> And thou, great god of Aqua Vitae!
> Wha sways the empire of this city,
> When fou we're sometimes capernoity,
> Be thou prepar'd
> To hedge us frae that black banditti,
> The City-Guard.

If poetry has a place in the life of the ordinary citizen, why should it not offer such practical advice?

In 'The King's Birthday in Edinburgh' Fergusson deliberately chooses an occasion which had been a common holiday throughout Britain since the Union. Claiming, 'I'm fain to think the joys the same/ In London town as here at hame', he then shows by increasingly bizarre detail that they are most definitely not the same:

> Now round and round the serpents whiz,
> Wi' hissing wrath and angry phiz,
> Sometimes they catch a gentle gizz,
> > Alake the day!
> And singe, wi' hair-devouring bizz,
> > Its curls away.

> Shou'd the owner patiently keek round,
> To view the nature of his wound,
> Dead pussie, dragled thro' the pond,
> > Takes him a lounder,
> Which lays his honour on the ground
> > As flat's a flounder.

Equally he has shown that his is no standard, laureate-produced, public poem: he has to take charge of the Muse, as incapable of holding her whisky as of directing his poem. The point could not be clearer: classical convention is irrelevant for the rendering of the particularities of individual or nation.

The introduction of a second definition is long overdue: 'to enlighten': 'to free from prejudice and superstition'. This is precisely what Burns does in a poem that is one of the great Scottish Enlightenment texts, 'Holy Willie's Prayer'. Specific in origin, the dismissal of William Fisher's charges against Gavin Hamilton, it develops into arguably the most effective demonstration in world literature of the limitations and dangers of the closed mind. James Hogg would follow suit with *Memoirs and Confessions of a Justified Sinner*, likewise, though with much more benign irony, John Galt in *Annals of the Parish*.

Burns's Holy Willie is pathetic in his limitations: the 'pillar in thy temple' loses even physical self-control in the face of the liberal, enlightened challenge:

> O Lord my God, that glib-tongu'd Aiken,
> My very heart an' soul are quakin',
> To think how we stood, sweatin', shakin',
> > An' pissed wi' dread,
> While Auld wi' hingin lip gaed sneakin',
> > And hid his head.

But, devious in his logic (witness his willingness to endure 'hough-magandie' if that is God's will!), he is also awesome in the sheer force of his bigotry:

> Lord in the day of vengeance try him,
> Lord visit them wha did employ him,
> And pass not in thy mercy by 'em,
>   Nor hear their prayer;
> But for thy people's sake destroy 'em,
>   And dinna spare.

Without saying a word in his own voice, Burns demonstrates the need for enlightenment by allowing a mind immune to enlightenment to reveal itself.

Burns's poetry reflects the influence of key concepts in Scottish Enlightenment thought, such as Benevolence and Sympathy. Half a century before him, Francis Hutcheson, in 'Concerning Moral Good and Evil', had stressed the virtue of showing benevolence towards rational and moral beings 'in the most distant planets'. Adam Smith's *Theory of Moral Sentiments* (1759) popularised the notion that the capacity for feeling is an index to virtue and emphasised the important element of sympathy. Burns ranges widely in his exemplifications of sympathy. In 'Death and Dr. Hornbook' the sociable peasant-farmer lends a sympathetic ear to Death, reduced to a figure of ridicule by the local amateur pharmacist whose incompetence makes Death redundant. Here the convention of the bargain with Death is given an ironic twist: Death needs sympathy from the listener and the defeat of his human rival before he can regain his rightful place. Burns has humanised Death and magnified Hornbook, whose malpractice is so notorious that he can be relied on to achieve for them the evil ends of malcontents. Death is not the enemy, Burns says, it is human corruption.

The process of demystification and familiarisation is taken further in 'Address to the Deil'. The ongoing need for this is evident from Walter Scott's concern as late as 1831 that George Sinclair's *Satan's Invisible World* was still widely influential, especially in rural areas. Burns's Deil, familiarised within the community, is anything but the awesome figure of the Miltonic epigraph, ' "O Prince, O chief of many throned powers,/ That led th' emabttl'd Seraphim to war" '; rather, he is the local nuisance, familiarly addressed as 'Auld Hornie, Nick, Clootie, Auld Hangie'. Demystified, the Devil is treated as a crony and warrants the speaker's sympathetic concern:

> But fare-you-weel, auld Nickie-ben!
> O wad ye tak a thought an' men'!
> Ye aiblens might – I dinna ken –
> > Still hae a stake –
> I'm wae to think upo' yon den,
> > Ev'n for your sake!

Even the Devil does not deserve to be consigned to eternal torment, and if he would only reform it would benefit not just himself but all mankind. Here is a Christian egalitarianism of a remarkably liberal kind which confronts the certainties of orthodox Calvinism with the ultimate possibility.

One final definition: 'to enlighten': 'to elevate by knowledge'. Is this not precisely what Burns does in his finest achievement, 'Tam o' Shanter'? The demystification continues, with the devil and witches, like humans, feeling the need to party (and dance, and sweat), but here the focus of the familiarisation is Tam, 'heroic Tam' our representative. This poem is the zenith of Burns's universalising on the basis of the particular; it is local (think of how we are guided along Tam's route) and it is universal in respect of Tam's responses: the fascinated observer of Cutty Sark is safe until instinct triumphs over reason and in his sexual excitement he cries out, betraying his presence, and threatening his survival. And how does Burns render the ordinary man's encounter with the supernatural? – Courtesy of the trappings of classical epic. Here the vernacular poets' democratising of poetry reaches its culmination. With Tam as hero, the epic is democratised; and Tam is 'elevated' into a universal figure courtesy of Burns's knowledge of human nature.

Much is made of Burns's radical politics. I would contend that the subtlest, and arguably most effective, expression of Burns's radicalism is to be found in the radical use of poetic forms. In 'Tam o' Shanter' a process initiated by Ramsay, developed by Fergusson, reaches its culmination. High art-low art distinctions crumble before the expressive needs of the individual writer; and, paradoxically, out of the particularised rendering of experience there emerges universal truth.

NOTE

[1] David Hume, *An Enquiry Concerning Human Understanding*, 1748. 'Of the Different Species of Philosophy', section 1

ROBERT BURNS AND THE ENLIGHTENMENT

Ɛ⁄Ꝛ

RALPH RICHARD MCLEAN

The trip which Robert Burns made to Edinburgh in the winter of 1786 has long been held up as the moment where the genius vernacular poet came into contact with pedantic anglicising critics. In the subsequent attempts to enshrine the egalitarian credentials of the bard as well as his superior intellect, the literati of Edinburgh were transformed into little more than pantomime villains, whose treatment of Burns as a rustic sideshow only exposed their own ignorance of his true abilities. Far from 'sticking it to the man' however, Burns had a far more complex and subtle interaction with the guardians of Scotland's enlightenment culture. While he certainly had a turbulent relationship with them, his difficulties were arguably only symptomatic of a free exchange of ideas, and served to power the motors of intellectual discussion.

The standard trope which has been used in the past to demonstrate Burns's superiority over the literati he encountered there has been for critics to point to the absence of Scotland's 'A-list' Enlightenment thinkers, David Hume, who had died in 1776 and Adam Smith, who was too ill to attend. Effectively the argument goes that only these two men would have possessed the intellectual arsenal capable of engaging Burns, which in turn would have made his stay in Edinburgh more worthwhile. This scenario would have been at best unlikely; for Hume, although he took an interest in promoting Scottish poetry, was more obsessed with championing neo-classical standards of Scottish literary identity, which resulted in him labelling minor poets such as Thomas Blacklock and William Wilkie as the Scottish Pindar and the Scottish Homer. Likewise Smith in his lectures on literary composition seldom used examples from the Scottish Canon, and instead focussed on

English writers, most notably Joseph Addison and Samuel Richardson. Indeed Smith believed that Jonathan Swift was the writer who had reached the pinnacle of compositional style. It would be folly to suggest that Edinburgh was bereft of quality conversation for the bard however. Dugald Stewart, the first biographer of Smith, and perhaps the ablest of the second generation of literati, was in Edinburgh at the time of Burns's visit. Stewart, who was an accomplished philosopher himself wrote highly of Burns, and specifically stated that he had been charmed by the quality of his conversations with him.

Even before Burns arrived in Edinburgh to promote his poetry, he had drawn deeply from the well of Scottish Enlightenment thought. And it was Smith who provided the richest nourishment. His groundbreaking work, *The Theory of Moral Sentiments* (1759), more than any other, exposed the poet to the world of Enlightenment thought and instilled in Burns a philosophical understanding of sympathy which would go on to become a hallmark of his poetry. Burns was quite open about the influence that Smith had over him, remarking in his *First Commonplace Book*, 'I entirely agree with that judicious philosopher Mr Smith in his excellent *Theory of Moral Sentiments*, that Remorse is the most painful sentiment that can embitter the human bosom.' Without this Enlightenment work, Burns may still have created poems such as, 'To a Louse' and, 'To a Mouse', but they would not have been constructed in the same way. 'To a Louse', for example, would still contain a great deal of comedy and humour, but may well have been robbed of its philosophical conclusion which gives the poem its real power. Burns's invitation 'To see oursels as ithers see us' is a moment for psychological reflection, and at the same time resonates with the Smithian idea of being able to put oneself in the position of another in order to express genuine sympathy for the suffering of another. It was primarily through an understanding and appreciation of Smith's investigations that Burns was able to add a psychological layer to his concept of sympathy. This psychological strain of critical thinking was not only an influence on Burns, it also stimulated major Enlightenment figures such as, Henry Home, Lord Kames, whose *Elements of Criticism* (1762) constructed a psychological system as a means for the individual to internally absorb literature and respond critically to it.

The most explicit instance of sympathy in a literary medium in Scotland is Henry Mackenzie's *Man of Feeling* (1771) in which the

main character Harley Cameron is placed in certain situations, some-
times quite improbably, which result in him shedding single tears of
sympathy; thus demonstrating a restrained sensibility acceptable to a
polite readership. At the time the book was a great success and was an
important icon for the literati of Scotland, for despite their notable
endeavours in the fields of history, literary criticism, economics,
sociology, anthropology, geology, chemistry, and law, to name but
a few, they had not been able to produce literature, either prose or
poetry that was of a comparable standard. Therefore, the *Man of Feeling*
represented an opportunity for the literati to shout about their literary
achievements. Burns too was a fan of the novel, and described it as a
book, 'I prize next to the Bible'. In a letter to Mrs Dunlop he outlined
why the work had affected him to such an extent, and at the same time
provided an insight into Enlightenment ideals that had touched his
heart.

> From what book, moral or even Pious, will the susceptible young mind
> receive impressions more congenial to Humanity and Kindness, Gener-
> osity and Benevolence, in short, all that ennobles the Soul to herself, or
> endears her to others, than from the simple affecting tale of poor Harley?[1]

Although the book has dated poorly for a modern audience, it was
clearly an influential piece in its day, and Burns found several key
enlightenment ideals enshrined in its pages. As well as the works of
Mackenzie, including, *The Mirror* and *The Lounger*, Burns demonstrated
in a letter to Sir John Sinclair of Ulbster that he was aware of some of
the Enlightenment works produced by other members of the literati.
In his capacity as book purchaser for a small club named the
Monkland's Friendly Society, Burns had bought Hugh Blair's *Sermons*,
William Robertson's *The History of Scotland*, David Hume's *History of the
Stewarts*, and *The Spectator*, as well as a number of literary works.[2] Even
the letter itself was indicative of an engagement in the wider Enlight-
enment community, for the man to whom Burns wrote the letter, John
Sinclair, was in the process of an ambitious project which would
provide information on all the Parishes in the country. *The Statistical
Account of Scotland* (1791–1797) was a grand social and economic
venture which had a huge impact in the country, and also illustrated
that enlightenment ideals were not solely located in the Universities or
found in books, but were located at all levels of Scottish society.

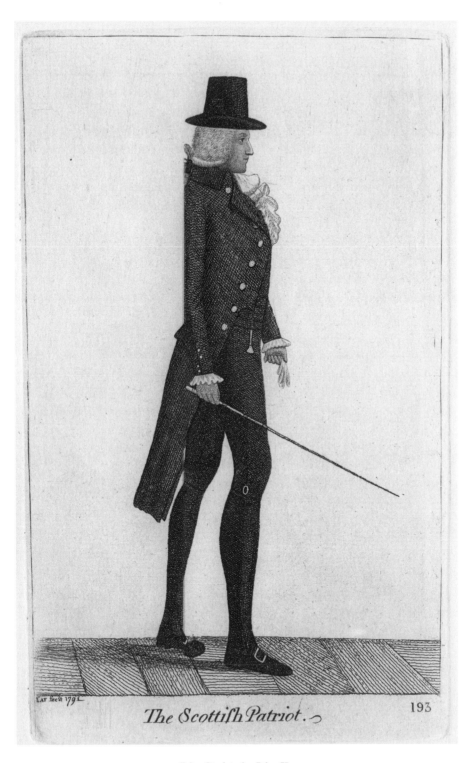

The Scottish Patriot.

193

John Sinclair by John Kay

William Robertson by John Kay

The idea of putting oneself in another's shoes was taken to the extreme in 'To a Mouse' where Burns extended his sympathy beyond the merely human realm to include all of God's creatures. The benevolence that Burns proffered to the mouse was not the condescending sympathy of an uninterested party, but rather the disinterested benevolence that was placed in man by a wise creator. There is no superior attitude to the lowly stature of the mouse, which is indicated by Burns's reference to 'earth born companion' and 'fellow mortal'. The principles of this conception of a disinterested benevolence had been disseminated in the early eighteenth century by Francis Hutcheson.

In this respect, Burns also owes a debt to Hutcheson, a man widely regarded as the 'Father of the Scottish Enlightenment', and Smith's teacher when he attended the University of Glasgow. Smith ultimately refined many of his mentor's philosophical inquiries, but he freely admitted the influence that, in his own words, 'the never to be forgotten Hutcheson', had wielded over him. Hutcheson was the first person in Britain to conduct a critical inquiry into the nature of aesthetics which he published as *An Inquiry into the Original of our Ideas of Beauty and Virtue* (1725).One of the central conclusions which he drew in the work was the belief that the best type of action which an individual could carry out was that which resulted in the greatest amount of happiness, with the worst actions being those that occasioned the greatest amount of misery. This philosophy was something which Burns articulated in his letters, but which also made appearances in his poetry. In a letter to Mrs. Dunlop Burns expressed himself in a manner similar to that of the Enlightenment philosopher: 'Whatever mitigates the woes, or increases the happiness of others this is my criterion of goodness; and whatever injures society at large, or an individual in it, this is my measure of iniquity.'[3]

Hutcheson, and his fellow Glasgow Professor, William Leechman who held the Chair of Divinity, were also important figures in educating a new breed of enlightened Presbyterian ministers who would go on to form the moderates in the Church of Scotland. Theologically Leechman was an important figure at Glasgow for he taught the generation of moderate ministers who would eventually be on familiar terms with Burns. Men such as John M'Math and William M'Gill attended his lectures, and praised his enlightened brand of theology which demonstrated an appreciation for literature and encouraged free intellectual enquiry, while at the same time promoted a love of Christian truth and piety. At the time of his appointment Hutcheson enthused that he would 'put a new face upon Theology in Scotland'.[4] In many ways Leechman was able to do this with his students, which was of great significance in the West of Scotland where the covenanting tradition was still a powerful force to be reckoned with. The education of a new breed of minister in the West of Scotland provided a bulwark against the more extreme forms of Protestant preaching, and provided the opportunity to establish a more moderate brand. It would be imprudent to claim Leechman as one of the great Enlightenment thinkers of Scotland, however, he did demonstrate a range of original thinking, and the fact that he educated a generation of Scottish clergymen and inculcated them with enlightened ideals, created the type of religious moderatism to which Burns was exposed in his youth. That Burns would have been influenced by the enlightened moderate clergy is hardly surprising given his upbringing. His father was a man stimulated by the moderate teachings and would regularly engage his sons in religious debate, thereby putting into practice the free exchange of ideas cultivated by the enlightened clergy.

As Liam McIlvanney has previously identified, New Light, or moderate Presbyterianism was one of the most important intellectual influences on Burns, and a movement which exposed him to Enlightenment ideals not only propounded in Scotland, but at a wider European level.[5] When dealing with the Enlightenment in Scotland, one must always be acutely aware of the unique position it held within the general European Enlightenment. Instead of being in opposition to the repressive forces of the Church in the way that the French Enlightenment operated, the Scottish system ran in conjunction with the Church, and in many respects was actually the engine that powered it. Therefore, in several important instances, the impulses of the Scottish Enlightenment emanated from the establishment, rather than in reaction to it. The moderates in the Church adhered to certain key principles of which Burns would have approved. These principles included benevolence, tolerance, private judgement, and defiance of tyranny. It was through the encouragement of exercising private judgement that Burns came to form his own critical response to the Church of Scotland, and crystallize his opinions on the division between the moderate and evangelical split in the country. Such a free intellectual inquiry permitted him not only to criticise the moderate regime where he felt there to be hypocrisy, but also in some cases to admire certain elements of the evangelicals style, even though he rejected many of their hard line stances over religious matters. This complicated relationship that Burns had with the two sides can be detected most clearly in 'The Holy Fair' where all the preachers in some way fail to inspire their congregation. Some fail through their lack of warmth and wisdom, while others attempt to terrify their charges into subservience which serves no purpose.

The moderate regime in Scotland held sway over a powerful cultural agenda, and when Burns arrived in Edinburgh, there was still enough of an intellectual presence in the city which was capable of engaging with him. Adam Ferguson and Hugh Blair, as well as Dugald Stewart and Alexander Dalziel all met him, and indeed it was at Ferguson's home where the famous meeting between Burns and Sir Walter Scott took place. Burns's relationship with Blair in particular has remained at best problematical. For too long the perception of Blair as a pompous interfering pedant meddling with the Bard and his writings has obscured any genuine investigation into a meaningful two way interaction. James DeLancey Ferguson, in a statement typical of one who perceives such a relationship between the two, believed that only the 'ungainly integrity of his genius saved Burns from the emasculation at the hands of Blair and his ilk.'[6] Much has been made of the efforts of the literati to offer Burns poetic advice when he was at Edinburgh, which understandably irritated him. The predominant enlightenment figures in Scotland during this period were in possession of either a theological or a legal background, and they were not slow in offering him the benefit of their own learning. In almost every instance Burns rightly ignored these genuine, if misguided, attempts to 'improve' his poetry. It was no surprise then that Blair, who had held the Regius Chair of Rhetoric and Belles Lettres at Edinburgh University, and had a British, and growing European reputation as an arbiter of taste and composition, also offered his opinions to Burns. The moderate clergyman suggested seven improvements which Burns could make to his poems, and of these suggestions Burns adopted two. The most famous of these is line 103 in 'The Holy Fair', which Blair argued read weakly as, 'wi' tidings of Salvation'. He believed that Burns ought to be able to contrive some other rhyme which he did by altering 'Salvation' to 'Damnation'. There are two points here which are frequently overlooked when appraising Blair's relationship with Burns. Primarily emphasis is given to the fact that Burns rejected five of Blair's suggestions, however, given that the majority of the literati proffered improvements only to have them declined, the fact that Burns even adopted two of them indicates that he had more than a passing respect for the Edinburgh professor. Secondly, that Blair could read 'The Holy Fair', a poem which criticised moderate preaching styles as much as it did evangelical, and mention only a word change in the poem, suggests that Blair was not entirely devoid of irony and humour. All the more remarkable on the grounds that Blair had written extensively on pulpit eloquence in his highly successful publication, *Lectures on Rhetoric and Belles Lettres* (1783). Burns also acquiesced to Blair's request that 'The Jolly Beggars' be omitted from the Edinburgh edition of his poems owing to the dubious content matter. Sadly he also advised against publishing a now lost poem, 'The Prophet and God's Complaint' in the same edition on similar grounds. Before one starts cursing Blair's interference for adding to the list of lost Burns poems, it is necessary to remember that Burns himself had left 'The Jolly Beggars' out of the Kilmarnock edition. Therefore this has the ring of sound commercial guidance advising him not to include anything that would alienate a potentially lucrative market.

That Blair had a reputation for vanity and pomposity is not disputed, even his close associates had picked up on it. His attitude certainly never escaped Burns either. In his *Second Common Place Book*, Burns observed, 'In my opinion Dr Blair is merely an astonishing proof of what industry and application can do. Natural parts like his are frequently to be met with and his vanity is proverbially known among his acquaintants.' Nevertheless, Burns was not blind to his abilities, and he acknowledged that Blair was, 'justly at the head of what may be called fine writing . . . In short, he is truly a worthy and most remarkable character.' He was also capable of great magnanimity, which he demonstrated when Burns attended a dinner party at Blair's house. When asked which places he felt had given him the greatest gratification, Burns opted to say the High Church, but instead of choosing Blair as his preacher of choice, selected his colleague and successor in the Chair of Rhetoric and Belles Lettres, William Greenfield. In order to reduce the embarrassment of what Burns admitted later was a painful moment, Blair generously seconded Burns's intimation.

The often quoted term, 'Heaven-taught ploughman' which Henry Mackenzie bestowed upon Burns is also symptomatic of a more intricate exchange between the literati and the bard. On one level the depiction of Burns as 'Heaven-taught' reduced a complex individual to a one-dimensional construct in order to serve an enlightenment agenda that had become overly focussed on finding the noble savage. It was Rousseau who had first hypothesised the existence of the noble savage, which subsequently resulted in a search to find such an individual or indeed group. The Scottish literati were particularly guilty of this, locating the noble savage not only in the guise of the highlander, but also in the poetic works of Ossian, a supposed third century bard who came from a primitive culture, yet wrote with a sensibility and sublimity that would have delighted a reader in the eighteenth century. It would appear that Burns had been sacrificed by the literati to the Gods of the Enlightenment in order to ensure that the noble savage would rise again; however, there is a more subtle exchange going on here than would appear at first glance. Burns was shrewd enough to realise that if he wanted the patronage of the literati, which was necessary to help promote his new edition, and in turn secure more sales, he would need to appease the establishment in some way. Effectively the 'heaven-taught' ploughman was a marketing ploy which provided the literati with an opportunity to promote one of their cherished, albeit misguided, enlightenment ideals, while at the same time it supplied Burns with a gimmick that would initially garner attention, but would ultimately lead to a more cogent focus on his very real product. Burns himself was not averse to playing up to this reputation when he thought that it could offer him some advantage. Indeed it would appear to be a partly cultivated image on his part, which he alluded to in his *First Commonplace Book*. In seeking inspiration to compose an air in the 'old Scotch style', Burns invoked his muse: 'I hope my poor, country Muse, who, all rustic, awkward, and unpolished as she is, has more charms for me than any other of the pleasures of life beside'. Here even in 1785 there is evidence of Burns playing with his image. Burns's ability to 'play the game' allowed him in a sense, to succeed where Robert Fergusson had run into problems. His reaction against the literati, most notably in the highly amusing yet highly impudent, 'The Sow of Feeling' attacked the sensibility of the literati to such an extent that it effectively put an end to any potential patronage they would extend to him. In the case of Burns, people inevitably began to see through this synthetic identity, mainly owing to the deep learning which the supposedly 'heaven-taught' ploughman

F I N G A L,

A N

ANCIENT EPIC POEM,

In S I X B O O K S:

Together with feveral other P O E M S, compofed by

OSSIAN the Son of F I N G A L.

Tranflated from the GALIC LANGUAGE,

By J A M E S M A C P H E R S O N,

Fortia facta patrum. VIRGIL.

L O N D O N;
Printed for T. BECKET and P. A. DE HONDT, in the Strand.

M DCC LXII.

Fingal bookcover by James MacPherson

expressed in his poetry. John Logan, writing in the *English Review* pointed to the fact that Burns had a deeper knowledge of the English poets than some of the English authors themselves. Dalziel, the Greek professor at Edinburgh University likewise alluded to Burns's more than passing acquaintance with English prose and verse.

In his assessment of Enlightenment culture, David Daiches, labelled it confused and complex, and although the period was in a sense a 'Golden Age' of literary and intellectual enquiry, it was a distinction that came at the price of national schizophrenia.[7] Daiches is right to identify the enlightenment as complex, but as a result of this complexity he boils down the complicated interactions which do not fit a standard pattern of national identity into the one dimensional label of national schizophrenia. Under his classification Burns himself would be one of the most pronounced sufferers, for he wrote poetry from the local, Scottish and British perspectives, celebrating identities in one circle which would appear incongruous in the next. Janet Sorenson has argued that this situation was only acceptable to the literati because of Samuel Johnson's displacement of class difference for national difference, which gained credence in Edinburgh, and therefore made Burns safe for consumption.[8] However, the literati were themselves negotiating the paths between a Scottish and a British identity, and would hardly have been likely to dismiss a genuine Scottish product that would bolster their own sense of Scottish identity within Britain on a purely class basis. The fault of the literati was their attempt to force the square peg of the bard's poetry into the round hole of enlightenment sensibility, and the cult of the noble savage; and was not the result of any perceived attempts to disenfranchise Burns from the top table of enlightenment.

In any case the Enlightenment reached deeper into Scottish culture than simply existing in the rarefied strata of polite Edinburgh society. Burns was also exposed to this environment, and in many respects felt more at home here, than hobnobbing with the literati. This second tier of Enlightenment still included eminent thinkers capable of engaging Burns, not only intellectually, but also convivially. The most notable of these figures was William Smellie, the editor of the *Encyclopaedia Britannica* (1768–1771) and the author of a two volume *Philosophy of Natural History* which became a set text at Harvard University. Burns described him warmly as that 'Old Veteran in Genius, Wit and Bawdry' and it was through Smellie that Burns came to be a member

William Smellie by John Kay

of the Crochallan Fencibles. This circle also included prominent figures such as William Dunbar, William Nicol and Alexander Cunningham, all men capable of enlightenment thought, despite the criticisms of Duglad Stewart who dismissed them as, 'not very select society.' Although Burns may have had more kindred spirits among these enlightenment figures, he was nevertheless capable of traversing both groups. Thus, just as he was able to move between different layers of identity, so too was he adept at moving between different registers of enlightenment.

This ability of Burns marks him as a true proponent of the enlightenment. In a sense Burns was both of, and not of, the enlightenment. This should not be taken to mean that Burns was labouring under some kind of schizophrenia, but rather is indicative of a complex individual who engaged in a myriad of interests and pursuits, sometimes working in perfect harmony, sometimes appearing to create conflict with one another. Burns engaged with the enlightenment establishment in Scotland, particularly its brand of moderate religion and free intellectual enquiry, and was not averse to adhering to their ideas when they proved acceptable to him. Likewise, the literati of Edinburgh were not unappreciative of his poetic efforts. Where the tension lay was over the fact that each wanted different things from the other. It was in this social milieu, and part of the ethos of the Enlightenment itself, that each could accommodate the other.

NOTES

[1] Robert Burns, *Letters of Robert Burns*, G. Ross Roy, (ed.) (2 vols, Oxford, 1985), II, p. 25.

[2] Burns, *Letters*, I, pp. 108–9.

[3] Burns, *Letters*, I, p. 419.

[4] Francis Hutcheson, Glasgow University Library (GUL) MS Gen. 1018.15

[5] Liam McIlvanney, *Burns the Radical: Poetry and Politics in Late Eighteenth-Century Scotland* (East Linton, 2002), pp. 123–44.

[6] James DeLancey Ferguson, 'Burns and Hugh Blair' *Modern Language Notes* 45 (1930), p. 446.

[7] David Daiches, *Robert Burns*, p. 1.

[8] Janet Sorenson, *The Grammar of Empire in Eighteenth-Century British Writing* (Cambridge, 2000), p. 155.

NIBBLING AT ADAM SMITH

❧

*A mouse's sma' request and the limits of social justice in the Scottish
Romanticism of Robert Burns*

MURRAY PITTOCK

What was Robert Burns? Do we still have a problem with this
question? Is it because of its protean answers: a ploughman poet, a
peasant poet, a model for the Scottish bourgeoisie, an exemplar of
liberty, the messenger of autochthonous proletarian value to the USSR
and China in the 1960s, the writer of lieder to the nineteenth-century
Germans, the connexion with the old country to their American
contemporaries, the last decadent representative of a great alien
tradition to TS Eliot, a major Romantic to poets and critics in the
Anglo-American world before 1945, a dialect poet of limited abilities
after it; a radical Friend of the People, a Scottish nationalist with
unfortunate British tendencies, a British nationalist with understand-
able Scottish tendencies, a misunderstood advocate of corporate
Labourism, a prophet of Red Clydeside before the industrial revolu-
tion, a freemason, a Jacobin, a Jacobite, a Nasmyth pin-up or a rugged
peasant poet, the guardian of Scottish song tradition or its manip-
ulator, a couthy comic or a dangerous subversive? Is the reader's Burns
above? Why do discussions of Burns-even scholarly discussions-often
hang their arguments on over-familiar quotations, almost as if they
were a timeworn Immortal Memory on the circuit rather than a fresh
encounter with a major writer? Would Wordsworth be assessed with
reference to one contemporary review, often quoted out of context?
Would Byron? To pursue this example, the Mackenzie review from the
Lounger continues often to be quoted in assessing Burns. Is it because
once the phrase 'heaven-taught ploughman' is enunciated we can all
relax in the knowledge of the argument to follow? But even if we limit
ourselves to Mackenzie's review, we should surely be asking about the

reference in it to Burns as Milton's Shakespeare in his 'wood-notes wild'; and we should be asking too about the popularity of *L'Allegro* in the late eighteenth century, what it signified, and what too was the relation of Mackenzie's thought to Smith's, and both of theirs to Burns? And we should also perhaps, as Kenneth Johnston began to do in the 1990s, examine Burns' collections in terms of his prefaces, as indeed would be a commonplace in Wordsworth's case.[1]

I do not mean to suggest that these things are never done: at Glasgow in particular-and elsewhere-there are distinguished Burns scholars who are doing them; but in order to confirm Burns in the front rank of writers of global significance in the Romantic era, we all have a responsibility to raise the level of critical debate. At the joint conference of the American and British societies of Romantic studies in Bristol in 2007, there were no papers on Burns in 300 or so presentations, a not untypical situation. This must change. Scholarly concern for Burns must globalize. The Arts & Humanities Research Council-funded Global Burns project (www.gla.ac.uk/departments/globalburnsnetwork/) aims to contribute to that in the scholarly field, by supporting, encouraging and enhancing an international conference and publications programme on the poet. At the same time, if Burns scholarship must spread, so must Burns Suppers, because Burns is not only a great Romantic poet but an ambassador of Scottish culture, and both Burns as scholarship and Burns as performance need to be spread globally. This is why, indeed, Burns is the peg on which the Homecoming 2009 agenda hangs, and why he is worth getting on for £200M a year to the Scottish tourist industry.

2009 is also the year of another anniversary: the 250th anniversary of the publication of Adam Smith's *Theory of Moral Sentiments* (1759), a text which I shall be arguing both deeply influenced Burns and was strongly interrogated by his poetry. Burns first read *Moral Sentiments* before 1783, possibly as early as 1777, if Kinsley's attribution of a paraphrase from it in 'A Penitential Thought', and his dating of that fragment, is accepted. In 1789, he read *Wealth of Nations*, and his own library contained the 6th edition of *Moral Sentiments*, first published in 1790. Burns mentions Smith explicitly in 'Of all the numerous ills that hurt our peace' and 'Epistle to Glenconner' and uses *Moral Sentiments* implicitly in 'Address to the Unco Guid' and the 1787 Woods Prologue, paraphrasing from it in 'To a Louse'. It has been long recognized that Smith's *Moral Sentiments*-indeed, like Mackenzie's

The Author of the Wealth of Nations

34

Adam Smith by John Kay

Man of Feeling-was an important text for Burns. But in order to fulfil his role as a poet, Burns had to find the space to interrogate and resist such influential texts-a condition indeed that Andrew Noble notes in the Canongate notes on 'To a Louse', and which Raymond Bentman also articulates in saying that 'running in and out of Burns's works is a desire both to agree with and to question the Enlightenment thinkers' reliance on reason'.[2] And there was a reason for this.

One of the key goals of the Scottish Enlightenment can be summed up in the phrase 'the teleology of civility', the foregrounding of the idea of civility as a model when that model was not merely an ideal, but a practical reality in what was now in post-Union Scotland the aspirational comparator of English society, in terms of wealth, culture, manners and even language, where Addison's *Spectator* essays had served to establish the parameters for a standardized middle-class English, which in itself presaged 'the carefully depoliticized domain of civil society' to which the emergent Scottish public sphere aspired intently in the aftermath of the 1745 Rising. As Thomas Miller points out, 'the first university professors [in Scotland] to teach English taught the English of the *Spectator*', which Burns admired while regretting it was 'so thoroughly and entirely English'. As James Sibbald put it in 1802, the poetic legacy of Allan Ramsay, to whom Burns was so much indebted, was couched in 'the familiar dialects of the meanest vulgar'; for Thomas Sheridan, studying and speaking English will make Englishmen of all the islands. Education and standardization were believed to go together, with the 'essay as a univocal instrument for instilling sensibility'.[3] What was called 'delicacy of sensibility and exactness of propriety' had their objective correlative in a single language through which both could be expressed. In Smith's *Moral Sentiments* violent events and images (implicitly linked to Scotland's past) were converted into the structures of sympathy, where mutual recognition was greatly aided by mutually recognizable language, both of word and body. This requirement implied shared notions of civility and a shared standard language. It might be doubted whether anyone could truly sympathize with a Gaelic or even a Scots speaker: the vernacular might invoke the colonization of pity, but not sympathy, and indeed this aspect of the limitations of the arguments of *Moral Sentiments* is explored in Maria Edgeworth's fiction.[4]

Smith's moral sentiments implied a unitary public space and

language: 'the amiable virtue of humanity requires [he wrote], surely, a sensibility, much beyond what is possessed by the rude vulgar of mankind . . . the great and exalted virtue of magnanimity undoubtedly demands much more . . . the amiable virtues consist in that degree of sensibility which surprises by its exquisite and unexpected delicacy and tenderness'. By contrast, 'if our own misery pinches us very severely, we have no leisure to attend to that of our neighbour: and all savages are too much occupied with their own wants and necessities, to give much attention to those of another person'. Sympathy in this case can only flow in one direction, towards the poor and backward from the rich and sophisticated, for 'every savage . . . can expect from his countrymen no sympathy or indulgence'. But this is not all, for in a telling passage Smith associates sympathy with commonality of language, not only social development:

> The rules of justice may be compared to the rules of grammar; the rules of the other virtues, to the rules which critics lay down for the attainment of what is sublime and elegant: composition . . . A man may learn to write grammatically by rule, with the most absolute infallibility; and so, perhaps, he may be taught to act justly.

Consistency and uniformity of language are thus just as important to the 'impartial spectator' of conscience as is sympathy itself,⁵ for who can be an impartial spectator while ignorant of the syntax of justice? And yet, although Burns quotes Smith-or paraphrases him very nearly, as Alexander Broadie has pointed out- in 'To a Louse' (Kinsley 83) ('O wad some Pow're the giftie gie us/*To see oursels as others see us*') he speaks the words of disinterested impartiality while actually speaking in the voice of a man who is not attending to the moral sermon of the preacher about that 'Power', but instead voyeuristically ogling a young woman in the front pews from behind: his is no grammar of justice, but a frank sexual interest and class envy posing as egalitarianism. The difference in rank between the louse, lady and speaker is a also a difference in language: the louse may be addressed as the 'crowlan ferlie' [creeping wonder] who might settle on an 'auld wife's *flainen* toy'[flannel cap] or 'squattle' in a 'beggar's haffet' [nestle in a temple], but 'Miss's fine *Lunardi*, fye!' brings us much closer to the world of Scottish 'standard' English, the language of the 'Misses' of Burns' world. By contrast, the louse sits at the bottom of the class pile without speech-living in 'plantations' as do the speechless slaves transported under (as Nigel Leask has pointed out) 'the guinea stamp', but different from them in that he is free to roam beyond the limits-'horn' (outlawry) and 'bane' set by society- the language of the comb is also the language of legal outlawry and social rejection. The louse is a 'ferlie', a wonder, because he escapes the class system which to the gazer is realized in terms of the lack of precisely that social mobility and free intimacy which the insect can command. To caress a young woman of position would be to take a 'freedom' with her: part of the puzzle for the speaker is that the lowest of the low, the louse in its overcrowded plantations, exiled from all society by 'horn' and 'bane', 'Detested, shunn'd, by saunt an' sinner', has that freedom, and can 'strunt rarely'. So Burns here challenges Smith's idea of moral sentiments as a proxy for a standard universalizable humanity, able to communicate as well as spectate, thus converting Scottish and social difference into British unity: class and language in their different ways divide the speaker from both louse and lady. Though he invokes the Smithian conscience, his is the gaze of voyeuristic envy, not that of the disinterested spectator, something like the role of the Scottish peasantry in the British state in fact. Hume's own 'Of National Characters' (1753) had implied that 'a unified [British] national identity will eventually coalesce as local attachments and habits give way to wider-reaching national sympathies'; Smith's theory of sympathy provided a basis for imaginative writing which celebrated such mutual British reconciliation. By the time *Theory of Moral Sentiments* entered its 5th and 6th edition, Smith was attempting to objectify refinement as a value, in an 'ethics' which 'valorized the virtues of assimilation' as against 'the awkwardness of a provincial dress'. This was the lesson absorbed by English-but paradoxically not entirely by Scottish-Romanticism. 'He who speaks two languages has no country', wrote Hazlitt, at about the same time that Scott was encouraging the use of Scots at Abbotsford and suggesting that both Scottish and English pronunciations of Latin should be taught at the new Edinburgh Academy.[6]

How could this work for Burns, for whom 'the appelation of a Scotch Bard, is by far my highest pride'? In the Kilmarnock Preface he makes it clear that unfamiliar languages are 'a fountain shut up' and 'a book sealed', against which he offers 'the sentiments and manners' of the 'native language' of Ayrshire and Scotland: yet of course, from the beginning he is also far from 'The Simple Bard unbroke by rules of

Art' of 'Nature's Bard' because of his extensive ability to cross register and language, so often misunderstood in interpreting – say – 'Tam o'Shanter'. Burns was anything but natural, anything but simple and direct. Influenced by Smith, he nonetheless interrogated the claims Smith made, because only thus could he have space to develop what he called 'counterpoise to the struggles of a world', a place to articulate difference, critique, reservation concerning the unitary language of a British public sphere and the shared polite subjects of its enquiry in intellectual discourse, and in physical sympathy the expressions of sentiment which were intense without ever breaking the bounds of propriety, the language of Clarinda. In challenging the hierarchy of registers-Bakhtin's heteroglossic hierarchy-Burns contested not only the linguistic unity of emergent British culture, but also the assump-tions of social rank and aspirational speech it had begun to embody. Instead, 'A Scottish Bard, proud of the name' proclaimed himself a ploughman who nonetheless was touched by 'Poetic Genius' to sing 'my native Soil, in my native tongue': yet the accessories to this are among the greatest images of English literature. Burns celebrates the 'rural scenes and rural pleasures' under cover of the *'mantle'* from *Lycidas*, the greatest English pastoral (and one of the earliest poems in English to integrate an image of the bard); his 'wildness, artless notes' enjoy a proximate derivation from Milton's Shakespeare: Just as Fergusson took 'Mirth' from *L'Allegro* so 'While the Plowman neer at hand,/Whistles ore the Furrow'd Land' from the same poem is Burns' paradoxical debt to Milton: in his lowest manifestation, his class and even colonial abjection before the Gentlemen of the Caledonian Hunt, he conceals his debt to the metaphors of a great predecessor by posing in them: as a ploughman speaking in a rustic tongue, how could he understand Milton, or sympathize with him? Yet he does,and can keep it private too: he is the 'uncouth Swain'; his *'Dorick* lay' of course both has the Theocritan license of vulgarity (a clear denominator of Theocritus' tradition) and the canonicity Theocritus has gained. Burns understands his auditors, but not they him, and this is the space in English-speaking British culture in which Scots (and sometimes Gaelic, of which Burns uses a number of terms) and Scotland's bard can live, remaining national, paradoxically, because they can use English poetry without it being recognized that they have done so, for in social prejudice sympathetic reading is annulled. And how deep this blindness can go: hundreds of allusions to the English canon were identified by Kinsley, and more have been found since: but it doesn't stop Burns being taken at face value as a 'dialect writer' by eminent scholars whose blushes deserve to be spared by not being named here. As Gramsci put it in discussing cosmopolitanism: 'as a metropolitan culture expands its sphere of influence, ambitious individuals from marginal groups learn to identify themselves with the dominant culture and become alienated from their social experience and cultural traditions'. We continue to live in the shadow of this process, which long ago Burns resisted.[7]

His battle was a contemporary one. When in 'Is there for Honest Poverty' (K482), published in the *Glasgow Magazine* and then the United Irish leaning *Northern Star* of Belfast successively in 1795 (a year of serious food shortages across western Scotland),[8] Burns alludes to the 'coward-slave', possibly begging for food-the 'hamely fare' is denied to the unlucky outcast whom we 'pass by', the 'we' are the Smithian children of commercial and sympathetic exchange for whom indeed 'the rank is but the guinea's stamp' in a system which ultimately rests on the branding stamp of the Guinea slave. At exactly the same time, Mungo Park in his *Travels in the Interior of Africa* was casting doubts on Smithian definitions of sympathy in his examination of the case of the slave who could sympathize with his hunger better than he with her because it was to her a normal, not an exceptional condition, but her miseries were not lessened by its normality. For Smith, 'honesty' is the norm in the world of commerce; for Burns, the 'honest man', like his Jacobite predecessor (the song shares the air of 'Tho Georthie Reigns in Jamie's stead') is a witness not to commercial exchange, but the solidarity of poverty, 'honest Poverty' which bears 'the gree', the prize of existence itself. The hunger of 1795–6 was a radicalizing hunger, coming as it did in the context of the collapse of Galloway cotton-spinning in 1793 and the declining rate of increase in real wages evident in that and following years. Radical contacts between small towns (many with handloom weavers) and dispossessed country dwellers increased. In Edinburgh, a repeat of the 1736 Porteous Riots was feared, and the climate was evident from the fact that in 1792 eleven thousand signed a petition to abolish slavery. The language of Burns' song was more than pertinent.[9]

In 'To a Mouse' (K69), Burns intensifies his exploration of the theme of rural dispossession, combining local event and the legacy of the

Sentimental era with a universal stance suited to his emerging prophetic status as the 'Simple Bard, unbroke by rules of Art'. The animal in question is many different things: a Sentimental object like Smart's cat Jeoffrey, the inheritor of a tradition of political fable reaching back to Robert Henryson and beyond, an avatar of the misery of the poet, and on some level a Wordsworthian solitary, the victim of a changing countryside. By the 1790s in Scotland 'best practice in harvesting technique was to cut the stubble so short that no corn was left for "gleaners and other pilferers" ', a further infringement on traditional rights. As Chris Whatley argues, 'Gleaning was the subject of mounting attacks, physical, legal and ideological, as property ownership in the countryside was consolidated in Scotland' (Whatley in Harris (2005), 29). The event is a moment in the speaker's life as a tenant farmer, which is poor as that of the mouse he encounters in part because Scottish leases, as Burns argued to the writer (solicitor) James Burness, 'make no allowance for the . . . quality of the land' compared with the British norm, and thus 'stretch us much beyond what . . . we will be found able to pay'. It was this situation which helped to bring Burns to the brink of emigration to Jamaica, all too alike the unhoused mouse of the poem: indeed, he wrote in 1788 to Mrs Dunlop that his conditions of living were such that he 'could almost exchange lives at any time' with farmyard animals.[10]

The initial language of 'To a Mouse' is unhoused, the register of the rural poor: the bard's voice is the voice of a ploughman's pity, of a tenant farmer with no wider horizons: 'WEE, sleeket, cowran, tim'rous *beastie* . . . Thou need na start awa sae hasty'. Yet this voice deceives us, and the first stanza, where ploughman meets mouse on a level, is succeeded by a second voiced by the benevolent bystander of Enlightenment theory. Instead of the agent who speaks to the mouse in local speech (for no Ayrshire mouse could be supposed to attempt standard English), a voice intervenes, who, in words close to Adam Smith's (and Pope's, Goldsmith's and Thomson's) is 'truly sorry Man's dominion/Has broken Nature's social union'. The 'social union' of all creatures is disrupted explicitly by human oppression of the mouse, and implicitly by human tyranny over others, the agricultural poor, bonded once again to the mice as *'fellow-mortal'* (l. 12) by virtue of the suffering both experience and by their difficulty in communicating it, even though they both display it: indeed, the idea that social union implies a union of language is present even today in Inuit protests over the Canadian Social Union. In a letter to the bookseller Peter Hill, Burns compared oppression of the poor to cats at 'a plundered Mouse-nest', his standard English indicative both of sympathy and of the speech of the spectator, concealing his own role as the suffering subject. In 'To a Mouse', as in 'Tam o' Shanter', both agent and spectator are conflated.[11]

Like many suffering from enclosure and the lowland clearance spurred by rack-renting, the mouse's house is ruined, and it is indeed the ploughman's role in a system of social oppression to ruin it: hence 'the cruel coulter' parallels 'crush's beneath the *furrow's* weight/Shall be thy doom' in 'To a Mountain Daisy'(K92). In such a case, Burns' prophetic bardic role cuts in. He asks a question ('What then?' (l. 14)) critical to agricultural disruption. The mouse's thieving is of necessity, for 'poor beastie, thou maun live!' (l.14). The most obscure Scots of the whole poem is then adduced to express that need, in an expression which binds the mouse back into a social union with the farming community of Scotland and its speech more intense than any principles relied on by the Enlightened spectator: for after all, 'Man', that abstract entity, has already disregarded those.' A *daimen-icker* in a *thrave'* (an ear of corn in two stooks) is 'a sma' request' for those whose 'wee-bit *housie'* is 'in ruin' (ll. 15, 19): '*daimen*', as Thomas Crawford points out, is a south-west Scottish word;[12] so indeed is 'icker', recorded in Ayr, Dumfries & Galloway. Burns uses the obscure Ayreshirism deliberately: it itself is 'a sma' request' for a wider social union's patience with the language of the farmer, as well as with the hunger of the mouse. Moreover, 'thrave' itself has further connotations: in its relationship to 'thraw', it is linked to twisting (the action of binding the stooks), including moral twisting: the nature of things is twisted and crooked when the poor must go hungry so the corn can be gathered in. The reproach of the poor may also be more than moral, for the 'thraw mouse' was proverbial of ill-luck: 'if a "thraw mouse" was allowed to run round the feet or hands the limbs would lose their power ever afterwards' (see *Scottish National Dictionary*). We are on the edge of connotation here, but is there a sense in which the sympathy of the farmer can be seen as a fending off of any ill-luck which the mouse may bring in encircling him with its wretchedness and wants after he has almost accidentally destroyed it.

The fate of the Scottish peasant farmer, a declining class threatened with homelessness and exile is to be like the mouse, 'turn'd out, for a' thy trouble' (l. 33): being hungry and homeless is a better guide to sympathy with the mouse than any dependence on a rhetoricized 'social union', even though Smith by contrast posits 'a sensibility, much beyond what is possessed by the rude vulgar' as a necessity for the 'amiable virtue' of a 'sensibility which surprises by its exquisite and unexpected delicacy'. More robust, but equally delicate, the Scots of 'Mousie, thou art no thy-lane' (l.37) advances a companionship which restores a social union-one of all creation, not simply those of 'amiable virtue', the union of Isaiah, not of the Select Society. The bardic voice then turns to mediate between the Enlightened spectator who thinks only in abstract Scots English ('I'm truly sorry Man's dominion/Has broken Nature's social union') and the peasant farmer who intensely realizes the compassionate moment in the fellowship of autochthonous speech:

> The best laid schemes o' *Mice* an' *Men*,
>   Gang aft agley,
> An'lea'e us nought but grief an'pain,
>   For promis'd joy !
>
> Still, thou art blest, compar'd wi' *me!*
>   The *present* only toucheth thee . . .
>   (ll.40–5)

The immediacy of the ploughman's response and the detachment of the Enlightened spectator are alike inadequate, but the former is much closer to the prophetic reality manifested by the bard who uses poetry (the quotation from Blair) at the end of the poem, just as philosophy (Smith) was used at the beginning, to mediate the ploughman's epiphanic rodent through emotion recollected in tranquillity, yet imperfectly, for guessing and fearing (l. 48) remain, as they do to all. Man's fate is to see beyond the moment, but not to deny that moment by abstracting from it unsustainable generalities: these too are 'schemes' that 'Gang . . . agley'. The poetic voice mediates standard English and agricultural Scots through a light Scots which depends on embedded references to Blair's *The Grave* and Johnson's *Rasselas*, emblems alike of the end of all creation and the illusory but permanent quality of hope.

Hugh Blair by John Kay

Burns' interrogation of Smith stands at the core of a process for the recovery of national diversity in the Romantic era. Herderian emphasis on particularities of language and tradition gave way-perhaps for obvious ideological reasons linked to World War II-in post 1945 Anglo-American criticism to the idea of the Romantic imagination as a unified aesthetic object, its particularities of location discreetly veiled by the common language in which they were expressed. But it is this very common language which Burns interrogates, revealing its function as an ideological weapon in the service of social and political conformity. The national bard could, after all, do no less.

NOTES

[1] Kenneth Johnston, *The Hidden Wordsworth* (London and New York: Norton, 1998).

[2] *Robert Burns' Common Place Book*, Raymond Lamont Brown (ed.) (Edinburgh: S.R. Publishers Ltd, 1969 [1872]), 7 for 1783 mention of Smith; Andrew Noble and Patrick Scott Hogg (eds), *The Canongate Burns* (Edinburgh: Canongate, 2001), p. 132; Raymond Bentman, *Robert Burns* (Boston: Twayne, 1987), p. 45.

[3] Murray Pittock, 'Historiography', in Alexander Broadie (ed.), *The Cambridge Companion to the Scottish Enlightenment* (Cambridge: Cambridge University Press, 2003), pp. 258–79 for 'teleology of civility' and similar concepts; Thomas P. Miller, *The Foundation of College English* (Pittsburgh: University of Pittsburgh Press, 1997), pp. 11, 17, 136, 192; James Sibbald, *Chronicle of Scottish Poetry*, 4 vols, (Edinburgh: Sibbald, 1802), IV: p. xlv.

[4] Miller (1997), 190; Edgeworth, *Ennui* Chapter 8 for an example of this (v. discussion in Murray Pittock, *Scottish and Irish Romanticism*, (Oxford: Oxford University Press, 2008), p. 182–85; for Enlightenment thought as reconciliation in Smith, v. Luke Gibbons, unpublished paper to the Scots-Irish Leverhulme seminar, University of Strathclyde (2002) and also *Edmund Burke and Ireland*, (Cambridge: Cambridge University Press, 2003).

[5] Adam Smith, *Theory of Moral Sentiments*, D. D. Raphael and A. L. Macfie (eds) (Oxford: Clarendon Press, 1979), pp. 15, 25, 175–76, 204–5. Copy-text is 6th [1790] edition.

[6] Alexander Broadie (ed.), *The Scottish Enlightenment* (Edinburgh: Canongate, 1997), p. 285; Evan Gottlieb, '"Fools of Prejudice": Sympathy and National Identity in the Enlightenment and *Humphry Clinker*', *Eighteenth-Century Fiction* 18:1 (2005), pp. 81–106 (85–86, 89, 95, 97); Miller (1997), p. 201; Hazlitt, quoted at Pittock (2008), p. 23; *The Journal of Sir Walter Scott*, W. E. K. Anderson (ed.) (Oxford: Clarendon Press, 1972).

[7] *The Letters of Robert Burns*, J. de Lancy Ferguson and Ross Roy (eds), 2nd edn, 2 vols, (Oxford: Clarendon Press, 1985), Letter 90; Robert Burns, *Poems Chiefly in the Scottish Dialect*, (Kilmarnock: John Wilson, 1786), p. 1; *Poems, Chiefly in the Scottish*

Dialect, (Edinburgh: William Creech, 1787), p. vi; cf. Noble and Scott Hogg (2001), pp. 4–5, 169–70; Miller (1997), p. 11.

[8] Noble and Scott Hogg (2001); Christopher A. Whatley, 'Roots of 1790s Radicalism: Reviewing the Economic and Social Background', in Bob Harris (ed.), *Scotland in the Age of the French Revolution* (Edinburgh: John Donald, 2005), p. 23–48 (26). Kinsley notes that 'the rank is but the guinea's stamp' comes originally from William Wycherley's, *Plain Dealer* (1677).

[9] Christopher J. Berry, 'Adam Smith: Commerce, Liberty and Modernity' in P. Gilmour (ed.), *Philosophers of the Enlightenment*, (Edinburgh: Edinburgh University Press, 1989), pp. 113–32 (125) for Smith and 'honesty'; Whatley in Harris (2005), pp. 24–25; Harris, 'Political Protests in the Year of Liberty, 1792', ibid, pp. 49–78 (60).

[10] Ferguson and Ross Roy (1985), Letters pp. 14, 290; Noble and Scott Hogg (2001), pp. xi, 96. 'Simple Bard' is from the Kilmarnock Preface

[11] Ferguson and Roy (1985), Letter 325.

[12] Thomas Crawford, *Robert Burns: The Poems and Songs* 3rd edn, (Edinburgh: Canongate Academic, 1994[1960]), pp.xi–xii.

SEX AND SOCIAL COMMENTARY

☙

Robert Burns's Merry Musing

PAULINE ANNE GRAY

Robert Burns's untimely death at the age of just thirty-six, and the complicated process of collating his hitherto disorganised poetry and letters for the publication of his posthumous life and works, was beleaguered by the same controversy courted by the poet throughout his short, but eventful life. One of the most contentious aspects of this process was the careful editing and ultimate censorship of a number of Burns's letters and works considered unfit for public consumption, and potentially damaging to the poet's reputation. Documents and letters that were considered likely to provoke controversy surrounding the poet's religious and political beliefs, not to mention his fascination with the opposite sex which was often both enthusiastic and uninhibited, were either destroyed or suppressed. Included amongst these documents was a collection of bawdy songs, some of which Burns wrote himself and others that he collected for recitation at the Crochallan Fencibles; an Edinburgh drinking club to which he was introduced in 1787. Reserved, sanctimonious attitudes towards sex, gender and religion common in Burns's time rendered the bawdy aspect of his work taboo and so the collection, commonly known as *The Merry Muses of Caledonia*, was censored.

Thankfully, largely owing to the literary underground of the eighteenth and nineteenth centuries, a significant number of Burns's bawdy productions have survived; a testament to their undeniable, if somewhat peculiar worth as literary and cultural documents. However, it was not until the 1960s, following the success of the famous *Lady Chatterley's Lover* case and the consequent reassessment of literary eroticism's place in modern culture, that Burns's bawdy productions were officially published in the public domain. For this reason, Burns's bawdy verse has been relatively little explored by literary critics. Whilst it is true to say that even today the abundant sexual content and bawdiness of many of Robert Burns's satires and songs has the potential to cause offence, it is time for notions of the 'profane' qualities in his work to be reassessed in the light of his serious intellectual agenda as a writer. A close examination of a selection of Burns's bawdy verse adds to our awareness of the poet's gift for social realism, his deep psychological perception of society and human nature, and his use of sexuality as a means of cultural and social comment; to consider everything from the human condition to politics and religion.

In the political song 'Why shouldna poor folk mowe,'[1] often published under the more polite title 'When Princes and Prelates', Burns subverts the social hierarchy by pointing out that the so-called lower classes command a most powerful political weapon; what he considers to be their expert ability to reproduce. In this particular song, the power and significance of sexuality and human reproduction is symbolised by the success of the French revolution. And so, the common masses surmount the European ruling class, who are portrayed as sexually and ultimately politically impotent:

> By sea and by shore! The Emperor swore,
>   In Paris he'd kick up a row;
> But Paris sae ready just laugh at the laddie
> And bade him gae tak him a mowe. –
>
> (ll. 13–16)

> Chorus –
> And why shouldna poor folk mowe, mowe, mowe,
>   And why shoudna poor folk mowe:
> The great folk hae siller, and houses, and lands,
> Poor bodies hae naething but mowe.

Here the attacking European monarch is defeated and condescendingly advised to return home to copulate. The alliterative reference to the Emperor as 'laddie' obviously undermines his authority, but more than that, it posits the notion frequently expressed by Burns, and ever-present in folk culture, that common man is significantly more accomplished at sex than the upper class. For Burns, sex and reproduction are central to humanity, and so true authority lies with common man, united and made powerful by their sexuality. The abundant, rhythmic repetition in the chorus, 'mowe, mowe, mowe', emulates the bodily actions associated with copulation, bringing physicality to the fore. This is maintained by reference to the common folk as 'poor *bodies*'. However this expression is not intended to provoke pity. Rather, this is a defiant song that advocates the triumph of sex over social class, and so common man is depicted as comparatively content when considered alongside the troubled monarchs of Europe and their unsuccessful battles with republican France:

> When princes & prelates & het-headed zealots,
> All Europe hae set in a lowe,
> The poor man lies down, nor envies a crown,
> And comforts himsel' wi' a mowe.
>
> (ll. 1–4)

The turbulent, aggressive European political climate is emphasised by the usage of 'lowe', Scots for 'flame'. This sinister metaphor is followed by the significantly more serene notion of the common folk as a positive, constructive community, who derive comfort and satisfaction from sexual intercourse, a natural activity. And so we acknowledge the idea frequently posited by Burns throughout his work that pleasurable sex is a natural phenomenon to which every man has the right, and which ought to be embraced.

Whilst it is not uncommon for people acquainted with Burns's life, correspondence, and bawdy verse to derive that the poet advocates an unbridled enjoyment of sex, it is apparent from 'Why shouldna poor folk mowe' that his principles regarding the subject are not entirely without morality:

> Auld Kate laid her claws on poor Stanislaus,
> And Poland has bent like a bow:
> Mat the deil in her ass ram a huge prick o' brass!
> And damn her in hell with a mowe!
>
> (ll. 17–20)

KING, QUEEN, & DAUPHIN,

OF FRANCE.

Sic transit gloria mundi.

French Royal Family by John Kay

Burns here expresses his disapproval of what he considers to be unnatural sex. The above reference is to Catherine II of Russia (1729–1796) and her attainment of Poland. Catherine is the one monarch in the course of the song who utilises her sexuality to her advantage by using her lover, Stanislaus Poniatowski, as a pawn in her political games. Catherine of Russia, having placed Stanislaus on the Polish throne in 1763, then played an active part in the partition of Poland in 1772 and 1793 and Burns's disapproval of these underhand politics is expressed in sexual language. In this case, the sexual act is not a natural, positive action based on love or human impulse, but may be perceived as manipulation aimed at the attainment of power and material possession. The alliterative, phallic language used to describe the political defeat of Poland implies the political castration of her lover and an entire country by 'Auld Kate' who is driven by power, more so than sexual desire. Burns's punishment for what he believes to be a contrived, dishonest and therefore unnatural abuse of sex is extremely sexually violent, and alludes to what was in the eighteenth century often considered to be an unnatural sex act – sodomy.

It is interesting to note the morality that Burns applies to matters of human sexuality. Well known for his promiscuity and extra-marital affairs, he fathered at least twelve children to at least five women. And yet, in poems such as 'The Fornicator', which we will come to shortly, he is defiant in the face of public censure. Burns shows no remorse or disapproval of sex borne of passion and tenderness towards the opposite gender, conjugal or otherwise. It is the abuse of what he considers to be life's greatest privilege that the poet opposes. In support of this we might turn to Burns's correspondence where we encounter his opinions pertaining to what he considers another unnatural manifestation of sexuality – prostitution. In a letter written to his younger brother William on the 10th February 1790, Burns states, 'I give you great credit for you [*sic*] sobriety with respect to that universal vice, Bad Women.'[2] He goes on to say that:

> Whoring is a most ruinous expensive species of dissipation; is spending a poor fellow's money with which he ought clothe & support himself nothing? Whoring has ninety nine chances in a hundred to bring on a man the most nauseous & excruciating diseases to which Human nature is liable; [. . .] All this is independent of the criminality of it. –[3]

And so, we might consider it interesting that Burns adopts such a strong, somewhat haughty moral stance, given his own repeated rejection of social and religious restrictions pertaining to sexuality, and his detestation of the self-righteous and hypocritical nature of those who claim to uphold such restrictions.

From his writing, Burns's disdain for hypocrisy is clear, and particularly for that which he considers to be rife amongst the pious and self-righteous members of his community. It is, however, the duplicity of such people that the poet attacks in his writing, rather than their professed faith. Burns believes in equality of men – both religious and political – and so he reacts against the assumed superiority of 'the elect'. In a letter to Alexander Cunningham, Burns insists that 'of all Nonsense, Religious Nonsense is the most nonsensical'.[4] It is important to note that Burns clearly distinguishes between 'Religion' and what he calls 'Religious Nonsense', and then proceeds to attack the latter:

> They are orderly; they may be just; nay, I have known them merciful: but still your children of Sanctity move among their fellow-creatures with a nostril snuffing putrescence, & a foot spurning filth, in short, with that conceited dignity which your titled Douglases, Hamiltons, Gordons, or any other of your Scots Lordlings of seven centuries standing, display [am (deleted)] when they accidentally mix among the many-aproned Sons of Mechanical life. –[5]

This excerpt forces us to recognize the relationship between Burns's Religious and political predilection. The 'children of Sanctity' are likened to conceited members of the upper class, and as such are portrayed in an unattractive manner. The plosive phrase 'nostril snuffing putrescence' and the alliteration of 'foot spurning filth' communicate aggression, yet Burns cleverly manipulates these phrases, creating an almost humorous caricature of the self-righteous. In doing so, Burns uses irony to convey the opinion that it is the supposed 'children of Sanctity' who are somewhat undesirable, as opposed to the 'many-aproned Sons of Mechanical life' who may be considered to represent honest, hard-working, but also natural men; men who accept that they are subject to the automatic, involuntary forces that nature has put in place, but who are wrongly considered by the sanctimonious to be less moral, or of a lower class.

The self-righteous, on the other hand, are considered by Burns as unnatural, in that their religious fanaticism has caused them to suppress their human instincts (at least outwardly) and consequently effected narrow-mindedness and an 'illiberalized' heart. However, it is their inability to entirely escape human nature that ultimately renders them hypocritical. Burns communicates this notion by reference to the loss of his own childlike naivety, which culminates in the exclamation, 'How ignorant are Plough-boys! – Nay! I have since discovered that a *godly woman* may be a – !'[6] It is safe to say that, at this point, Burns' tongue is firmly in his cheek. However, it is significant that Burns's protest against hypocrisy concludes with what he considers to be the ultimate truth: no matter how self-righteous one is, one can't escape human nature. Even a '*godly woman*' is subject to carnal appetites, and not least sexuality, which Burns considers to be the most powerful natural instinct. And so, Burns uses sexual subject matter to emphasise social truths; the inability of the self-righteous to deny their natural sexuality, and the hypocrisy sprung from religious fanaticism.

The 18th century Scottish Kirk's disapproval of sexual desire is evident from the sermons zealously preached by Presbyterian ministers to the general public. It was not uncommon for sermons to then be published and circulated in print. Consequently, Burns would almost definitely have borne witness to one or another form of the Kirk's two-pronged assault on sin, and particularly on what were considered 'the sins of the flesh'. The following excerpt from a sermon by Reverend David Imrie published in 1748, *The necessity of the almighty power and grace of God to cure the infection of sin*, is an example of the fear-mongering both preached and published by some ministers, to deter their congregation from acting upon the 'sensual passions':

> And particularly, there is nothing that more weakens and enervates the soul, and renders it incapable of every thing that is great and good, than the vitious and irregular indulgence of the *sensual passions*. Where a vitious *habit* of this kind begins to *prevail* devotion is extinguished, and an indolence of spirit, and indisposition towards every thing that is noble and manly, seizes upon the soul and thoroughly possesses it.[7]

The Rev. David Imrie enthusiastically broadcasts the sadistic notion that 'sensual passions' are unhealthy, violent, soul destroying and ultimately evil. This view was not uncommon in the Presbyteries of

Burns's day, and so strict sanctions were put in place to 'regulate' the moral, and for that matter the sexual, behaviour of the community.

The Scottish Kirk's attempt to regulate the sexual behaviour of the community took the form of ritual public humiliation for those whose behaviour was considered to be sexually deviant. Fornicators and adulterers were therefore often sentenced to a spell upon the cutty stool, also commonly referred to as the stool of repentance. The cutty stool was usually a wooden structure that stood directly in front of the pulpit. Offenders were dressed in sackcloth and made to stand at the entrance of the church whilst the worshippers arrived. They were then led to the cutty stool before the sermon, where they would stand bare-legged and hatless, and be rebuked by the minister, sometimes for as many as thirty consecutive Sundays. Indeed, the fear amongst the community at the prospect of such shame and humiliation can scarcely be imagined, and it is widely believed that the threat of the cutty stool prompted numerous young, pregnant females to take their own lives or that of their child. Ultimately the Kirk, in their attempt to prevent sin, drove young girls to even greater crime.

It is widely believed that Robert Burns first came under the censure of the Kirk in 1784–1785 owing to his affair with a servant girl, Elizabeth Paton. This affair resulted in the birth of the poet's first child, Elizabeth or rather 'dear bought bess'. The session books of Tarbolton Kirk for the period of Burns's attendance there are unfortunately no longer extant, and consequently there is no formal record of the young couple having been publicly rebuked on this occasion, yet Burns alludes to the Kirk's disapproval in two poems inspired by the incident. In 'The Fornicator'[8] we acknowledge Burns's inability, or rather his unwillingness, to take seriously the punishment imposed by the Kirk for fornication, which Burns describes as 'the blissful joy of lovers':

> Before the congregation wide
>   I pass'd the muster fairly,
> My handsome Betsey by my side,
>   We gat our ditty rarely;
> My downcast eye by chance did spy,
>   What made my mouth to water,
> Those limbs sae clean, where I between
>   Commenced Fornicator.
>
> (ll. 9–16)

> Wi' ruefu' face and signs o' grace
>   I paid the buttock hire;
> The night was dark, and thro the park
>   I cou'dna but convoy her;
> A parting kiss, what could I less,
>   My vows began to scatter;
> Sweet Betsey fell – fal lal de ral!
>   I am a Fornicator.
>
>   (ll. 17–24)

Here we see the triumph of sexuality over religious orthodoxy. Burns and his lover stand side by side on the cutty stool. Instead of attentively receiving his rebuke, Burns is rather distracted by the 'bare-legs' of his 'handsome Betsey', an image that becomes at once highly sexualised by the poets reference to the parting of his lovers legs and his own watering mouth; symbolic of his sexual arousal. This is not the only time that we see Burns as distracted by the female form whilst in church. It is interesting to note that Burns's failure to fully participate in Sunday worship, in favour of daydreaming about women, is also apparent in poems such as 'To a Louse' and 'Epigram to Miss Ainslie in Church'. The poet does not seem ashamed to be standing on the cutty stool – at this point in time it seems of little consequence to him. Rather, he is preoccupied with thoughts of what caused him to be there in the first place – sex. The next stanza sees the poet pay the monetary fine which he caustically terms 'buttock-hire', and so the Kirk's compulsory fine for the act of fornication is ironically sub-verted, becoming money (or rather tax) for sex. Burns pays the fine with feigned 'rueful face and signs of grace' only for the couple to reoffend as soon as they leave church, reiterating the fact that this song is not remorseful in the least, it is a defiant and unashamed assertion of Burns's frequently posited belief that sex conquers all. And so, Burns's assertion that he is indeed a 'Fornicator' becomes a defiant affirmation of his sexuality as opposed to a label of debauchery and impiety.

Burns adopts a more serious tone to address the same incident in 'A Poets Welcome to his Love-Begotten Daughter; the first instance that entitled him to the venerable appellation of Father'.[9] This particular title reinforces the notion that the poet's daughter is indeed the product of love, with all of its positive connotations. However, it is important to note that the manuscript of this poem preserved in the

Rosenbach Museum and Library in Philadelphia provides evidence that Burns alternatively named this piece 'A Poets Welcome to his Bastart Wean'. That is not to say that this obviously more crude title is a literal reflection of Burns's thoughts pertaining to the birth of his daughter. Rather, it conveys the same earthy defiance identified in the preceding discussion of 'The Fornicator', with Burns's positive attitude towards the arrival of his daughter exuding from the poem itself:

> Welcome, my bonie, sweet, wee dochter!
> Tho' ye come here a wee unsought for,
> And tho' your comin I hae fought for
>   Baith kirk and queir;
> Yet, by my faith, ye're no unwrought for –
>   That I shall swear!
>
>   (ll. 13–18)

The defiance with which Burns rejects the Kirk's zealous disapproval of his begetting an illegitimate child is clearly and effectively conveyed. Whilst admitting that his child could have arrived under more advantageous circumstances, Burns establishes that 'by his faith' her being born, her existence, is of greater importance than the puritanical notions of the established Kirk and the society in which he lives. The phrase 'ye're no unwrought for', reiterates the poet's sincere determination in defending the birth of his daughter against the disapproval of the Kirk, whilst simultaneously introducing an element of warm humour by alluding to the physical exertion involved in the act of procreation, and so Burns, ironically and humorously, conveys his perceived drudgery in dealing with the Kirk session.

The song 'Yestreen I Had A Pint O Wine'[10] is commonly believed to have been inspired by yet another of Burns's fruitful affairs, this time with Helen Park. Very little hard detail is known about this woman including the date of her birth or the date and means of her death. She is thought to have been the niece of the owner of the Globe Tavern in Dumfries, a regular haunt of the poet, and it is here that she is assumed to have met and begun her affair with Burns, who was by this time married to Jean Armour. Helen fell pregnant and gave birth to Burns's daughter Elizabeth (1791 – 1873), commonly known as Betty, a matter of days before his wife Jean gave birth to his son William Nicol Burns.

In spite of the obviously complicated circumstances surrounding the affair, the notion of the depth of the poets' feelings and intimacy with 'Anna' is poignantly developed in the following stanza where his need for, and rejoice in their physical and emotional union is conveyed by religious metaphors:

> The hungry Jew, in wilderness,
> Rejoicing o'er his manna,
> Was naething to my hinny bliss,
> Upon the lips of Anna.
>
> (ll. 5–8)

Here we observe the idea of physical and emotional dependence. The 'hungry Jew' was provided with manna,[11] to act as physical and spiritual sustenance, and likewise, the poet's intimacy with Anna and his resulting pleasure is necessary to sustain him both physically and spiritually. In more general terms this might be considered representative of one view consistently posited by Burns throughout his work; that pleasurable sex is a gift from God that is both natural and essential to life.

The idea of sex as one of the most important and essential aspects of human life may also be acknowledged in stanzas three and four where we observe what appears to be the poets increasing intimacy with, and need for his lover, 'Gie me within my straining grasp/The melting form of Anna' (III, 11–12), not to mention another metaphorical assertion of the importance that he places upon their intimacy:

> Then I'll despise Imperial charms,
> An Empress or Sultana;
> While dying raptures in her arms,
> I give and take with Anna.
>
> (ll. 13–16)

Stanzas three and four see the poet undermine the political authority and importance of monarchy, in favour of the essential and life-giving union of man and woman, reinforcing the sentiment expressed in 'Poor bodies do naething but mowe'. The notion of sexual enjoyment is conveyed by the ambiguous, yet very erotic imagery present in the lines, 'While dying raptures in her arms/I give and take with Anna', which act as an extremely poignant, tender, and emotional depiction of the act of sexual intercourse as well as reinforcing the ideas of equality and mutual enjoyment that seem to be a recurring and important part of Burns's attitude towards heterosexual relationships both physical and otherwise.

Most interesting is the postscript to this song that appears in *The Merry Muses of Caledonia (1799)*. This was recorded in a hand other than that of Burns, yet it remains entirely possible, even likely, that it is the work of Burns himself. Indeed the following stanza does appear to be a strong representation of Burns's attitudes, something that is evident not only from his work, but from the way in which he lived his life:

> The kirk and state may join and tell;
> To do sic things I manna:
> The kirk and state may gae to h-ll,
> An' I shall gae to Anna.

And so here is a pointedly defiant rejection of any interference and attempted jurisdiction over human relationships and sexual activity by both religious and political orders.

It is clear from the material discussed and from the way in which Burns lived his life that the poet does not recognise the social and religious restrictions imposed upon the community as regards physical passion. Burns embraces sexuality as a natural, life-giving, pleasurable force necessary for the success of civilization. For him, sex is the ultimate expression of humanity; the undeniable unifying principle that binds and levels man, regardless off social class or creed. It is his openness to this reality, and his refusal to deny or suppress what he considers an essential component of human life that sets him apart from the predominant religious orthodoxy of his community, and renders the verse discussed controversial to 'polite' society. However, from the above it is clear that Burns's skilful use of sexuality as a means of cultural and social comment renders the poet's bawdy verse great poetry.

NOTES

[1] Carruthers, G. *Burns: Poems* (ed.) (Everyman: London, 2006), pp. 124–5.
[2] G. Ross Roy and J. DeLancey Ferguson Eds., *The Letters of Robert Burns,* vol. II, (Oxford, 1985), p. 14.
[3] Ibid.

4 Ibid., p. 146.

5 Ibid., p. 147.

6 *Letters II*, Letter 506, p. 147.

7 David Imrie, A. M. Minister of the Gospel at Dalton, *The necessity of the almighty power and grace of God to cure the infection of sin: Illustrated in A Sermon, preached before The Synod of Dumfries, At Dumfries, Oct. 11. 1748*, (Edinburgh, 1748), pp. 6–7.

8 *The Merry Muses of Caledonia*, facsimile edition produced by G. Ross Roy, (University of South Carolina Press; Columbia, 1999), pp. 3–4.

9 Carol McGuirk (ed.), *Robert Burns: Selected Poems*, (Penguin Books; London, 1993).

10 *The Merry Muses of Caledonia*, facsimile edition produced by G. Ross Roy, (University of South Carolina Press: Columbia, 1999), pp. 9–10.

11 In the Bible, Book of Exodus, Ch.16, manna was the food supplied by God to the Israelites starving in the wilderness.

ROBERT BURNS AND THE STIMULANT REGIME

❧

NIGEL LEASK

Despite longstanding disagreement about the medical symptoms lead-ing up to his untimely death in July 1796, much work remains to be done respecting Robert Burns and the medical scene in 18th century Scot-land. That Burns was himself a pointed commentator on the subject is evident in his poem 'Death and Dr Hornbook', a satire on the effects of William Buchan's best selling Domestic Medicine (1769) and the popularisation of medical expertise. Here 'Death' complains that he's been cheated of his dues by the self-taught village physician/ school-master 'Dr Hornbook', and threatens a terrible revenge;

> Ye ken Jock Hornbook i' the Clachan,
> Deil mak his king's-hood in a spleuchan!
> He's grown sae weel acquaint wi' Buchan,
>   And ither chaps,
> The weans haud out their fingers laughing,
>   And pouk my hips.[1]

In the present essay I'll focus rather on the role of 18th century medical theory in constructing Burns's posthumous reputation, and its influence on subsequent romantic writings about 'the infirmities of genius'. In this, as in other respects, the case of Burns possessed a seminal importance well beyond his native Scotland.

In July 1800 Charles Lamb wrote to Coleridge expressing sharp criticism of the recently published 'Life of Burns'; 'very confusedly and badly written, and interspersed with dull pathological and medical discussions. It is written by a Dr Currie. Do you know the well-meaning doctor? Alas, *ne sutor ultra crepitum!*[2] Coleridge had recently met Dr James Currie, an expatriate Scottish physician who had settled in Liverpool, and thought rather more highly of his biography of Burns. In his anonymously published 'Life' Currie did indeed bring considerable professional baggage to bear on his life of the Ayrshire poet by locating him in terms of a medical theory which Michael Barfoot has dubbed 'the stimulant regime'.[3] By this I mean a radical and materialist theory of the cause and treatment of disease known in the 18th century as the 'Brunonian system' after its inventor the Scottish physician Dr John Brown, which became popular in late enlightenment Edinburgh, and subsequently influenced the whole medical profession in Britain and overseas.

Currie's 1800 edition of Burns' Works, prefaced by the controversial biography of the poet, had gone through 5 editions and about 10,000 copies by 1805, making it the standard account of Burns for the romantic period. Apart from his own Scottish roots, Currie's claim to write the life of Burns the 'heaven taught ploughman' lay in his role as a professional observer and manager of the poor. He was the sort of reforming bourgeois intellectual who might have been invented by Michel Foucault if he hadn't actually existed: a leading abolitionist and Dissenting activist, he was a prominent member of Liverpool's Committee for Managing the Poor, a physician in the Liverpool Dispensary (a charitable hospitable for the poor), and was later instrumental in establishing both the Liverpool Fever hospital and Lunatic Asylum.

Although Currie held that at his best Burns 'rises . . . into a strain of grandeur and sublimity, which modern poetry has not surpassed',[4] he argued that the sword had consumed the scabbard, and that the poet's 'high-wrought sensibility which laid the foundations of his excellence' also explained the 'defects' which had brought about his premature decline into alcoholism and dissipation, precipitating his early death in 1796.[5] Underlying Currie's charges of moral weakness lay rumours of Burns's sexual irregularities, and his political radicalism, both played down in the 1800 biography. Despite his anonymity, Currie had himself been a prominent radical pamphleteer in the early 1790's, and in the reactionary political climate of 1800 preferred to cast a veil of silence over the recent 'war of ideas', especially as the philanthropic motive of the edition was to raise money for the poet's widow and surviving children.[6]

26 ℞ℱ
1786

John Brown by John Kay

Dr John Brown and the 'Brunonian System'

Like Robert Burns, Dr John Brown (1735–1787) hailed from a humble rural background, son of a weaver from Lintlaws in Berwickshire, and like the poet benefited from the Scottish parochial education system, although he was raised in a small community of Presbyterian Seceders rather than the Kirk. Both men had quickly discovered that professional self-advancement was dependent upon successfully negotiating the class-bound patronage network of 18th century Scotland. Despite their achievements, both poet and physician in the end fell foul of the system and died prematurely, in relative poverty and (in Brown's case, if not Burns') alcohol and opium dependence. Brown was a larger-than-life character whose 'Doric dialect' (according to his biographer Thomas Beddoes) was unintelligible to English ears, who admired David Hume's infidelity and scepticism, and who loudly proclaimed his anti-unionist politics, of both a Jacobite and republican stamp. Acquainted with Robert Burns's associates William Smellie and William Nichol (he never met the poet himself) in 1784 he founded a Masonic Lodge entitled 'The Friends of the Roman Eagle' and was elected 'Latin Secretary' to the eccentric Earl of Buchan's Society of Antiquaries, noted for its Fletcherite and classical republican leanings. Brown was also the grandfather of the painter Ford Madox Brown.[7]

After his breach with his mentor Professor William Cullen and failure to win recognition from the medical establishment in Edinburgh, Brown began to disseminate his ideas to students extra-murally, and in 1780 published his influential Elementa Medicinae, a work which caused bitter controversy, despite being published in Latin. Christopher Lawrence summarises its radical simplification of current medical theory; 'Brown used contemporary ideas of irritability and sensibility as the basis for a dualist theory of disease and a radically simplified therapeutics. He taught that excitability, a property of the nervous system, was the fundamental feature of living bodies. It was activated by environmental stimuli to produce excitement, the life force . . . For Brown, health was an equilibrium between stimulus and excitability. Insufficient stimulation caused asthenic diseases, with a deficit of excitement and a surfeit of unused excitability. Treatment for these diseases, by far the most common, was by stimulation, notably by the ingestion of opium and alcohol, a therapy Brown applied liberally for his own gout . . . The opposite of asthenic diseases were the less frequent sthenic disorders which required mild depletion. By eighteenth-century standards Brunonianism was sparing in its use of bloodletting and purging'.[8]

Asthenic diseases, we should note, particularly hypochondria, taedium vitae, melancholia and depression, seems to have been the particular bane of provincialized, under-stimulated, post-Union Scotland, as is evident from James Boswell's Journals, although Boswell didn't need his physician's advice to reach for artificial stimulation. Brown was notorious for overdoing the 'stimulant regime' on himself, and died an impoverished laudanum addict in London in 1788. His biographer Thomas Beddoes wrote that 'one of his pupils informs me that when he found himself languid, he sometimes placed a bottle of whisky in one hand, and a phial of laudanum on the other; and that, before he began his lecture, he would take forty or fifty drops of laudanum in a glass of whisky; repeating the dose four or five times during the lecture. Between the effects of these stimulants and voluntary exertion, he soon waxed warm, and by degrees his imagination was exalted into phrenzy.'[9]

James Currie as a Medical Writer

It's hardly surprising that James Currie appears to have been strongly influenced by Brunonian ideas, given that he'd been a medical student at Edinburgh University between 1777 and 1780, the years when Brown exerted maximum influence on younger members of the Medical Faculty, and particularly the Royal Medical Society, which Currie joined as a young man. Although he never mentions the fact, it's probable that Currie knew Brown personally. In his essay 'Brunonianism under the bed', Michael Barfoot suggests that many of the young medical students influenced by Brown's radical theories subsequently preferred to keep quiet about the fact as they climbed the professional ladder to medical respectability; 'a former allegiance to Brown, rather like Hobbes or Hume before him, may have been something that had to be denied even in private'.[10] Brown represented the materialist values and politics of Scotland's 'radical enlightenment', such as it was.

This helps explain why in his later writings Currie paints such a negative portrait of Brown, consistently less willing to admit the influence of Brunionism than his friends and Edinburgh contemporaries Thomas Beddoes and Erasmus Darwin, grandfather of the more famous Charles. (Both physicians came under the sway of Brunonianism whilst studying at Edinburgh.) In fact Currie later criticised Brown for theoretical inflexibility as well as 'dangerous generalisations' in rejecting standard nosologies (classifications of disease), while praising his former teacher Cullen for resisting Brown's materialism.[11] In 1795 Thomas Beddoes published a new translation of the Latin Elementa prefaced by a rather ambivalent biography of Brown, in order to raise a subscription for his impoverished family. It's worth noting that Currie's edition and life of Burns – which he embarked upon the year after the publication of his friend Beddoes's medical biography of Brown – was undertaken for identical reasons, and cast a similarly critical light on its subject. Indeed, despite obvious formal debts to Boswell's Life of Johnson, I'm convinced that Beddoes' biography of Brown was a major influence on Currie's 'Life of Burns'. Brunonians, as Roy Porter has noted, emphasised the importance of detailed case histories, or 'the individual's constitutional diathesis', in diagnosing disease, and were particularly concerned by the balance between 'the healthy requirement for excitation of a particular constitution, and the quantum of stimulus being received or generated'.[12] As we'll see, this concern is evident in Currie's treatment of Burns, (as Lamb noted) and there's also evidence of direct and even verbal borrowings from Beddoes' 'Brunonian' biography of Brown.

Long before embarking on his famous edition of Burns, James Currie was well regarded as a medical author. As a student he'd composed an Essay on Hypochondria which he read to the Manchester Literary and Philosophical Society in 1781. Hypochondria was the pathological form of melancholy, the former characterised by 'gloom, timidity and selfishness', while the latter is characterised by 'a grandeur of sentiment and sublimity of fancy' [Memoirs, I, 441]. But anticipating his judgements on Burns, Currie suggests that 'those grand aspirations of the human mind which give sublimity to the poet, and enthusiasm to the patriot, might perhaps be considered a species of melancholia' [Memoirs, I, 447], an important idea for romantic theories of genius.

The most important statement of Currie's philosophical development is his long article on Thomas Reid's Essays on the Active Powers of Man published in the *Analytical Review* in 1788. Currie here writes as an active partisan of the Scottish Common Sense philosopher, whose work, he was glad to report 6 years later, was 'gaining ground in England, though till very lately it seems not to have been understood' [Memoir II, 319]. Via Reid, Currie arrived at a thoroughly orthodox voluntarist conclusion in refuting the determinism and materialism of Hume and Priestley, albeit one supported by a formidable philosophical scaffolding; 'motives support liberty in the agent, or they have no influence at all. Rational beings, in proportion as they are wise and good, act according to the best motives . . . a free action is not an effect without a cause [contra Hume], since it is caused by a being who has power and will to produce it'.[13]

Given that Burns scholars still regard the effect of Currie's 'Life of Burns' on the poet's posthumous reputation as being like a bucket of cold water poured on the still-glowing embers of his genius, it's appropriate that his major medical treatise was entitled Medical Reports, on the Effects of Water, Cold and Warm, as a remedy in Fever and other Diseases.[14] Currie's advocacy of 'cold affusions' to cure fever was linked to his work with the poor and insane, in the Liverpool Fever Hospital and on the Committee for the Management of the Poor, and clearly marks the influence of the 'stimulant regime' on his own medical practice. Currie argued that 'fever prevails chiefly amongst the poor', the new proletariat of Britain's urban/industrial/ military complex, and he feared that contagion might break out in hospitals, factories, prisons, war and slave ships, anywhere the poor were concentrated and exploited. [MR I, p. 16]. Appropriately enough, he also described Robert Burns as being 'liable to fever of body, as well as of mind'. [Currie I, 219].

Currie recommended – quite literally – pouring cold water on the incipient problems of the new class of urban poor, with a view to allaying bourgeois fears of plebeian revolution. He reasoned that 'the stimulating action of cold, though short in duration, is powerful in degree. In the torpor of convulsion, when weaker stimuli are unperceived, the affusion of cold water on the naked body will often excite the dormant sensibility, and introduce a new action throughout the nervous system'. [MR I, 74] He did allow for 'affusion' with cool rather than cold water in certain cases, but condemned hot water bathing as a symptom of decadence. The Roman taste for hot baths coincided with the decadence of empire; 'in the bagnios of Imperial

Rome, the last of the Romans, the followers of Zeno and of Cato, sought to sooth their sorrows, and were melted down into slaves. The powers of their minds became enfeebled, the vigor of their frames decayed, and they lost for ever the bold impression of freedom and virtue'. [MR I, 126]

Although Currie's 'cold affusion' is clearly inspired by Brunonian ideas, his description of its power to 'introduce a new action throughout the nervous system' draws on a a rather different, voluntaristic rather than mechanistic, theory of agency which looks forward to romantic notions of free will. He approved of Erasmus Darwin's theory in Zoonomia, in which the movement of volition was represented as being from the inner organs to the body's surface, and of sensation conversely from the surface to the inner organs.[15] 'To increase the force of voluntary actions must therefore be to lessen positively, as well as relatively, the actions that arise from sensations, and the converse is equally true'. [I, 147] Sudden application of cold water to the body's surface galvanises the inner voluntary force by making it match the shock received on the surface. Rather than seeking a pharmaceutical cure for the feverish body by introducing alcohol or laudanum, Currie's stimulant regime offers to supplement the body's organic, but debilitated powers. In Currie's revision of Brown's system, therapy seeks to remedy the weakness of the patient's voluntary powers, invigorating it to new efforts, rather than simply readjusting it to its environment by chemical stimulus.

Despite the fact that he tolerated Brown's 'encouragement of a more liberal use of wine and opium' [MR I, 159] in the treatment of some conditions, Currie was also largely responsible for the belief that alcohol abuse was the principal cause of Burns's early death. Currie nowhere mentions that the poet's febrile system had hardly benefited from 'cold affusions' at Brow on the Solway Firth in summer 1796, as recommended by his physician Dr Maxwell. As James Mackay comments 'part of the treatment recommended by Maxwell consisted of wading up to the armpits in the icy waters of the Solway – a treatment that was singularly inappropriate for a man in the last stages of emaciation and debility, and in the grip of the incurable heart disease endocarditis'.[16]

Given Currie's previous medical writing, it's remarkable that his 1800 'Life of Burns' now rejects the stimulant regime, which is now largely blamed for the poet's downfall. Earlier passages of the 'Life' develop

Burns's own description of his depression in his correspondence; 'a constitutional melancholy, or hypochondriasm that made me fly solitude' [Currie I, 45]. In her insightful essay 'The Politics of Hypochodriasis', Leith Davis plausibly identifies Currie's obsession with Burns's 'hypochondriasis' as a displaced commentary on the poet's transgressive politics, whether Jacobite or (after 1790) Jacobin: 'increasing emphasis on Burns' hypochondriasis serves to deflect the reader's attention from his shift from Jacobite to Jacobin politics'.[17] Davis however overlooks the downplaying of hypochondria or melancholy in Currie's analysis of Burns' condition in the 1790's, when the discussion of the poet's melancholy symptoms were largely replaced by the language of poetic sensibility, over-stimulation and weakness of volition.

Currie diagnosed Burns's pathology as characteristic of 'the temperament of genius'; [Currie I, 219] 'endowed by nature with great sensibility of nerves, Burns was, in his corporeal as well as in his mental system, liable to inordinate impressions, to fever of body as well as of mind'. [I, 219] This was a propensity that required moderation by 'the volition, that regulating power of the mind, which like all our other faculties is strengthened by exercise' [I, 240].[18] If the hypochondriacal gloom of a pre-revolutionary Burns veered towards Jacobite politics which might relieve the provincial taedium vitae of post-1707 Scotland, his symptoms after 1789 rather represent the overstimulated regime of the heady revolutionary years 1792–4, in the shape of political enthusiasm and inordinate sociability, followed by despair and drink in the revolutionary aftermath. Abandoning the solitary life of a farmer at Ellisland in order to adapt himself to the regimented drudgery of the life of an Excise officer entailed Burns's move into Dumfries, where (according to Currie) 'temptations to the sin that so easily beset him continually presented themselves; and his irregularities grew by degrees into habits . . . his appetites and sensations, which could not pervert the dictates of his judgements, finally triumphed over the powers of his will' [Currie I, 205].

At this point in his biography Currie's language becomes increasingly Brunonian as he describes Burns the radical overcompensating for his excessive – and now disappointed – political enthusiasm; 'perpetually overstimulated by alcohol in one or other of its various forms, the inordinate actions of the circulating system became at length habitual; and the process of nutrition was unable to supply the waste, and the powers of life began to fail'. [Currie I, 219] But turning against Brown's

advocacy of the stimulant regime, Currie describes the lethal attractions
of alcohol and opium; '[they] provid[e] a fictitious gaiety to the ideas of
the imagination, and [alter] the effects of the external impressions we
receive' [Currie I, 248]. Yet the effect of both is in the end narcotic rather
than stimulative, the gist of Cullen's objection to Brown's theory. Currie
signals his return to Cullenite medical orthodoxy by asserting that 'in
proportion to its stimulating influence on the system . . . is the debility
that ensues; a debility that destroys digestion, and terminates in habitual
fever, dropsy, jaundice, paralysis, or insanity. As the strength of the
body decays, the volition fails . . .' [Currie I, 252]. Currie's unwarranted
judgement on Burns' alcoholism (as mentioned above, the poet most
probably died of rheumatic heart disease, rather than any alcohol related
illness) gave great offence to his admirers, particularly the insinuating
question, raising the spectre of Burns's sexual transgressions; 'he who
suffers the pollution of inebriation, how shall he escape other pollu-
tion?' [Currie I, 224].

The Neuropathology of Genius

The philosophical, as opposed to medical, core of Currie's analysis lies
in his account of the weakness of the poet's will, symptomatic of the
dangers attendant upon literary genius; 'The fatal defect in [Burns's]
character lay in the comparative weakness of his volition, that superior
faculty of the mind, which governing the conduct according to the
dictates of the understanding, alone entitle it to be denominated
rational; which is the parent of fortitude, patience, and self-denial;
which by regulating and combining human exertions, may be said to
have effected all that is great in the works of man, in literature, in
science, or on the face of nature. The occupations of a poet are not
calculated to strengthen the governing powers of the mind, or to
weaken that sensibility which requires perpetual control, since it gives
birth to the vehemence of passion, as well as to the higher powers of
imagination. [Currie I, 236]. After this it would take all the ingenuity of a
Wordsworth to restore the image of the romantic poet as healthy, water-
drinking, and well-adjusted to a salubrious (and rural) environment.

Quite apart from his scruples concerning poetic genius itself, Currie
here sought to exorcise a particularly Scottish pathology of mind that
he associated with the materialism and deterministic ethics of both
David Hume and his admirer John Brown, a state of being dependent

Ioannes Bruno M.D.
Hercule! Opium minime sedat.

John Brown by John Kay

27

on the stimulant regime. Currie's description of Burns's protean, mobile character – illustrating Hume's account of the mind as merely a 'kind of theatre' through which ideas and impressions pass in aleatory surges – stretches the biographer's descriptive vocabulary to its utmost limits; Burns is kind, brave, sincere, compassionate, but he's also proud, irascible, and vindictive. [Currie I, 235] Burns has aggravated his nervous condition by misapplying stimulants; endowed with all the talents, education and passion of the Scottish peasantry, he'd failed to subject his over-energetic sensibility to a controlling will. Yet Burns's predicament is also symptomatic of the crisis afflicting Currie's radical generation and its discourse on genius at the close of the revolutionary decade. It's especially notable that Coleridge (in contrast to the remarks of his friend Charles Lamb) described Currie's 'Life of Burns' as 'a masterly specimen of philosophical biography'.[19] About the same time he wrote; 'Virtue & Genius are Diseases of the Hypochondriacal and Scrofulous Genus – & exist in a peculiar state of the Nerves, & diseased Digestion – analogous to the beautiful Diseases that colour and variegate certain Trees. – However, I add by way of comfort, that the Virtue and Genius produce the Disease, not the Disease &c . . .'[20]

Currie's Burns biography represents one influential attempt to regulate literary genius in the wake of the revolutionary decade. A more famous attempt – and one in which Coleridge collaborated, despite his private musings on the proximity of creativity and madness – was the 1800 Preface to Lyrical Ballads, with Wordsworth as senior partner. The fact that both poets read Currie's 'Life' in the Autumn of 1800, when they were composing the famous Preface, has passed largely unnoticed by critics.[21] Bearing this fact in mind, it is easier to see that the 'Preface's' definition of poetic creativity is in part a response to the stimulant regime which Currie has supposed to be so fatal to Burns's genius, and which might prove equally so to poets in general. The 'Preface' proposes that modernity (urbanisation, war, work discipline and the rapid circulation of print) had created what the authors call 'a degrading thirst after outrageous stimulation'.[22] Like Currie's description of the effects of alcohol and radical politics on Burns' genius, modern life has 'unfitt[ed] [the mind] for voluntary exertion to reduce it to a state of almost savage torpor'. The resultant 'craving for extraordinary incident', with the concomitant fashion for 'frantic novels, sickly and stupid German Tragedies, and deluges of idle and extravagant stories in verse' [LB p. 249] has vitiated modern literature. The polemical task of the 1800 Preface is to make good its claim (and note the language) that 'the human mind is capable of excitement without the application of gross and violent stimulants'. [LB p. 248]

To a greater extent than Currie, whose medical discourse signals a return to Cullenite orthodoxy, this represents a refinement rather than a rejection of the Brunonian remedy for the asthenic condition of modernity. That's to say that the Preface is far from proposing to counteract the 'savage torpor' of modern literature by advocating tranquil pastoral verse of the kind associated with Burkean political quiescence, but rather by imitating 'a selection of the real language of men in a state of vivid sensation' (my italics). This 'real' and 'permanent' language' is associated with 'low and rustic life' as exemplified in Burns' poetry; moreover, it is 'a far more philosophical language than that which is frequently substituted for it by Poets' [LB p. 245].

By distinguishing legitimate 'poetic excitement' from 'outrageous stimulation', Wordsworth and Coleridge tried to recover a disciplined, internal power of imagination, regulated by the intervention of memory ('emotion recollected in tranquillity'), thereby rescuing the affective economy of poetic genius from the dangers of the stimulant regime. Currie has confused the two in suggesting that 'the occupations of a poet are not calculated to strengthen the governing powers of the mind, or to weaken that sensibility which requires perpetual control, since it gives birth to the vehemence of passion as well as the higher power of imagination' [Currie I, 236]. I'll close with the suggestion that Currie's neuropathological analysis of Burns (which, I've argued, itself masked a critique of Brown's materialism), not only prompted the most influential theoretical discussion of poetic creativity in the Romantic period, but, beyond that, stirred up anxieties about the healthfulness of genius that simmered through Decadence into the Freudian era.

NOTES

[1] *Poems and Songs of Robert Burns*, James Kinsley (ed.), 3 vols, (Oxford: Clarendon Press 1968), I, p. 81, ll.79–84.

[2] ['Let the cobbler stick to his rattling', from Pliny's *Natural History*] Donald A. Low, *Robert Burns: The Critical Heritage*, (London: RKP, 1974), p. 112.

[3] Michael Barfoot, 'Brunonianism under the Bed: An Alternative to University Medicine in Edinburgh in the 1780's', *Medical History*, Supp. no. 8, (1988), pp. 22–45, 45.

[4] *The Works of Robert Burns; with an Account of his Life, and a Criticism of his Writings. To which are prefixed, Some Observations on the Character and Condition of the Scottish Peasantry*, 4 vols, (Liverpool, 1800) I, p. 315. Henceforth Currie in text.

[5] William Wallace Currie, *Memoir of the Life, Writing and Correspondence of James Currie*, 2 vols., (London, 1831), 1, p. 251. Henceforth *Memoir* in text.

[6] R. D. Thornton, *James Currie: The Entire Stranger and Robert Burns* (Edinburgh and London: Oliver & Boyd, 1963).

[7] See Christopher Lawrence, 'John Brown', DNB; Michael Barfoot, 'Brunonianism under the Bed'.

[8] DNB 'John Brown'.

[9] John Brown, *The Elements of Medicine. A New Edition, revised and corrected with a biographical preface by Thomas Beddoes, M.D.* 2 vols., (London 1795), I, p. lxxxvii.

[10] Barfoot, p. 27.

[11] James Currie, *Medical Reports, on the Effects of Water, Cold and Warm, as a remedy in Fever and other Diseases*, 2 vols., (London: Cadell and Davies, 1798– 1805), I, pp. 73, 197.

[12] Roy Porter, 'Brunonian Psychiatry', *Medical History*, Supp no 8, (1988), pp. 89–9, 93.

[13] *Analytical Review*, II, (1788), pp. 266, 269. See my essay 'Robert Burns and Scottish Commonsense Philosophy' in Gavin Budge (ed.), *Romantic Empiricism: Poetics and the Philosophy of Common Sense, 1780–1830* (Lewisburg: Bucknell University Press, 2007), pp. 64–87.

[14] The first volume of *Medical Reports* was published in 1798 (the second had to wait until 1805) by Cadell and Davies, who also published Currie's *Works of Burns*. Henceforth MR in text.

[15] But note that Darwin insisted that his use of the word 'voluntary' is the opposite of 'common language; . . . in this work the word volition means simply the active state of the sensorial faculty in producing motion in consequence of desire or aversion; whether we have the power of retarding that action, or not' [Erasmus Darwin, *Zoonomia; or, The Laws of Organic Life*, 2 vols (London 1794–6), I, p. 416. This is quite different from Reid's account of will power as glossed by Currie, cited above.

[16] James Mackay, *A Biography of Robert Burns*, (Edinburgh: Mainstream 1992), p. 619.

[17] Leith Davis, 'James Currie's Works of Robert Burns': the Politics of Hypochondriasis', *Studies in Romannticism*, 36 (Spring 1997), pp. 43–60, 52.

[18] Currie here echoes Beddoes' analysis of John Brown; 'he was endowed with uncommon susceptibility to impressions . . . this quality is the foundation of all moral and intellectual superiority; but unhappily, the strong feelings and bold resolutions of Brown were not improved into steady principle. He never seems to have taken pains to form a system of conduct advantageous to himself, and just towards others'. [Beddoes (ed.), *Elements of Medicine*, I, p. xciv.]

[19] 24th July, 1800, letter to Thomas Poole, quoted in Low, *Critical Heritage*, p. 108.

20 *Collected Letters of S.T.Coleridge*, E.L. Griggs (ed.), 6 vols, (Oxford University Press, 1956–71), II, p. 902.

21 See my essay 'The Shadow Line': James Currie's 'Life of Burns' and British Romanticism', in *Romanticism's Debatable Lands*, Claire Lamont and Michael Rossington (eds) (Basingstoke: Palgrave Macmillan, 2007), pp. 64–79.

22 Wordsworth and Coleridge, *Lyrical Ballads*, R. L. Brett and A. R. Jones (eds), 2nd edn, (London and NY: RKP, 1991), p. 249. Hereafter LB in text.

BURNS ABROAD

❧

ROBERT BURNS AND SLAVERY

છ૭

GERARD CARRUTHERS

Scotland's national bard is often taken to be the forward-looking champion of human 'brotherhood'; and yet, also, Robert Burns let it be known that he had intended to sail to Jamaica to take up a position helping manage the slave economy. Apparently, he had proceeded so far with this affair as to timetable his voyage from Greenock on 10th August 1786 on board the *Nancy*, a brig that regularly traversed the Atlantic from the Clyde to the Caribbean and back with personnel and freight, including sugar, which was associated with the Slave Planta- tions. Scotland had no such notorious port as Liverpool or Bristol where African slaves, men, women and children were chained in the most appalling captivity before a crossing that took some weeks, with sometimes a third or more of the slave 'cargo' dying en route, mostly from disease or sometimes from severe physical abuse (though either way as the result of determined mistreatment). The sailings from the Clyde associated with the Slave trade were quicker and so suitable for the carriage of more precious human lives: the whites who traded in their human traffic or sugar or tobacco, which in the latter half of the eighteenth century represented a profitable interlocked economy from the United Kingdom to South Carolina to Antigua and Jamaica. Glasgow or even Scotland's part in the slave economy is less nakedly apparent, but perhaps more insidious than was the case in the ports of England.

There are the very matter-of-fact, even pleasant, illustrated adverts for the sailings of the *Nancy* repeatedly posted in the newspaper, the *Glasgow Advertiser* in the late eighteenth century, which attest to the 'banality of evil'. Almost certainly, Burns saw these adverts in the *Advertiser* and this was what put the idea of a potential new life into his head. Why did he

For SAVANNAH-LA-MARR, JAMAICA,
to call at ANTIGUA,

THE Brigantine NANCY, ANDREW SMITH, Mafter, will be at Greenock ready to take in goods, 25th, inftant, and will be clear to fail by 10th Auguft.

For freight or paffage, apply to James Brown, infurance-broker, Glafgow, or to the Mafter at Greenock.

Glafgow, 12th July, 1786.

Graham Fagen after The Glasgow Mercury, *6th–13th July 1786*

want to emigrate? On the face of it he had decided to run off with Mary Campbell ('Highland Mary') after being rejected by Jean Armour who in obedience to her father's wishes had abruptly stopped all relations with the poet. This was in spite of the facts that Jean was in the early stages of pregnancy and that Robert and Jean had plighted their troth by signing their names together in a Bible, in token of an irregular but legally binding betrothal. In early 1786 Jean's father, James, supposedly went to the extraordinary lengths of having a lawyer formally cut the names from the Bible and so dissolved the marriage contract. Burns, never one to be long without female solace turned to the servant girl, 'Highland Mary', with whom he had probably been dallying while courting Jean in any case and, seemingly, he resolved to start a new life with her in Jamaica. In May Mary was sent ahead to wait for Burns in Greenock; in July the poet signed the Burns family farm at Mossgiel entirely over to his brother, Gilbert; in July and August Burns and Jean were publicly rebuked in church on three consecutive Sundays for fornication; in September Jean gave birth to twins (during which month Burns yet again and repeatedly postponed his trip to Jamaica); in October Burns heard that Mary had died at Greenock. By this last month, Burns's book, *Poems, Chiefly in the Scottish Dialect* (which had been published in Kilmarnock at the end of July) was a huge literary hit in Ayrshire and beyond, and the great and the good in the west of Scotland had begun to notice the poet. In early September 1786 Burns wrote to John Richmond, who was probably helping to open up the prospect of literary fame for Burns in Edinburgh. A legal clerk, typical of the aspiring bourgeois class with whom Burns associated throughout his early manhood, Richmond had a residence in Edinburgh (as well as in Ayrshire) and it was at his house in the capital in which Burns first stayed for a time from November of 1786 as he began to plan his 'Edinburgh' edition of poems to appear in 1787, an enlarged version of his 'Kilmarnock, collection. Burns wrote to Richmond:

'I am still here in statu quo, tho I well expected to have been on my way over the Atlantic by this time. – The Nancy, in which I was to have gone, did not give me warning enough – Two days notice was too little for me to wind up my affairs and go for Greenock. I now am to be a passenger aboard the Bell, Captn Cathca[rt] who sails the end of this month. – I am under little apprehension now about Armour. – The warrant is still in existence, but some of the first Gentlemen in the country have offered to befriend me; and besides Jean will not take any step against me'[1]

All of this is somewhat strange. Burns had claimed previously and does so again in the passage just quoted that Jean's father has a warrant to throw him in gaol (though this may have been melodrama on Burns's part). It is far from clear how James Armour could have accomplished this, legally. Burns also seems to obfuscate on another matter, since might easily have reached Greenock, a distance of some forty miles, in a day, and we know for fact he had already signed Mossgiel over to his brother. So he had nothing much in the way of affairs to 'wind up', as he puts it. Conceivably Burns had actually taken cold feet about his proposed voyage some time before he heard of Highland Mary's death (the reason often given by biographers for Burns finally aborting his Jamaican plan). Even if the notion of James Armour taking out a warrant for Burns's arrest is the poet being fanciful it is perhaps psychologically revealing. He felt persecuted, or at least disrespected. It is quite clear that Burns, a tenant farmer who was also a man of some clear accomplishment and learning, expected himself to be seen as a catch by James Armour for his daughter. As so often was the case throughout his life, Burns had a very clear idea of where he was in the social pecking order, and thought himself to be the equal, at least, of the Master Mason, Armour (when he wanted to impress people later on, Burns claimed that his Father-in-Law was an architect).

It was a severe shock for the exceptionally class-conscious Burns to be looked down upon by the Armours, and this, arguably, explains what might be taken to be a fantasy of Burns: that he may as well be regarded as a rootless, buccaneering kind of man – the kind who might well go off to make his fortune in Jamaica. In Burns mind this maybe at once confirmed his damned, dark reputation in James Armour's eyes, but also included the possibility, of returning with improved financial means to parade in front of those who had previously snubbed him. The emphasis here though must be on the fantasy since numerous whites (especially Scottish clerks or book-keepers as Burns was intending to be returned no better, or even worse off. I tend to side with those commentators who see Burns as never seriously intending to emigrate.[2]

For K I N G S T O N   J A M A I C A , to call at any of the
Windward Iflands, as freight may offer,

THE Brigantine B E L L, J o h n C a t h c a r t , Master, will be ready to receive goods at Greenock, by the 20th inftant, and clear to fail by the end of September.

For freight or paffage apply to John Hamilton, or Captain Cathcart, Greenock, to James Buchanan, Glafgow.

The Bell is a new British-built veffel, about 200 tons, and has excellent accommodation for paffengers.

2d Auguft, 1786.

Graham Fagen after The Glasgow Mercury, *10th–17th August 1786*

But this is not to have Burns off the hook, to enable us to say, 'Oh, he never really wanted to be part of the disgusting West Indies economy.' On the contrary, in this episode of his life Burns, I would argue, is guilty of a failure of sympathy, a failure in imagination. And there is corroborating evidence for this view in his poetry. At some point during April and July 1786 Burns wrote 'On a Scotch Bard Gone to the West Indies' in which the poet projects himself being tearfully missed when he leaves Scotland and projecting a kind reception in the West Indies:

> Jamaica bodies, use him weel,
> An' hap him in a cozie biel:
> Ye'll find him ay a dainty chiel,
>   An' fou o' glee:
> He wad na wrang'd the vera Diel,
>   Tho' owre the Sea![3]

'Jamaica bodies', are presumably the whites (who will treat him well) and provide for him a cozy shelter. We have here a somewhat comical poem, but not an ironic one. Burns thinks of living 'cosily' amidst the slave economy? This thought is appallingly compounded in the same stanza when Burns talks of himself being harmless, as someone who would not even 'wrong the Devil 'owre the Sea.' The problem, precisely, is that the Devil most certainly was at work over the sea in the plantations in Jamaica.

Burns, actually, is remarkable in this work for how little attention he pays to the African slave and we can contrast him somewhat unfavourably with a number of contemporary Scottish writers in this regard.

Robert Burns's rather insipid 'The Slave's Lament' (1792) has provided an otherwise disappointed politically correct readership for the Scottish Bard with a slender thread with which to tie him to the Abolitionist cause. Burns's sympathy for the plight of the Senegalese captive in this song first published in James Johnson's *Scots Musical Museum* was subsequently and gratuitously magnified with the claim that the tune chosen by Johnson (in collaboration with Burns) was 'an original African melody', but this is untrue. This claim was first made, unaccountably, by the song-historian William Stenhouse in 1853 and continues to be parroted by some Burnsians.[4] Actually, even the attribution of the words to Burns merits some re-examination and it is possible that Burns merely collected the song when scraping the barrel to send Johnson material; it is also possible that Johnson aware of the poor quality of the piece attempted to give it added weight by attributing it to Burns. It is fairly pallid stuff:

It was in sweet Senegal that my foes did me enthral,
  For the lands of Virginia, – ginia O;
Torn from the lovely shore, and must never see it more,
  And alas! I am weary, weary, O!
    Torn from &c.

All on that charming coast is no bitter snow and frost,
  Like the lands of Virginia, – ginia O;
There streams for ever flow, and there flowers for ever blow,
  And alas! I am weary, weary, O!
    There streams &c.

The burden I must bear, while the cruel scourge I fear,
  In the lands of Virginia, – ginia O;
And I think on friends most dear, with the bitter, bitter tear,
  And alas! I am weary, weary, O!
    And I think &c.[5]

Surprisingly unnoticed is a much more interesting engagement by Burns (albeit in a sub-textual instance) with the 'African Question'. This occurs in his poem 'The Ordination', first drafted in 1786, but revised in late 1787, as it lampoons the 'Auld Lichts' or Calvinist evangelicals in their theological battles with the Moderate Presbyterians in Ayrshire. Burns allows the 'Auld Licht' voice expression of its favourite darker Biblical texts, including those that revel in murder and whoring. He also has this voice appeal:

> Come, let a proper text be read,
>   An' touch it aff wi' vigour,
> How graceless Ham leugh at his Dad,
>   Which made Canaan a niger[6]

Here, we have the myth of monogenesis (that humanity began as one race and somehow later became racially distinctive), comprising part of the litany of 'Auld Licht' ignorance. Clearly, what Burns looks forward to in 'The Ordination' is the casting off the Old Testament mentality in Presbyterian Ayrshire. With typical psychological comedy, Burns has an Auld Licht lament, "Nae mair by Babel's streams we'll weep,/To think upon our Zion."[7] The implication is that in a long historical comfort-zone of being cast-out seemingly (though in fact theologically dominant in the Scottish kirk for most of the eighteenth century), the Auld Licht mentality in its scriptural hubris is actually desensitised to real cultural displacement, be it that of the Israelite or the African slave, according to Burns. Satirically, heroic, feminine, true Calvinism is seen towards the end of the poem hitting back at the forces of Moderatism 'banishing' and 'cowing' these, where liberal use is made of the whip also:

> See, see auld Orthodoxy's faes
> She's swingeing thro the city!
> Hark, how the nine-tail'd cat she plays!
> I vow it's unco pretty,
> There, Learning, with his Greekish face,
> Grunts out some Latin ditty;
> And Common Sense is gaun, she says,
> To mak to Jamie Beattie
> Her plaint this day.[8]

As recent work by Iain Whyte has shown, the Scottish Presbyterian church in the second part of the eighteenth century, whether Auld or New Licht, was often strongly Abolitionist. Burns, then, is being somewhat partial in tarring the Auld Lichts with the imputation of a

---

For Kingston and Savannah-la-Mar J A M A I C A
The Ship *Roselle*, CAPT. Hogg,

Burden 300 tons, now lying in Leith harbour, will be ready to take in goods by the 10th November, and will positively fail on the 15th December. For freight and paffage apply to Meffrs William Sibbald and Co. Leith.

N.B. The *Roselle* has excellent accommodation, and will take paffengers for the Windward Iflands, to be landed at Antigua or St. Kitts: the paffage money will be paid here.

WANTED a few Apprentices for the fhip, ftout lads, not under 16 years old.

Graham Fagen after The Edinburgh Evening Courant, *Saturday October 21st, 1786*

pro-Slavery mentality; for instance, one of the key Auld Lichts he lampoons specifically by name in another of his Calvinist satires, 'The Holy Tuilzie', is John Russell, who was to be party to a particularly impassioned Abolitionist petition from the Presbytery of Irvine in 1792 (not everyone lashed by Burns's pen necessarily deserved it, at least not all the time).[9]

In 'The Ordination', Burns further sets up a false opposition (certainly so far as the slave question was concerned) as 'Common Sense' complains to James Beattie, the man in his own time perhaps even more so than Thomas Reid, associated with the philosophical school of that name. Beattie is the Scottish Enlightenment *philosophe* most enduringly abolitionist (and here, if previously he had been bettered in terms of pure epistemology by David Hume, he emerges in much better light than his old philosophic foe, some of whose comments on black people are simply indefensible and perhaps all the more so for a man of Hume's prodigious intellect). Around 1778, Beattie had written but not published his 'Discourse on Slavery with particular reference to the plight of the Negroes' and in a letter to his friend William Forbes ten years later, in May 1788, Beattie rails against those who attempt to argue 'the licitness of the Slave-trade from the scriptures of the Old and New testament.'[10] One month later, he is, however, pessimistic about the traffic in slaves, fearing that 'it cannot be accomplished soon.'[11] Much of the reason for Beattie's pessimism would seem to be the theological strength within the politically powerful Church of England in the 1780s in favour of Slavery, which was probably at least as potent at this time as the Abolitionist strain within the same communion. As Colin Kidd has recently shown also, Beattie in the polished published version of his *Elements of Moral Science* (1790) was, while whole-hearted and vocal in his anti-slavery stance, timid when it came to the business of detailed scriptural critique, believing without question that the first man, Adam, had been white and that the black people had become so because of environmental conditions.[12] Beattie 'argued' here too that 'the negro' in his indigenous context most certainly had a soul but had only 'a very imperfect idea [. . .] of a supreme being and a future state'.[13] 'Common Sense' clearly still had some way to go to in practice to speak out univocally against slavery. In 'The Ordination' Burns is right to applaud implicitly Beattie's broad Abolitionist stance, but his seeming confidence that the forces of enlightenment and of reaction can clearly be delineated in matters of theology, culture and humanity, and especially with regard to the theory of monogenesis partakes somewhat of wishful and distorted thinking. Beattie was less than intellectually clear-sighted on the matter however much his heart beat commendably in favour of Abolition. It would be interesting to know the extent to which Burns's tantalising sub-textual material on the issue in 'The Ordination' shows, actually, conscious awareness of Beattie's problem on racial belief and an attempt at transference on to the hapless 'Auld Licht' fall-guy. We are into deep waters here, with soundings not previously registered in Burns criticism, which require further trawling.

Let us take a final example of Burns's engagement with slavery, this time in 'Is there for honest poverty' (or 'A Man's a Man). First of all I want to point to a strange historical 'accident' in this song first published in 1795. Burns has earned praise for penning a supposedly proto-Socialist anthem which ends with the lines:

> That Man to Man the warld o'er,
> Shall brothers be for a' that.[14]

The reason that Burns mentions the 'world' is because at this time when Britain is at war with France, had he said 'Europe' (which is really what he most probably had in mind) he might well have been gaoled. The idea of a series of confederated or even united republics of Europe (and including the same within Britain for England, Ireland and Scotland was what the French had in mind in the 1790s for their re-mapping of the continent. There is, arguably an implicit anti-monarchist stance in the song. 'The honest man . . . is king o' men' writes Burns in his text, and as a number of critics have noted Burns also cleverly embeds something of the phraseology of Thomas Paine's *The Rights of Man* in his poem.[15] Both of these things might well be spotted, but a defence lawyer could quite easily argue that there is nothing explicitly seditious in these devices. On the other hand the explicit French egalitarian idea, 'Its comin yet for a' that/ That Man to Man [Europe] o'er,/Shall brothers be for a that' would have counted as out and out sedition so far as the British authorities were concerned, and it is most likely that any contemporary court of law at this time would have concurred.[16] It is a nice irony that the changing of the text to 'world' has led to the inflated idea of Burns's democratic sensibility, when in fact he was attempting, understandably, to disguise this. Another textual fold, all too little noticed, is the line in the opening stanza of the song, 'The coward-slave, we pass him by,/we dare be poor for a' that!'[17] I am not suggesting that Burns is referring to African slaves explicitly, or perhaps one should say *realistically* here, but he is certainly using the idea of African slavery as a metaphor. People are enslaved and enfeebled with their desire for power and rank, and, as Burns says, 'The rank is but the guinea's stamp/The man's the gowd for a' that' which carries, arguably and as Nigel Leask has suggested, the connotation of the stamp burned by iron into the slave's skin.[18] Burns's logic is that another type of debased human condition is to be found at the top of the human social hierarchy just as much as at the bottom. This is quite nicely done. But, I would argue, it shows again, even as it is poetically imaginative, a somewhat limited, Eurocentric position on Burns's part. People can indeed be slaves to the wrong thing, but to use this metaphor at a time of real, appalling, miserable actual slavery is rather insensitive. It is even possible to suggest that Burns's 'coward-slave' touches on a contemporary idea that slaves become increasingly debased morally (so far, so logical, we might say) but that this is demonstrated also in a cowed or cowardly attitude where they do nothing to help themselves. (This rhetoric of increasing and irredeemable torpor of humanity, in fact, is quite prominent in eighteenth century moral discourse surrounding slavery)

One might justifiably say, of course, that this perspective is to make hugely arrogant assumptions about the choices available to most slaves. With or without this connotation, we find in 'Is there for honest poverty' (as with 'The Ordination') a disturbingly sub-textual (and so relegated) engagement with the slavery issue so that if we're looking to fill out Burns's politically radical or progressive CV then this is one area with which we really cannot do too much.

What has been said above will perhaps be seen as a little negative by some people, those, particularly, who dislike any kind of considered criticism of Burns. And there are many: such as the man who telephoned me two months ago and introduced himself by shouting down the line, 'Ye're nae freend o' mine'. When I asked why, he replied that I was 'questioning Burns'. I replied that this is what I, as a professional academic, am paid to do, which, of course, cut no ice. Let me attempt, then, to plead for Burns something I equally often do alongside the questioning. We might simply suggest that Burns had little interest in the slave issue and it is up to the individual, writer or otherwise, to what extent he or she wants to be politically active or expressive. Burns's straying into the territory of slavery in his work is piecemeal and far from entirely happy, but, equally, it may be that Burns would liked to have said more but felt constrained since from the late 1780s he is a government employee (more vocal Abolitionist Scottish writers such as Alexander Geddes, William Campbell or William Yates were not so encumbered).[19] It is quite noticeable how as we enter the 1790s many Abolitionist writers are silenced (the afore-mentioned Campbell perhaps among them) because of the scare-mongering yoking of a cause that until then was finding very wide support across the spectrum of political and religious opinion in Britain, with the democratic sensibility of the early French Revolution, a despicable manoeuvre of the reactionary right at this time.

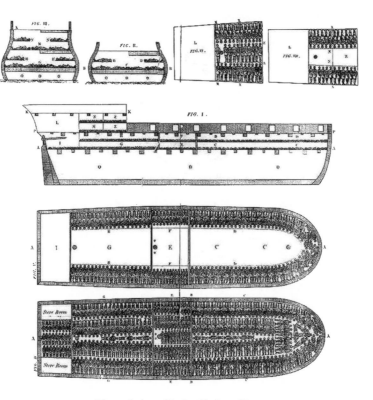

Plans of slave ship by Graham Fagen

That Burns, a man of undoubtedly genuine humanitarian spirit, is largely silent or maybe even confused on the Abolitionist issue should be a sober lesson to us all in how, for various potential reasons, we can lose sight of the big socio-moral questions that face us. We should not be complacent. We live in a world where United Nations figures show us that slavery of one kind or another (and perhaps of even greater variety of strain than in the eighteenth century) is at least as endemic and virulent as in the time of Robert Burns. If Burns, arguably, did not do enough, too few of us who have come after him have done anything effective either.

NOTES

[1] *The Letters of Robert Burns* Vol. I [1780–1789] J. De Lancey Ferguson (ed.); 2nd edn, G. Ross Roy (ed.) (Oxford: Clarendon Press, 1985), pp. 49–50.

[2] For a very interesting imagining of how Burns's life might have transpired in the West Indies, see Andrew O. Lindsay, *Illustrious Exile* (Leeds: Peepal Tree Press, 2006). I am grateful to Andrew Lindsay and also Norrie Paton for helping me tweak my own thoughts on the whole episode of Burns's planned immigration.

[3] James Kinsley (ed.), *Burns: Complete Poems and Song Burns* (London, Oxford & New York: Oxford University Press, 1971), p. 192.

[4] William Stenhouse, Illustrations of the Lyric Poetry and Music of Scotland originally compiled to accompany the "Scots musical museum" [by James Johnson] and now published separately, with additional notes and illustrations (London and Edinburgh: Blackwood, 1853), p. 353.

[5] James Kinsley (ed.), *Burns: Complete Poems and Song Burns* (London, Oxford & New York: Oxford University Press, 1971), p. 515.

[6] Ibid., p. 171.

[7] Ibid., p. 172.

[8] Ibid., p. 173.

[9] Iain Whyte, *Scotland and the Abolition of Black Slavery* (Edinburgh: Edinburgh University Press, 2006), p. 77.

[10] William Forbes (ed.), *An Account of the Life and Writings of James Beattie* [1806]. (Bristol; Thoemmes Press, 1997), p. 228.

[11] Ibid., p. 230.

[12] Colin Kidd, *The Forging of the Races: Race and Scripture in the Protestant Atlantic World, 1600–2000* (Cambridge: Cambridge University Press, 2006), pp. 100–1.

[13] Ibid., p. 101.

[14] James Kinsley (ed.), *Burns: Complete Poems and Song Burns* (London, Oxford & New York: Oxford University Press, 1971), p. 603.

[15] Ibid., p. 602.

[16] Ibid., p. 603.

[17] Ibid., p. 602.

[18] Ibid. I am extremely grateful to Nigel Leask for highlighting this idea to me, around which he will publish in the future.

[19] Poet, polemicist and pioneering biblical critic Alexander Geddes is particularly noteworthy for his powerful, ironic prose contribution, *An Apology for Slavery* (1792), usefully reprinted in Paul Keen (ed.), *Revolutions in Romantic Literature: An Anthology of Print Culture 1780–1832* (Ontario: Broadview, 2004), pp. 334–6.

FICKLE MEN

೪

How Robert Burns never met James Boswell (and neither met Toussaint Louverture)

MITCHELL MILLER

1. '. . . almost in the same Parish': Living in parallel

Of all the non-events of the Scottish Eighteenth century, the meeting between Robert Burns (1759 -1796) and James Boswell (1740 -1795) is surely one of the most intriguing. Born in the same region of Scotland and identifying with the same locality,[1] their respective contributions to literary culture left a very different world of letters to the one they found. Through, respectively, vernacular poetry and the modernisation of the biography, both men explored themselves and the world that surrounded them, possessing that virtue extolled many generations later by another precocious Scot, John Grierson, of 'documentary value'; Burns through the record of song and verse and Boswell through applying what Frederick Pottle describes as 'great powers of imaginative realisation' to remembered events.[2] They were close contemporaries, dying within two years of each other and for much of their final years, rarely more than 50 miles apart, often less than three. Yet until a floorboard springs open in the Burns cottage, or a secret box tumbles out of the loft at Malahide to reveal some documentary smoking gun, history records no meeting between them. Their orbits overlapped, both were 'clubbable' men but they never intercepted each other, a state of affairs which, given their social and physical proximity seems absurd. But it is true.

We do know that Burns had attempted to secure a meeting, writing to Boswell's cousin, Bruce Campbell in November 1788:

I inclose you, for Mr Boswell, the Ballad you mentioned; and as I hate sending waste paper or mutilating a sheet, I have filled it up with one or two of my fugitive Pieces that occurred. – Should they procure me the honour of being introduced to Mr Boswell, I shall think they have great merit – there are few pleasure my late will-o-the-wisp character has given me, equal to that of having seen many of the extraordinary men, the Heroes of Wit & Literature in my Country; & and as I had the honour of drawing my first breath almost in the same parish with Mr Boswell . . . but to have been acquainted with such a man as Mr Boswell, I would hand down to my Posterity as one of the honors of their Ancestor.

In *Burns, Boswell and the French Revolution* where this extraordinary passage is quoted, Thomas Crawford tells us that Boswell noted this overture with pleasure, but did not pursue an appointment, nor comment specifically on the enclosures Burns had sent with the letter. For followers of Boswell's writings, a body of work based in substance, if not repute, on journals and letters, there is something familiar to the Burns charm offensive – something we are used to seeing going *from* the Boswell writing desk rather than to it. The deliberately effacing tone and Burns' thrifty excuse for enclosing poems for Boswell's consideration, not to mention the panegyrics are very Boswellian effusions. Did Boswell recognise the traces of the *modus operandi* he had used to ingratiate himself with literary figures, thinkers and leaders of opinion, seldom with any palpable sense of shame or embarassment?[3] Was the role reversal implied in being himself targeted as a man of influence and utility – the Johnson spot – a little too much? That is mere conjecture; the bare facts indicate that Boswell, despite being fond of the bucolic verses of Allan Ramsay (trying without success to interest Johnson in them) was simply not interested in vernacular poets.

This is the line taken by Crawford, and makes sense, given Boswell's oft-expressed attitudes. His experience of the elocution craze of the mid-eighteenth century, when young Scotsmen of note attended lectures by the like of David Garrick and Thomas Sheridan left them keen to purge their Scotticisms; Burns retained not only the Scotticisms but the Scots.

Such a literary explanation has a satisfying Occam's razor edge to it, though the application of a little role play presents some further possibilities. Burns and Boswell were from Ayrshire and this links them (as did their profound enjoyment of their own sexuality). But it also, surely, presented many more divisions, all the more keenly felt as they were based on accents and common references familiar from birth. Most obvious was that Boswell was born in the big house and Burns in a snowdrift, a huge class division not easily surmounted. Burns hob-nobbed with aristocrats and Boswell with the sons of Lichfield booksellers; but Burns' aristocratic patrons largely contained their literary ambitions within the bounds of patronage whereas Boswell was a fellow practitioner, full of his own opinions on good and bad poetry. In any case, Lichfield booksellers were *Lichfield* booksellers – safely English, safely distant, safely clean-handed and greatly ameliorated by Johnson's time studying at Pembroke and reliance on the *approved* access points to literary society and his subsequent position in polite London society. Johnson did not have inside knowledge of the same territory the self styled 'old Goth' claimed his lordship over, and who knows what gossip the licentious younger Auchinleck inspired around the parish. Nor, as Crawford points out, would Johnson reproach him by iterating the occasionally grim experience of an Auchinleck tenant. Both as idea and specimen, Burns was connected to a social reality that challenged many of the myths Boswell cultivated about himself; least forgivable, it drew him back into the over-familiarity of the Scots parish that he had felt entrapped and encumbered him. Burns felt that too; but he did not feel it on the same latitudes. The parish contained and upbraided Burns but it dragged the young Boswell down, its legacy here exploding out of a passage from his interview with Rousseau, recorded in 1764, when he was in his early twenties:

> There he felt the thistle. It was just as if I had said 'Howt Johnie Rousseau man, what for hae ye sae mony figmagaries? Ye're a bony Man indeed to mauk sicna wark; set ye up. Canna ye just live like ither fowk?' It was the best idea could be given in the polite French language of the rude Scots sarcastical vivacity.[4]

They both knew how significant a reversion to Scots from English – or polite French – could be; the hidden meanings it contained. We need little reminder of how aware Burns was of the double edge his Scots gave him, or the power of its reductive tone that laces his best satirical poems. Boswell's greater achievements were in English prose, but his Scots identified him. When Fernilea of Skye greeted Boswell of Auchinleck with 'fare fa' you?'[5] it was demonstratively a courtesy through acknowledging his guest's own language. And it was in this sarcastical Scots that the parish reminded Boswell before the fine silks and laces of his London outfits he was *seigneur* of the dykes, byres and thistles of Auchinleck. Boswell's return to Scots in the passage above is remarkably forceful here, bursting out of a delicately written account and clearly powerful enough (when transliterated into French) to astonish the sublime Rousseau. Twenty four years later, we have Burns, the vernacular wizard angling for an appointment. Was this just too close for comfort? Did Boswell fear such proximity?

Such fictions, plausible or not, easily spiral into cod-psychoanalysis; maybe Boswell, latest in a long line of Auchinlecks resented the celebrity afforded to the hired help from down the road? Perhaps he took umbrage over a son of the northern incomer Burnes (who was apparently as serious and austere as Lord Auchinleck) becoming the star of Scots letters — or what that rise represented? These are of course mere speculations; to return, again, to the facts, if James Boswell ever met Robert Burns then clearly Boswell never recorded it and Burns never celebrated it. If they had, the encounter may have given us a Boswellian interview of considerable cultural and national significance;

> One might say that he was passionately reasonable . . . he carried his principles to the merest trifles. For example, he used to wear his watch suspended from a button on his coat, because that was more convenient. As he was precluded from marriage he kept Mistresses, and made no secret of it. He had a number of sons . . .[6]

Not Burns of course, but from the interview with Rousseau, where the 'wild Philosopher' discusses Abbe de St Pierre and essentially describes what he takes to be his own virtues. As well as providing proof that he did not need to hang his talents on a Johnson, it gives a sense of what such a treatment may have been like, fuel to happy, but possibly unconstructive speculation. Boswell's interviews count among his best and most valuable writing, as artful as they are factual. We not only hear what Rousseau said, but get some sense of his humours and his attitude as he says it. In a later interview with Mrs

Rudd the notorious con-artist with whom Boswell dallied, we are treated to an atmospheric description not just of her but her surroundings – the books on her shelf, the cut of her clothes, the feel of the room, an accrual of documentary value. Burns has been spotted, described, drawn, painted and idealised from many directions, but the absence of a Boswellian Burns, scooping up all of those superficial, significant details is surely to be regretted.

This wish is easily reversed. If Burns, the analyst of mores and pretence, author of 'A Man's a Man' and detector of louses had met Boswell, a peacock of the first order, the literary record may have been greatly enriched. Of course, Burns did write about Boswell as 'him wha led o'er Scotland a'/The meikle Ursa-Major.' But that is Boswell as a character, a cipher in popular literature that lacks the absurd, volatile warmth of the persona inhabiting the *London Journal* or the *Tour to the Hebrides*. Becoming characteristic was again, something both men hold in common beyond a common accent and dialect. Their ultimate fate was to feature as *dramatis personae* in cautionary tales as to the dangers of the libertine lifestyle also unite them, at least in common folklore if no longer the historical record.[7] Their disarmingly frank depictions of sexuality in eighteenth century Scotland – as contained openly in Burns' poems, and furtively in Boswell's autobiographical writings – raise the status of the reproductive act from sin to existential question. Burns took sex on as a social and political position (no pun intended) as expressed in his poetry. It was an expression of common feeling and he focused a great deal of attention on what sentiments and notions his desires moved inside him, how it helped him be human.[8]

With Boswell it was a little less straightforward. Sex was confined to his journals (although he spoke of it frequently), his audience never any bigger than a few intimates or his imagined descendants,[9] keen to examine every pore of their ancestor. In the *London Journal* Boswell insists on his sexual prowess and may have exaggerated his achievements in this field, but is brutally honest in how demeaning and destructive his back-alley encounters could be.[10] He is nevertheless touching in his description of the affair with Louisa, though his reaction to catching a venereal disease from her is to immediately think of his wounded dignity (and the money he loaned her) and his response is cold and hypocritical. Louisa (in reality the actress Miss Lewis) was also an impossibly fanciful, romantic adventure that was purely of the moment; there could have been no question of turning her into the new Lady Auchinleck. It confirms that for Boswell promiscuity was an escape from his own obsessions and compulsions, as well as the cast iron disciplines of his youth. His desperate run to an Edinburgh prostitute after witnessing (on his own, fascinated insistence) a particularly horrific hanging at the Grassmarket that would not get out of his head, epitomises his medicinal approach to sex as a corrective to his own frailties, crying 'take it out!' as he seized upon her.

Whereas Boswell identified sex with descent and disgrace, Burns contended that sex had (again, no pun intended) levelling power, was energising rather than somatic. The differences may be more readily detected in the deployment of euphemism and innuendo. In Burns' poetry this expresses the breadth and richness of feeling his sexual curiosity opened him up to, in short, his bawdiness opened the mind. For Boswell, locked into a repeating pattern of sin, suffer, repent, sin again (that is drink, hangover, repent, drink again; or sex, gonorrhea, repent, sex again; or drink/sex, hangover/gonorrhea, repent, drink/sex . . .) euphemism played quite the opposite function. Words gave him room to manoeuvre and confined the chaos of his sexual activities into prosaic forms and idioms. He extended this to the Word itself, turning than once, to religion to excuse his infidelities. In a moment from the *Edinburgh-Lichfield Journal* of 1776, an Anglican service provides an epiphany which, he thinks, squares the circle and absolves the guilt:

> I was much pleased with the Cathedral service here, having never heard the music so solemn and so accordant with the words. I was quite elevated, but sensual connexions with women, particularly with the lady with whom I had been twice lately in London, came across me. I thought thus: "These are Asiatic satisfactions, quite consistent with devotion and with a fervent attachment to my valuable spouse."[11]

As Pottle notes in his introduction, 'Promiscuity' seemed to Boswell unpleasantly naked and direct in its meaning, but 'concubinage' was Asiatic, and ergo Biblical – 'If it was morally wrong, why was it permitted to the most pious men under the Old Testament, nay, specially blessed with fruitfulness? Why did our SAVIOUR say nothing against it?' As this prospective father of nations furled himself in the protective leaves of the Old Testament, Burns' asserted in 'Address to the Unco Guid', that natural sympathy was a superiorbasis of moral consciousness, showing far greater courage than Boswell, forever searching for a flimsy theological excuse to pursue his desires while maintaining his outward respectability. Boswell was the man about town; but Burns could at least argue he was just being a man.

2. '. . . you forgot yourself, and became a man.' Sympathy vs Empathy

Both Boswell and Burns shared an admiration for the works of Dr Johnson, who moulded aspects of them their fathers never could. Johnson figures surprisingly large in Burns' reading. He knew, and clearly disparaged the work of Elphinstone, the Edinburgh-born, London schoolmaster who counted Johnson as a friend and translated Martial from the Latin. He writes entertainingly of him in a Clarinda letter, dated 12th January 1788;[12]

> The poetry of Elphinstone can only equal his prose notes. I was sitting in a merchant's shop of my acquaintance, waiting somebody; he put Elphinstone into my hand, and asked my opinion of it; I begged leave to write it on a blank leaf, which I did, –

> TO MR. ELPHINSTONE.

> O thou, whom poesy abhors!
> Whom prose has turned out of doors!
> Heardst thou yon groan? proceed no further!
> 'Twas laurel'd Martial calling murther!

A few months later he writes to Mr Hill, the Edinburgh bookseller from Ellisland in 1789 to ask for a copy of *The Dictionary* to be bundled in with his order. It is clear he had already read it and thought it the best available. We also know he read *The Lives of the English poets* sometime before 1790, inspiring a poem about Johnson expressing his disappointment at the Cham's attacks on the poet Hampden for his republican leanings. He may well have read Johnson's *Journey to the Western Isles* as well as Boswell's *Tour*. Burns' conception of the English language was thus directed and shaped by Johnson. It was not a legacy Burns accepted unreservedly, wondering in a letter to Miss Dunlop in 1788 whether its formality led to emotional and intellectual dishonesty.

There is an affectation of gratitude which I dislike. The periods of
Johnson and the pauses of Sterne may hide a selfish heart. For my part,
Madam, I trust I have too much pride for servility, and too little prudence
for selfishness. I have this moment broken open your letter, but

> Rude am I in speech,
> And therefore little can I grace my cause
> In speaking for myself –

so I shall not trouble you with any fine speeches and hunted figures. I shall
just lay my hand on my heart and say, I hope I shall ever have the truest,
the warmest sense of your goodness.

And there Burns declares his approach to language, one Johnson
made possible though he would scarcely have approved. The rise of
sentiment and the post-Reformation notion of the 'natural man' which
Rousseau created and Burns cultivated is contained in this short note.
Burns develops it in other letters – many of them to women –
criticising 'the language of gratitude' as prostituted to 'servile adulation
and designing flattery'. Such accusations were and are regularly hurled
at Boswell by his many detractors, particularly the notion that his
alleged hero worship of Johnson was in fact a design to cut him down
to size.

While both men placed a different degree of trust in the formalities
of language neither was content to merely make do with the standards
Johnson had set. Before he ever met Johnson, we find Boswell
admiring, but not uncritical of the Johnsonian style. This changed
somewhat after he made Johnson's acquaintance in 1763. In Decem-
ber that year he writes to his confidante Temple from Utrecht of
Johnson's superiority to Hume and how he retained 'the full dignity of
an English period', for which he surely felt an empathetic longing,
based on his own desperate, and frequently vain efforts to maintain his
own.[13] In the form of Johnson the mannerism hides not servile
adulation but a bombastic and energetic nature (which is perhaps,
through the distortion into gentility, ultimately the *de facto* result).
Modern readers have certainly struggled with Johnson's writings,
hobbled as they are by the 'classical fetters' Boswell describes as early
as 1763; when early Johnson is already out of date.[14] But he evolved,
having in Boswell's opinion, thrown his fetters off by the time of the

Idler and seeming much more nimble a writer by the *Journey to the Western Isles.*

But it is as a character, his intellect forcefully expressed through exclamations and outbursts that the bear-like Johnson most appeals to a Boswellian or a Burnsian. Burns probably approved of Johnson's commonsensical defence of the poor against richer moralists who wanted to curtail their pleasures, what he termed 'the sweeteners of their existence'.[15] This very character that attracted Boswell was, from the earliest meeting in 1763, partly his own literary creation. The vivid, indomitable Johnson that first appears (publicly) in the pages of the *Journal of a Tour to the Hebrides* is the result of the ongoing development of the Johnson character in the pages of the private journals, an outgrowth of Boswell's own desire to examine and understand his nature. The Johnson homunculus thus appeals to our own desire for self-insight, and more superficially, a desire to know the person holding the pen, for direct contact with the *man* not the book, the self over the works. The *Life of Johnson* changed biography because it examined its subject's motives, passions and the exercise of his will, and in so doing permanently blurred the flimsy barrier between the public and the private person. As Adam Sisman remarks in his recent biography of the biographer, 'Though Johnson himself had championed values rejected by the Romantics, his passionate intensity was a trait they cherished'.[16] The lumbering, scrofula ravaged bulk that housed a remarkable brain has a Romance, a Frankenstein, Gothicism that continues to appeal. In Burns' formative years as a poet Boswell foreshadowed these Romantic landscapes with the *Journal of a Tour to the Hebrides*, instrumental in turning the Scottish Highlands from wasteland to arcadia, furnished with many Roussean instances of man in nature.

Through his associations with Rousseau and writing *The Account of Corsica* (1768) Boswell became greatly interested in the idea of the noble savage, responding to it in characteristically peacock fashion by gadding about London dressed as a Corsican 'chieftain'. But, as Crawford points out, it was the Corsican General Paoli's cosmopolitan nature and fine manners, less than his rude, Corsican barbarism that led Boswell to become a champion and an intimate. He was never the natural man, never subscribed to Paine's assertion that the 'NOBLE shrinks into a dwarf before the NOBLE of nature'. He believed that property, subordination and social order were essential to protect civilisation, and thus its liberties, a position which seems to have developed as early as 1763. In his interview we see him taking an oppositional stance with Rousseau, bolstered by frequent conversations with Johnson that had assured his faith and his basic assumptions. He tested also, notions of common humanity through physical means, describing how he 'seised his hand. I thumped him on the shoulder. I was without restraint' whenever a Roussean saying pleased him.[17] The subsequent puncturing of Rousseau's postures on 'common humanity' is another instance where the representation of a self – Rousseau's – proves more powerful than the works, up to and including *The Confessions*. As a moment in European literature, it deserves to be much more famous than it actually is, and perhaps only a wise fool such as Boswell could have managed it-

> BOSWELL. If you were in Scotland, they would start off by calling you 'Rousseau, Jean Jacques, how goes it?' with the utmost familiarity.
> ROUSSEAU. That is perhaps a good thing.
> BOSWELL. But they would say 'Poh! Jean Jacques why do you allow yourself all these fantasies? You're a pretty man to put forward such claims. Come, Come settle down in society like other people'; and this they will say to you with a sourness which, for my part, I am quite unable to imitate for you.
> ROUSSEAU. Ah. That is bad . . .

This is followed by Boswell's abrupt launch into the Scots of his tenants and father as mentioned above – a point well scored by the 23 year old law student. The method of scoring it however, had already been suggested by Johnson, this from the *London Journal,* 22 July 1763;

> He insisted on subordination of rank. 'Sir,' said he, 'I would no more deprive a nobleman of his respect than of his money. I consider myself as acting a part in the great system, and do to others as I would have them do to me. Sir, I would behave to a nobleman as I would expect he should behave to me were I a nobleman and he Sam. Johnson. Sir, there is one Mrs Macaulay in this town, a great republican. I came to her one day and said I was quite a convert to her republican system, and thought mankind all upon a footing; and I begged that her footman might be allowed to dine with us. She has never liked me since.

Ultimately Boswell took this anecdote from Johnson as a message from his own Guardian Angel. It was sufficient proof of the importance of social distinctions and separations. Burns meanwhile, exposed the social structures that made it difficult even for a great republican Lady to sit down with her footman. He negotiated the rocky terrain of rank and precedence, lampooned hypocrisy under his nose and over his head – and yet, he too essentially accepted its existence and tackled it as a mountaineer would. His sentiment wanted to break the mountain, but his head looked to conquer it.

What is clear from exchanges such as this, beyond Johnson's gloating, is that even great republicans had their foibles and Smithian sympathy its limits.[18] But Smith might also have pointed out to either his pupil Boswell or his reader Burns, one very obvious, inescapable fact; There was more than just protocol preventing the Lady taking supper with her footman. Mrs Macaulay *paid* her footman to wait on her.

3. ' . . . sae mony figmagaries': Politics

In a letter to Miss Chalmers, dated 14th March 1788, we find Burns once again. coming over all Boswell;

> I have discharged all the army of my former pursuits, fancies, and pleasures – a motley host! and have literally and strictly retained only the ideas of a few friends, which I have incorporated into a life-guard. I trust in Dr. Johnson's observation, "Where much is attempted, something is done." Firmness, both in sufferance and exertion, is a character I would wish to be thought to possess: and have always despised the whining yelp of complaint, and the cowardly, feeble resolve.

Such moments of resolution are familiar in Boswell, who made them as regularly as others breathe, and always with a rider of self-reproach. One of his most self-loathing self-analyses surfaces in the *London Journal*:

> There is an imperfection, a superficialness in all my notions. I understand nothing clearly, nothing to the bottom. I pick up fragments but never have in my memory a mass of any size.

Of course, Boswell also trusted in Dr Johnson's observations, much more directly and intimately than Burns. In an undated memorandum, written just before he departed to Utrecht to study law and after a few months as a new friend and confidante to Johnson, Boswell's paternal and literary models merge:

> Set out for Harwich like Father, grave and comfortable . . . Go abroad with a manly resolution to improve, and correspond with Johnson. Be grateful to him. See to attain a fixed and consistent character, to have dignity. Never despair. Remember Johnson's precepts on experience of mankind. Consider there *is* truth. Consider that when you come home with a settled composure you will enjoy life much, without exhausting spirits and setting yourself up as a buffoon or a jolly dog . . . You're your own master . . .[19]

He never was, entirely. Burns perhaps did rather better than Boswell in meeting his resolutions, though the letters of both men show their greater capacity for finesse over consistency. Boswell seems altogether more aware and apprehensive of this fact, and no writer has explored their self-deficiencies as ruthlessly. As David Daiches remarked, Boswell was made for the age of Freud, and in forging his 'self' into a literary tool, was able to lay the groundwork for a sympathetic relationship which came to fruition when twentieth century audiences came into contact with the hidden trove of papers at Malahide:

> There are few readers of the journals who can not help feeling at some point and in some sense *de te fibula*, that the story is somehow about themselves . . . One might say that it is not Boswell's character that was so unusual, but the way he displays and exploits it.'[20]

In his essay On *Sympathy* Smith remarks 'If we saw ourselves in the light in which others see us . . . a reformation would generally be unavoidable.' This seemingly obvious statement sent Burns looking to his louses and Boswell to creating a huge body of prose that examines, minutely, the influences, affects and evolutions of his own thoughts and feelings, often through putting himself in the guise of others. He recreated himself as Johnson, or Sheridan or Burke, and in those moments saw himself more clearly. These records of Boswell's struggles with his own mind give us a comprehensive history of its development – and above all, why it seems so self-contradictory. We might wish we had something similar from Burns, who gives us clues in his letters but is always on project.

But as 'fickle men' go, Burns and Boswell are surely, exemplary specimens. This is not entirely their fault, being variously claimed from different ends of the political spectrum (though if they are a puzzle they bear the brunt of responsibility). Both men displayed traits that were variously, Jacobite, Romantic, Republican, Hanoverian – even Marian,[21] sometimes within the space of a few words. They contended with a number of what Boswell's hypothetical peasant-assassin calls 'figmagaries' and frequently confuse us in their responses to them. Viewed from a 21st century perspective this can easily be mistaken as insincere. At times they may have been, but then ideology in the eighteenth century could be fluid, certain opinions dangerous. Burns was careful to protect himself and protest where necessary, his moderacy, particularly in the months after the revolution in France:

> I know of no party here, republican or reform, except an old Burgh-Reform party, with which I never had anything to do. Individuals, both republican and reform, we have, though not many of either; but if they have associated, it is more than I have the least knowledge of, and if such an association exist it must consist of such obscure, nameless beings as precludes any possibility of my being known to them, or they to me.[22]

Similarly, Boswell appears on the surface the epitome of the landowning Tory, out to block emancipation for his own interests. But as an advocate he migrated towards the hardest luck and hardest-up cases and felt empathy with anyone who showed frailties or caprices he recognised in himself. He protected landlord's rights but believed they should be exercised responsibly. Rousseau may have detected a 'despot tendency' in Boswell when he tested him with his parable of the dog and the cat,[23] but if despot he was, he was decidedly gooey at the centre. It would take the bulk of the nineteenth for the great political creeds to establish distinctive ideological frame-works and firm up the party lines. Being 'whiggan' in 1707 was different from the whiggery of 1776, which looked and felt different from a Whig of 1848. As Pottle notes in his commentary on Boswell's Account of Corsica; 'On occasion the eighteenth-century man of sensibility will appear to slip back into the ideas and actions of the Middle Ages. And there are times when he will seem to be looking into the nineteenth or the twentieth century. Intensely, absurdly caught between the past and the future'. A fitting description of Burns or Boswell.

What had become more certain to such absurd individuals was that liberty had a direct correlation to property; beyond this basic fact the details were very much up for grabs and that seems to have suited Burns and Boswell just fine. They are to some extent a *litmus* for the reactions of their respective classes to these huge political and social pressures. Greatest of all was the realignment of the dominant social class. The rise of the bourgeoisie put Burnses and Boswells alike on unsure footings. The seigneurial powerbase of the Auchinlecks was being eroded, though Lord Auchinleck's career as a leading jurist and even his son's as a mediocre one provided one way of maintaining political and social influence. For the Burnses, the earthquake moved mere scraps of land and altered their position within the parish, the trajectory from ploughman to exciseman being another instance where occupational solutions mitigated against potential disenfranchisement.

And there was politics. The respective biographies of Jamie and Rabbie are framed by five violently prosecuted political upheavals that followed the Treaty of Union, ranging from the very local to the international. The influence of the last of them, The French Revolution, has been expertly parsed in Crawford so will be mentioned mostly in passing, rather than recycled, while the importance of the first – the 1715 Jacobite rebellion – and the third, the '45, are illuminated in Pittock. The second upheaval has almost passed unnoticed, and as it took place very close to Ayrshire is surely deserving of further research. It happened in neighbouring Galloway with the 1724 insurrection of the levellers against the system of agricultural enclosure that removed common pastures in favour of larger, privately owned 'parks' that allowed cattle to be reared in greater density. This was a flashpoint in the oft-overlooked Lowland Clearances, analysed by Marx in *Das Kapital* as an essential process that set the conditions for the industrial revolution.[24] The 'parking lairds' of Galloway became the target of direct action, organized by committees of tenant farmers and pastoralists, what James Steuart described in the 1767 book, *An Inquiry into the Principles of Political Oeconomy as* 'the superfluous

mouths' who must be displaced, and sent to the cities to swell the
resources of commerce – confirmation that in the eighteenth century,
the 'progressive' agenda was not always the most compassionate.[25]
Landowners were taking advantage of new cross-border trading
opportunities post-1707 to breed cattle for export to England. The
large enclosures of two miles square allowed cattle sufficient pasture to
be bred and fattened for the chophouses of England. Forming a
cellular structure under 'captains', groups of 'levellers' flattened the
dykes that set the new park boundaries. An extreme element known as
the 'Houghers' went further, actually killing the cattle that belonged to
these landowners. The organisation of the Levellers was in many
respects, their most striking feature, benefiting from the traditions of
local militias raised against the Jacobites in 1715, a call to which
Gallovidians warmly responded the South West was strongly anti-
Jacobite and still acting out the tensions and upheavals of the
Covenanter wars. Burns would find himself embroiled in the tail
end of this tradition when France threatened to invade. Although the
Levellers were anti-Stuart they were equally anti-Steuart, and there
were more important economic allegiances for the government to
acknowledge. Its response – to send in the Dragoons – would have
been hauntingly familiar to anyone old enough to remember the
'Killing Times' of the 1680s.[26]

The revolt was quickly, but bloodlessly extinguished. It is almost
unthinkable that a landowner like Boswell would not have heard of the
events and remembered them with a shudder. That at least, would
have united him with the elder Auchinleck; but the Covenanter link
would have been abhorrent to Boswell alone (he identified strongly
with David Boswell, the 17th century Auchinleck who refused to sign
either of the Covenants). Boswell was also, in sympathy if not always
in practice, a Jacobite and he would have been a natural target for
Leveller committees. If Burns, son of a northern incomer picked up on
this snippet of local history from his mother's family, who came from
Maybole, then little is said of it, and his own Jacobitism might have put
him at odds with this popular movement. In any case, the mark of the
Levellers would have been detectable. Just as the ravages of the
Covenanter wars left kirks derelict and the ruin of burnt cottages
to haunt the landscape, the failure of the levellers to arrest enclosure
ordered it, perhaps even providing the dyke vaulted by Tam o' Shanter
and Meg. It certainly re-ordered the social world in which Burns was

raised, moving populations and motivating the aspiring to climb the ladder. But as to what either Burns or Boswell thought of the Levellers, history is silent.

The Levellers incident punctuates the span of years between the two Jacobite rebellions the '45 being the third major political rupture of Burns and Boswell's lives. Boswell was an infant during the period and Burns not quite arrived; neither fought in it but both developed an obsession with its aftermath. Taboo as a subject, requiring Johnson to clarify to Sheridan what claret he used to drink King James' health, Jacobite sympathisers looked backwards into history to find a way to express their sympathies, or, as Murray Pittock, who has thought more about Jacobitism in literature than most shows, sideways, into causes such as Corsica, where 'fratriotism' allowed Boswell to espouse pro-Stuart sentiments in the guise of defending little Corsica's liberty.[27] Even the interview with Rousseau allowed Boswell to praise George Keith, the Lord Marischal, exile from 1715 on whose behalf Frederick the Great was willing to wage war.

The figure of Johnson also provided a more distinguished *alter ego* through which Jacobite sentiments could be forwarded without risking reputation and livelihood declaring for it. Nevertheless, contemporaries noted the Jacobite taint, which made Boswell's political ambitions difficult to achieve. Pittock is probably correct in asserting it caused 'gross offence'[28] not easily overcome. Sisman also notes a the remarkable episode with George III, when, having gained access to his levee, Boswell asks the Hanoverian King whether he should refer to Prince Charles Edward Stuart as 'Prince' or 'Pretender'. This was bad enough, but Boswell, with almost incredible innocence, left a trail of such political blunders. One of these involved Henry Dundas, whom he attacked in a pamphlet in 1784 over the decision to reduce the number of the Lords of Session. Calling it a betrayal of the 1707 terms of Union Boswell's pamphleteering helped thwart the Bill, yet he then thought nothing of subsequently asking Dundas for help and advice. Burns was lucky enough to avoid entangling himself with the Dundas despotism but used the death of a Dundas to curry political capital, penning the so-so poem 'On the Death of Lord President Dundas' in 1787, this Dundas being the head of the Court of Session. Tied in as they were to the energies of national politics, these were most keenly felt at local level and a local hustings was the catalyst of Burns' failed approach in 1788. One of the enclosures in the Campbell

PATENT for KNIGHTHOOD.

150

Henry Dundas by John Kay

letter was almost certainly the *Fete Champetre,* in which the 'Ursa-Major' appears to illustrate Boswell's candidacy in the Parliamentary elections. The poem speaks directly to the electorate, wondering whom will they choose:

> . . . will ye send a man o law?
> Or will ye send a sodger?
> Or him wha led o'er Scotland a'
> The meikle Ursa-Major?

This looks on the face of it, complimentary, but may have stung Boswell a little as his opponents are described by professions he had failed at. He had of course, struck an entirely mediocre note as a man of law, and had prostituted himself to the court of Lord Lonsdale, the despot of the English northeast in the vain hope of an English constituency. He had failed also, to become a soldier in the guards in 1763; the friendship with Johnson being his one public success, and he was mocked even for that as lapdog and lickspittle. Maybe these lines pleased him, but maybe they also hurt? In any case, here was 'sarcastical vivacity' in action.

Allan Cunningham is in his 1855 edition, both punning and scathing in his analysis of Burns politics, effectively consigning Burns to *Private Eye's* 'A Cab Driver Writes' column:

> . . . the politics of Burns smelt of the smithy, which, interpreted, means, that they were unstatesman-like, and worthy of a country ale-house, and an audience of peasants. The Poem gives us a striking picture of the humorous and familiar way in which the hinds and husbandmen of Scotland handle national topics.[29]

'The Poem' was *The American War,* written in 1784 and so sensitive at the times, it was excluded from the *Kilmarnock Edition.* The revolutions of America and France, fulfilled the promise (or threat . . .) of the treatises and essays that formed Burns and Boswell's intellectual landscapes. As the rollicking satire of the American War suggests, the loss of the American colonies had a profound effect on British politics forcing figures of all stripes to take a position. Boswell and Johnson were famously divided on the matter, Boswell being enthusiastic on the rights of the colonists, Johnson far less so. His reasons were moral; the Americans had slaughtered the Indians just as the Whigs had the Jacobite Highlanders, and based their republic upon the institution of slavery.

4. Postscript: All Souls Rising?

In the pages of *The Drouth* we have questioned the verdict of the Lockerbie Trial, given a fair hearing to proponents of Hizbullah, come out against the universally popular Scottish play *Black Watch* and analysed the scandal surrounding Socialist MSP Tommy Sheridan. None of these controversial topics excited anything like the response to Gerard Carruthers' article on *Burns and Slavery*, which, for daring to note Burns' relative complacence on the issue stirred a minor media storm in the blog pages of *The Herald*. The rebuttals were angry, indiscriminate and indignant; how dare a two-bit journal suggest there was a chink in the saintly armour? The ensuing teacup storm emphasised the weight of expectation Scotland – or at least an irate section of it – heaps upon its national poet. What Carruthers found in Burns was an *absence*; the lack of any discernible track record on slavery beyond a poem of dubious attribution and its embroilment in poems dissecting the politics of the Kirk. Burns further emerges as someone content to compartmentalise what knowledge he had of slavery with the bounties offered by working on the Jamaican plantations. The tone of Carruthers' piece is puzzlement at how a man so convincing when writing of universal brotherhood could have such a blind spot? The tone of the angry bloggers was fury that anyone could doubt Burns' virtues would not naturally extend to opposing all forms of injustice, including slavery.[30]

Clearly we expect a great deal of Burns – almost as much as we do *not* expect of Boswell, although Boswell had much more contact with African slaves, ex or current, than ever a Burns did, and did, at least on a personal level, have a track record which can be reasonably assessed on slavery. He was good friends with Johnson's servant Francis Barber and defended him against rival Johnson biographer John Hawkins. His empathy was as genuine and heartfelt as Burns' sympathy was expansive. We assume in Burns it was colour-blind; we know that in Boswell's often was, but his politics were less impressive to us, especially over Slavery;

> For Slavery there must ever be,
> While we have Mistresses like thee

This is from *No Abolition of Slavery, or the Universal Empire of Love* (1791), written two years after the storming of the Bastille.[31] It is almost universally recognised as a terrible poem and fatally wrong-headed. Yet it strangely, has its merits each, like the man himself, almost immediately disqualified by some stupidity. It exposes the squalor of 'free' citizens in London (which he had seen firsthand on his meanders in the back alleys) yet contrasts against it, implausible images of slaves happy and well fed and clothed – and he may even have believed it. The sentiment expressed above tries to push the notion that all men are slaves because we are *all* slaves to love. Thus, if the bed-linen is clean and property rights safe, why risk the chaos and injustice of France to alter it?

The American Academic Howard Basker has accused Boswell of effectively derailing Wilberforce's Abolition Bill of 1791 because his *Life of Johnson* 'downplayed' Johnson's firm and unwavering opposition to slavery, which could have provided important propaganda for the Abolitionists.[32] Leaving whether or not the *LoJ* does is a moot point; it grossly overrates the power of the grossly accident prone Boswell to influence change, and seems to confuse multi-volume biographies with political pamphlets (nor does it take Johnson's many other biographers to task for failing to hand the Abolitionists a propaganda boost, at least one of whom – Hawkins – expressed a strong dislike of negros). Burns may be terse on slavery, but he has never been accused of political sabotage through omission. What Boswell's case shows is that it was possible to hold numerous contradictory positions all at once, especially when so much depended on sentiment, even if said sentiments were broadly and privately republican (and even if he had cause to abjure them). Also important to note here, is that republican-ism as a political position did not necessarily entail an abolitionist or even Universalist ethos.

We find no shortage of republics in Boswell and Burns' time. The Most Serene Republic of Genoa took military action against the Corsican cause Boswell espoused, while the Most Serene – but diminished, and always closeted – Republic of Venice, limped on until 1797, only just outliving both writers. Both were extinguished by the ascendancy of Republican France en route to the Napoleonic Empire, events which would pit revolutionary and evolutionary notions of liberty against each other for the best part of two decades. The Most Serene Republic of Poland and the Grand Duchy of Lithuania was anything but (in reality an elective joint monarchy), while Tiny San Marino outlived all of them and continues to enjoy its republican Serenity today. Each of these might fail to impress us today, as representing what republics 'should' be. Were we to visit the Republics of Machiavelli's Discorsi, where plebeian and patrician engaged in fruitful conflict (a position taken up in Henry Lord Kames essay on 'The Rise and Fall of Patriotism') we might find ourselves mightily disoriented by a heady cocktail of sincere political libertarianism, deep social divides and yes, forms of indenture tantamount to slavery.

Which leads us back to America. There were all sorts of ways in Boswell and Burns' time in which the cause of 'progress' could come across as unfeeling and as heartless as Steuart's discussion of 'superfluous mouths'. To support America in the 1780s meant to accept, or at least live with considerable cognitive dissonance over slavery in the colonies. Supporters may also, as the descendants of many Scots *emigres* in the southern United States did, identify one with the other, easily done if republican liberty is understood to correspond to economic prosperity and autonomy.

Republicanism was a complex business, as was attempting to live life by the notion of common humanity. And this is because the big question – one which Boswell and Burns both contended with, asks us to define the limits of such liberty. Did the founding fathers of the Americas think of African slaves when they wrote the constitution? Did the French Assembly? Who was in the club, and who, by definition, was out? One of the more dangerous brews mixed into every republican stew is the notion that a people contains something exceptional about them that their constitution must preserve, against the non-exceptional sorts outside their gates. This doctrine of exceptionalism should not be underestimated. Consider this episode, where Boswell reveals how content Corsicans were to allow the hated Genoese do their dirty work, and thus remain themselves in a state of fraternal purity;

TWO SHADOWS IN CONVERSATION

132

Lord Kames by John Kay

While I was at Sollacarò information was received that the poor wretch
who strangled the woman at the instigation of his mistress had consented
to accept of his life, upon condition of becoming hangman. This made a
great noise among the Corsicans, who were enraged at the creature, and
said their nation was now disgraced.[33]

'Wha sae base' to be a hangman? General Paoli was brave enough to
disagree, advancing the reasonable argument that; 'As we must have
Corsican taylours and Corsican shoemakers, we must also have a
Corsican hangman.' Boswell thought this dubious as tailoring was a
mean profession but its practitioners not untouchables – and Rous-
seau himself agreed 'it might have a good effect to have always a
Genoese for the hangman of Corsica.' In short, Rousseau's Corsica
would always need an 'other' to roke in the dirt for it – and, by
implication, should always fear the spectre of Genoese dominance to
preserve its sense of common cause. In a letter to Erskine, dated 1793,
Burns, protests his loyalty to the British state against France, and
neatly sums up a very republican form of arrogance;

> I have a large family of children, and the prospect of more. I have three
> sons, who, I see already, have brought into the world souls ill qualified to
> inhabit the bodies of slaves. – Can I look tamely on, and see any
> machinations to wrest from them the birthright of my boys, – the little
> independent Britons, in whose veins runs my own blood? – No! I will not!
> should my heart's blood stream around my attempt to defend it!

One wonders if Burns had seen the Holocaust or other modern
genocides, he would have written that, as slavery has ever since,
seemed less and less of a qualitative judgment on the enslaved. We
could damn these words if we chose – say that Burns implies there are
nations fit to be slaves, and those that are not, but it would be unjust to
assume Burns' talk of birthright meant he saw fit to deprive others of
theirs. Burns is also talking about what he would do in the event of an
invasion; Boswell's statement over Corsica is a much clearer example
of how the moral hygiene of the republican cause could in fact, mock
the very notion of common humanity and set down the possibility, if
not the actuality, of a reign of terror.

The Declaration of the Rights of Man and of the Citizen was published in 1789
and extended in 1793. It formed the basis of the first French

constitution, destroyed the legitimacy of the nobility, enshrined property as the basis of personal liberties and established the 'eminent domain' where public life did not intrude on individual rights to property and free pursuit of happiness, a boundary whose extent would be argued and contested for generations to come. One of these debates would be over its extension to slaves. The original declaration extended citizen rights to all 'free black' and 'mullatoes' in the colonies. *Les Amis Noirs*, a group of radicals and abolitionists argued that this should go beyond that to include the slaves; a greatly more powerful group of planters met in the Hotel Massaic, and said it should not, and the latter group proved victorious when the French government retracted the move in 1791. Neither Liberty, Fraternity nor Equality invalidated the receipts of French slave owners. The issue see-sawed when the Jacobins swept the moderates from power in 1793 and elected to pursue the ideals of the republic to the fullest, declaring an end to slavery, only for Napoleon to restore it in 1803. Republicanism, French or otherwise, may not have required slavery but where it existed it found it difficult to contend with. The third estate based its legitimacy on capital, and so tied itself into ethical knots over what happened when people were apportioned as a commodity and free trade demanded cheap labour. There were times when Liberty was bought and sold. Genoa sold Corsica to France in 1764 who then brandished their receipt at Paoli, backed up with armies and ordinance.

What is apparent is that these were times when moral conviction guided the application of *The Rights of Man* and Rousseaun ideals, not the other way around (it may be ever thus). It came down to Boswell's personal ethics in treating people of colour such as Francis Barber with dignity and respect, not abstract sentiment, which repeatedly failed those it was supposed to help. The master of Toussaint Breda, of the Arada people in West Africa was another person whose ethics bested his politics. He taught him reading and writing from an early age so that, just as Burns had, Toussaint read Rousseau and the other *philosophes*, and came to his own conclusions about sentiments of common humanity. The name he took, Toussaint Louverture is subjected to many translations – 'one who finds an opening', 'the wakening of all saints' or most concisely, 'all souls rising' being just some of them. Either of these would embody a very Burnsian sentiment, if not a very Burnsian practice. In finding his opening Louverture trounced three European powers, founded the second

TOUSSAINT LOUVERTURE

337

Toussaint Louverture by John Kay

American republic and the first founded on the premise that a 'negro' was the equal of a white. It started well and ended worse. Like the French Jacobins, Louverture lapsed into absolutism and draconian acts to protect the Republic of Sainte Domingue, and like Burns found himself fickle, suddenly becoming French under the threat of Bonaparte's intervention.

Those of course, were *his* choices, choices usually denied to slaves, women and peasants, the right to which he and his compatriots had to take for themselves. It was not in the gift of either a Boswell or a Burns to give it to them. What mattered was that Toussaint made these choices because he *could* engage with the same ideas as the biographer and the poet, ask questions of himself and his conduct, and likewise, be of independent mind.

NOTES

[1] But possibly not the same extent of knowledge. In his interview with Rousseau Boswell discusses his rather poor understanding of his own estates and tenants, not surprising given his repeated attempts to escape Auchinleck altogether.

[2] Frederick Pottle, Introduction to *The London Journal* 1762–1763, Penguin Books 1950. Pottle's edition of the *London Journal*, originally sent in weekly packets of quartos to Johnston of Grange during the London adventure went a long way to rehabilitating Boswell as more than the 'witless stenographer' of popular repute.

[3] Boswell's interviews with celebrated literary figures such as Voltaire and Rousseau, as well as his own well-documented engagement with Johnson are of course, near legendary, just one reason why many scholars were willing to believe in the infamous Goethe and Kant Hoaxes, which imagined Boswellian encounters with the poet and the philosopher.

[4] Louis Kronenberger, *A Johnson and Boswell Reader* (Viking Press, 1969), p. 432

[5] From *To The Hebrides,* incorporating *The Journal of a Tour to the Hebrides*, (Birlinn, 2007), p. 266.

[6] Kronenberger, p. 422.

[7] See Nigel Leask's chapter in this volume.

[8] Pauline Gray deals with the issue in her chapter.

[9] Various editors and writers of Boswell have confirmed he envisioned his journals being kept for ready-reference in the family archive. His mortified descendants begged to differ.

[10] The degree of Boswell's actual frankness over his sexual encounters is dealt with in Murray Pittock's *James Boswell*, AHRC Centre for Irish and Scottish Studies, 2007. He argues, convincingly, that Boswell's honesty was an exaggeration – that rather than admit to Saturday evenings alone, occasional encounters with prostitutes out of sight of the watch became an almost nightly adventure.

[11] James Boswell, the Edinburgh Lichfield Journal 1776, p. 294.

[12] J. Logie Robertson, The Letters of Robert Burns.

[13] Letter dated 7th December 1763.

[14] London Journal, p. 132.

[15] Kronenberger.

[16] Adam Sisman, *Boswell's Presumptious Task* (Bloomsbury, 2006), p. 337.

[17] Ibid., Kronenberger, p. 419.

[18] It is likely Boswell and Burns were aware of attempts to develop a science of rank and social distinctions, most directly by James Millar, whose *The Origin of the Distinction of Ranks* first appeared in 1771.

[19] From 'the Inviolable Plan', a memorandum Boswell wrote to himself on 16 October 1764.

[20] David Daiches, 'Boswell's Ambiguities' in *New Light on Boswell* (Cambridge University Press, 1991), p. 6

[21] Showing affection to the memory and cause of Mary Queen of Scots – in a sense, Jacobitism-lite.

[22] Letter to Robert Graham of Fintry dated 1793

[23] Rousseau tells the story of his cat and dog as a parable. In it the dog is inclined to give his paw every time the cat strikes him. Those who prefer dogs to cats are, to Rousseau's mind, more given to despotism than lovers of cats.

[24] Karl Marx, *Das Kapital*, quoted here from selections in The Viking Portable edition, (Viking Press 1983), pp. 357–8.

[25] James Steuart, *The Principles of Political Economy* (Edinburgh, 1767).

[26] Oddly enough there is very little published on this episode in Scottish history and no books currently in print.

[27] Boswell had corresponded with James Steuart on the issue of Corsica, noting in his preface to *The Account of Corsica* (1768); the 'candour and politeness with which Sir James Steuart received the remark which I have ventured to make in opposition to a passage concerning the Corsicans, in his 'Inquiry into the Principles of Political Oeconomy.'

[28] Pittock, p. 79.

[29] Allan Cunningham, *The Complete Works of Robert Burns: Containing his Poems, Songs, and Correspondence,* 1855.

[30] Which is not to say that as expressed through his poems they cannot. The point is that the man himself leaves little evidence of being interested in the issue.

[31] James Boswell, *No Abolition of Slavery, Or, the Universal Empire of Love,* 1791.

[32] From a paper delivered at Dr Johnson's House, 14 July 2006.

'I ONCE WAS A MAID'

&

The Female Narratives of Burns

THOMAS KEITH,

I once was a maid, tho' I cannot tell when,
And still my delight is in proper young men;
Some one of a troop of DRAGOONS was my daddie,
No wonder I'm fond of a SODGER LADDIE.[1]

Robert Burns (*Love and Liberty*)

Much time and attention have been paid to the women to and for whom Burns wrote his love songs – trying to match the actual person with her fictionalized counterpart (who usually appears under a different name or none at all) became such a popular endeavor that books have been written about the subject.[2] While many of Burns's love songs were written about particular women Burns knew, very few contain much by way of describing those women physically. Instead they are portrayed generally; called lovely, fair, etc. Many have agreed with Hugh MacDiarmid's assessment that the lines 'I sighed and said among them all/ ye are na Mary Morison' were among Burns finest, though no where does the song give any idea of what Mary looked like.[3] The scenarios in which these women are involved tend to be stolen moments, worship from afar, parting, or promises of love and protection.

There is also an entirely different group of women Burns wrote about. Nameless, faceless, and having no known specific models from life, these are the women to whom Burns gave a *voice* in song. Writing in the female narrative is rarely mentioned with the roster of masculine traits attributed to Burns, and yet it is a significant factor in Burns's character and important to the understanding of Burns as a writer. On the one hand, the women Burns extoled and honored in his love songs all are young, all possess physical beauty, most possess implied moral purity and all are silent. On the other, the women who *speak* in Burns's lyrics are variously guidwives, maids, hizzies, crones, gossips, carlins and quines whose beauty or lack thereof is not much at issue, whose moral purities and ages run the gamut, and who are anything but silent. Burns shows more than a touch of the dramatist in his song collection and often in his poems – his ability to see the world through the eyes of others and turn those perspectives into monologues and dialogues is extraordinary. Like any good dramatist Burns found a way to bring a sense of truth to their feelings and motivations so that he could write 'I once was a maid' with authority.

Scottish, Irish and English ballads are littered with the bodies of women who died for love. In fact, most died for what would now be considered trivial reasons, but still they were hanged, burned, drowned, or beaten primarily for being women. The few times Burns tried his hand at ballads, he steered clear of the violence and gore, turning instead to the comedy of 'Kelliburn Braes' or the magic of 'Tam Lin.' His interest lay in folk songs – the details of character and character motivation Burns developed in the female narratives in his lyrics demonstrate the growth of his dramatic instincts.

Of the roughly 325 traditional tunes to which Burns wrote lyrics, there are seventy in which the speaker is female and another fifteen in which a woman engages in dialogue. Burns is always present in these songs, at least he never completely disappears; his personality and poetic style come through to one degree or another. However, in nearly every case a distinct female character emerges and dominates the narrative.

In Burns's female narratives that can be categorized as love songs, the romantic feelings are those of women as expressed by women. Some of these include 'Ca' the Ewes,' 'Laddie, Lie Near Me,' 'Jamie, Come Try Me,' 'Ye Banks and Braes of Bonnie Doon,' and 'Ay Waukin O.' The latter is a good example of the many songs for which Burns wrote the lyrics based on words from source material, either oral or printed, creating a new lyric for an old melody.[4] In the case of 'Ay Waukin O' Burns used two songs, 'Simmer's a pleasant time' and 'The Day Begins to Peep,' and a chorus fragment, 'O wat, wat – O wat and weary!' from David Herd's manuscripts.[5] It can be rightly argued that Burns wrote many of his female narratives in part because his source was a fragment or song title that was already in the female voice. That is certainly true in many cases, but it is also most often true that the resulting creation has structure, imagery, and emotional impact not found in the sources.

'Ay Waukin' O' (*Poems*, II, 510) also demonstrates the simplicity of most of these – what one might call – 'reverse' love songs; a young woman expresses her desire for intimacy and companionship and mourns the lack of it. Consistent with Burns's style, a connection with the natural world is established in the first stanza. In 'Ay Waukin' O' we are told that summer is in full bloom, as is the young woman's desire, and a rushing waterfall corresponds to the intensity of her feelings. The chorus and the last two stanzas fill out the scene: the young woman is awake in the middle of the night, restless, frightened and weeping from loneliness. Burns allows us into her emotional private moments – the character who expresses her honest feelings is more intriguing than the one who remains a passive or silent object of abuse, lust, or, as was so often in Burns's case, adoration.

One of Burns favorite themes runs through many of the songs about country lassies involved in rural courtship: the virtue of choosing of love over material gain. In 'My Collier Laddie,' 'The Country Lass,' 'The Gallant Weaver' and 'Tam Glen' each of the female narrators articulates her determination to marry the young man she loves, refusing an arranged marriage and the prospect of coupling with a wealthy man for whom she has no feelings. While the outcomes in most cases are not revealed, by channeling his own romantic ideals through these female characters, Burns is giving them a kind of power that women of that time may have possessed but which was rarely, if ever, expressed publicly or artistically.

The young woman in the song 'Tam Glen' (*Poems*, II, 435) is given especially detailed imagery – in this gently comic monologue, a love-sick country girl goes to her sister under the pretense of asking for advise when in fact what she really wants is for her sister to confirm the decision she has already made.

> My heart is a breakin' dear, Tittie,
>   Some counsel unto me come len'
> To anger them a' is a pity,
>   But what will I do wi' Tam Glen? –

'To anger them a',' i.e., her family, is not a danger, or a mistake, but merely a pity. She has decided that she can make a go of it in poverty and be happier with Tam:

> There's Lowrie the laird o' Dumeller,
> 'Gude day to you brute' he comes ben:
> He brags and he blaws o' his siller,
> But when will he dance like Tam Glen. –

Who is this girl? She's already danced with Tam, or seen him dancing, and, not all that indirectly, is revealing that she has sexual feelings and that those feelings for Tam factor into her decision. She tells how her mother has warned of flattery and deception in men and in response she asks rhetorically 'But wha can think sae o' Tam Glen[?]' She tells of how her father tried to bribe her with money to forsake Tam and then asks her sister:

> But if it's ordain'd I maun take him,
> O wha will I get but Tam Glen?

Now it is destiny and no matter what the young lady does she will have to marry Tam – at least this is how she strengthens her argument to get her sister to say what she wants to hear. She relies on the Presbyterian belief in predestination which she then mixes with superstition: at a Valentine party she throws the dice three times and each result tells her that she will marry Tam Glen. She then relays how she carried out one of the most complicated courtship rituals from Burns's poem 'Halloween', and the result is incontrovertible evidence that Tam will be her lover. In a last act of desperation she switches from begging to bribing her sister for the approval she seeks:

> Come counsel, dear Tittie, don't tarry;
> I'll gie you my bonie black hen,
> Gif ye will advise me to marry
> The lad I lo'e dearly, Tam Glen. –

She loves him, of course, but it took her eight verses to say it. Her temperament is convincing; enough to embolden any young woman who might have heard her story, not to mention any young man.

Mary Morison is eternally at her window; Bonie Mary will always have her silver tassie; and Mary Campbell is forever looking virginal in heaven. All three are well known from Burns's pantheon of love-interests. It begs the question as to whether the woman who narrates 'Cock Up Your Beaver' is named Mary.

Burns's bawdy songs showcase some of the funniest and most outspoken female characters he created. Good examples are the female voices in 'Nine Inch Will Please a Lady,' the bawdy version of 'Duncan Gray,' 'The Jolly Gauger,' and especially 'Wha'll Mowe Me Now?' (*Poems*, II, 903) which, as it turns out, is double-edged, holding as much pathos as it does humor.

In the first verse the speaker tells that she has lost the blush in her cheeks and her slim waist and curses a soldier she describes as a 'loon' and whom she blames: 'The sodger did it a'.' What she blames the soldier *for* is repeated after all six verses and found in the chorus where she asks, 'Wha'll mow me now?' and informs that the soldier has 'banged [her] belly fu'.' Not an attractive or happy scene to start with. She does use the soldier's pistol and ammunition belt as a metaphor for his genitals and that is mildly amusing, but this woman's course, uncensored speech doesn't carry the lightness that allows us to readily laugh at the dialogue of the women in 'Nine Inch Will Please a Lady' or the sweetness of the woman who sings 'Daintie Davy.'

In the next three verses Burns, through his female narrator, makes angry and explicit arguments against the injustice that springs from class distinctions and poverty – themes unmistakably close to Burns are here expressed through graphic sexual imagery.

I want to clarify an exception to that. The most important image of the song isn't really graphic unless one knows the word *mowe*. Most Scots dictionaries give the definition in this context as 'to copulate'[6] or 'to have intercourse.'[7] The more accurate and direct translation of the word 'mowe' would be 'fuck.' But even when one knows that meaning of the word, the meaning is only an echo or a shadow when the word one is actually hearing is 'mowe' – not as familiar to most people and without the harshness of the word 'fuck.' Using the word 'mowe' softens the graphic nature of the line and allows the repetition of the chorus to be more effective.

In the second verse she tells how she must 'thole the scornfu' sneer of many a saucy quine.' She then draws the class distinction between herself and another woman, dramatically, crudely showing their common humanity, and bringing them both down to earth:

> When curse upon her godly face!
> Her cunt's as merry's mine.

She draws an even more vivid and insulting picture in the third verse with 'Our dame hauds up her wanton tail,' – the woman of means offers herself up for sexual gratification whenever she feels like it, while our speaker, who has identified herself as 'a young thing,' is judged and suffers name-calling for assuming the same freedom.

More exposition is woven into the fourth verse in which the woman of privilege has sex for her own greedy pleasure while our speaker, who has *now* identified herself as 'a poor thing,' is again subject to insults, this time because she's 'mowing for [her] bread.' She is angry about her poverty and angry about the position it puts her in sexually; if she is not a prostitute *per se*, she is at least desperate enough to exchange sex for food and shelter. Verse five:

> Alake! sae sweet a tree as love,
> Sic bitter fruit should bear!
> Alake! that e'er a merry arse,
> Should draw a sa'tty tear.

Burns has it both ways, so to speak, in showing the woman's vulnerability: in the first lines she conceives the symbol of 'the tree of love' denying her the sweetness she expected from life; her other romantic metaphor is the image of her own rear-end weeping tears.

In the final verse she becomes furious again, damning the soldier for denying his fatherhood, and finishing with a sentimental and political flourish:

> Or lea's the merry arse he lo'ed,
> To wear a ragged coat!'

That is, he goes off to join the army as a conscript. The most powerful part of this woman's musical monologue is the chorus, repeated after each verse. It is not incidental or accidental that our anonymous heroine does *not* ask: 'Who'll help me now?.' 'Who'll feed me now?,' 'Who'll take care of me now?,' or 'Who'll love me now?' It is with a rhetorical mixture of irony, sarcasm, and fury that she asks, 'Who'll fuck me now?'

Bawdy? Yes. Funny? Yes. Whatever her name is, she is among Burns most complex and intensely emotional female characters. Burns clearly had a strong connection to this woman; whether bragging, confessing, exalting or defending, he wrote about his own sexual life, directly or indirectly, in many of his song lyrics.

On the lighter side, 'Oh Whistle and I'll Come to ye, My Lad,' 'Johnnie Blunt,' 'I'm O'er Young to Marry Yet,' 'O An Ye Were Dead Gudeman,' and 'Last May a Braw Wooer,' among other Burns songs, all depict comic scenes wherein the female speaker is in control.

Undoubtedly based on a chorus and fragments published as early as 1769 (*Dick*, pp. 415–416), Burns took his turn at the tune 'O Whistle and I'll Come to Ye, My Lad' (*Poems*, II, 700) in 1793 and the results present a strangely familiar couple of young lovers. It may have been originally a fiddle tune because most recordings of the song until very recently have been sung at high speeds by sopranos with such rounded vowels that understanding the words is nearly impossible.

The young female speaker of 'O Whistle' can be thought of as either coy and flirtatious, or as bossy on the verge of promiscuous. Both of those conclusions may be readily inferred from the title and the chorus:

> O whistle an' I'll come to ye, my lad,
> O, whistle an' I'll come to ye, my lad;
> Tho' father an' mother an' a' should gae mad,
>   O, whistle an' I'll come to ye, my lad!

And yet there is certainly room for a more practical interpretation of her character when one considers that the next word out of the girl's mouth is 'but.' She says:

> BUT warily tent when ye come to court me,

A simple enough instruction and generally speaking, under such circumstances, a word to the wise should be sufficient. However, she feels the need to continue:

And come nae unless the back-yett be a-jee;

Fine – there will be a signal, easily understood by anybody; when the back gate is left open a wee bit, that's the cue to come calling. Still, she's going to paint the whole picture to make sure he's got it:

> Syne up the back-style, and let naebody see,
> And come as ye were na comin to me –

– and, just in case he didn't catch that –

> And come as ye were na comin to me. –

To be fair, the repetition at the end of each verse is of course built into the structure of the tune. When arriving at the end of that first verse, one has to wonder to whom she is talking. Is he stupid? He requires awfully detailed instructions. He's not stupid; he's dumb-struck. There is no condescension in the young woman's tone, rather she is motivated to be very precise – the need for discretion is urgent and essential and she has the challenge of conveying that to a young man who now understands, perhaps contrary to his prior experiences, that an attractive girl is attracted to him and wants to meet with him in private. The verses are about her attempts to get him to snap out of his reverie or at least maintain some semblance of composure. She continues in the second verse:

> At kirk, or at market, whene'er ye meet me,
> Gang by me as tho' that ye car'd nae a flee;

That's a helpful instruction: 'when we're in public, act disinterested, don't give us away.' Then there's the 'but' that comes in every verse:

> But steal me a blink o' your bonie black e'e,

'Don't be too cool, or so cool that you're cold. Just keep a little private flirtation going.' That's a bit of a mixed message for this fellow who isn't very adept at being nonchalant, so her instruction in the second verse comes with a 'but' and a 'yet':

> But steal me a blink o' your bonie black e'e,
> Yet look as ye were na lookin to me –
> Yet look as ye were na lookin to me. –

For this young man those requests may be the equivalent of trying to rub his stomach and pat his head at the same time. But, after another chorus, she forges ahead with a more sophisticated assignment:

> Ay vow and protest that ye care na for me,
> And whyles ye may lightly my beauty a wee;

She tells him to go so far as to verbalize his disinterest in her to others in public – a risky thing to suggest – and even to make light of her beauty, which is naturally followed by the 'but':

> But court na anither, tho' jokin ye be,

Perhaps she's gone too far now –

> For fear that she wyle your fancy frae me –

Burns gives this character more than one motivation, more than one obstacle and a definite conflict, and in doing so elevates her to the status of a complex, self-aware individual.

Whether it is to the French lyricist Berenger, or the writers of Tin Pan Alley in New York in the early twentieth century, or to the image of Burns dressed up as Elvis which was posted in the Glasgow underground in 2003, there have always been comparisons made between Burns and popular song writers and popular music from different eras and places. In the case of 'Oh Whistle . . .' there may be evidence of a direct Burns influence. Exhibit A: a young woman instructs a love-sick young cowboy in this lyric written in 1942 by Oscar Hammerstein, II for the Broadway musical *Oklahoma!*:

> Don't throw bouquets at me
> Don't please my folks too much,
> Don't laugh at my jokes too much,
> People will say we're in love.[8]

The most popular of Burns's dramatic female narratives has surely been the simple and tender 'John Anderson, My Jo,' in which the wife in an elderly couple reassures her husband that they will face not only old age together, but eternity. Another dramatic song, 'Logan Braes,' gives voice to the wife of a soldier. She sings to the River Logan as she wonders about the fate of her husband, laments her loneliness, and finally curses the war mongers over whom, to her intense frustration, she has no control:

> O, wae upon you, Men o' State
> That brethren rouse in deadly hate!
> As ye make monie a fond heart mourn,
> Sae may it on your heads return!
>   (*Poems*, II, 690)

The misery of women trapped in arranged marriages is a familiar theme in the folk songs of many countries. Burns dealt with the subject in several songs, including 'My Tocher's the Jewel,' but in 'To Daunton Me' (*Poems*, 398) he brought together a perfect combination of complex emotions, lyric structure, resonant imagery, and a haunting melody. The tune 'To Daunton Me' was printed as early as 1694 and had been used for Jacobite-themed lyrics (*Dick*, 411).[9]

In the first verse the unnamed speaker draws a stark contrast between herself and her husband with symbols of fertility (blood, flowers, and the depth of the ocean) and symbols of death (winter, snow and ice):

> The blude-red rose at Yule may blaw,
> The simmer lillies bloom in snaw,
> The frost may freeze the deepest sea,
> But an auld man shall never daunton me –

Burns's choices in this lyric demonstrate his dramatic talents at their best. Instead of telling the details of her story leading up to this moment as exposition – her fears for the future or didactic raging about the injustice she suffers – the woman simply repeats her determination that 'an auld man shall never daunton [her]' and illuminates that resolve with factual statements. This is a good example of why the folk song form suited Burns more than the ballad form. In the ballad form the *narrative* is the essential part of the lyric from which the drama springs. In this song, the character's emphatic and desperate perspective, told in the present tense, is what reveals the pathos of her dilemma. Hence, the drama of 'To Daunton Me' comes out of the character, not the narrative.

Burns uses tension to propel the story forward as the speaker further steels her determination to remain undaunted. Her willfulness is kept consistently throughout the lyric, supported by steady, driving rhythms within the stanzas and within the lines, as in the next two verses, with contained rage, she lists the old man's amenities:

> For a' his meal and a' his maut,
> For a' his fresh beef and a' his saut,
> For a' his gold and white monie,
> An auld man shall never daunton me. –

In the third verse she adds an additional determination that her self – her heart and soul – cannot be bought or sold no matter how much the auld man has paid:

> His gear may buy him kye and yowes,
> His gear may buy him glens and knowes,
> But me he shall not buy nor fee,
> For an auld man shall never daunton me. –

That is an especially bold statement as it comes rather close to acknowledging that she has, in a sense, been prostituted against her will.

Through her physical description of the auld man in the last verse, she adds additional weight to her indignation at the injustice she is facing and draws a grotesque portrait of the man she is declaring she has refused:

> He hirples twa-fauld as he dow,
> Wi' his teethless gab and his auld beld pow,
> And the rain rins down frae his red blear'd e'e,
> That auld man shall never daunton me. –

Finally she identifies the repugnant object of her future specifically as '*that* auld man.' Without traditional storytelling, the female narrator

of 'To Daunton Me' sings a dramatic monologue which has motiva-
tion and conflict and tells a poignant story.

Burns's writing that can be technically categorized as dramatic – the
cantata 'Love and Liberty,' the allegorical dialogues of 'The Twa Dogs'
and the 'The Twa Brigs o' Ayr,' the prologues written for the Dumfries
Theatre, as well as monologues such as 'Holy Willie's Prayer' – further
demonstrate his dramatic interests, and there is ample evidence in his
letters[10] and elsewhere[11] that he had ambitions to write plays. The
women he created in his song lyrics are just a few examples of how
Burns's vivid imagination, keen powers of observation and sensitivity
to human nature came to bear on his growth as a lyricist and, in
hindsight, show his dramatic instincts to be solid, if not fully realized.
Faced with the challenge of writing in the female narrative, Burns
embraced it and created a gallery of female characters unique in
eighteenth, and even nineteenth, century literature.

NOTES

[1] James Kinsley, (ed.), *The Poems and Songs of Robert Burns*, 3 vols. (Oxford, 1968), I,
p. 198. Henceforth, *Poems*.
[2] Robert Ford, *The Heroines of Burns and Their Celebrating Songs*, (Paisley, 1906); Rev.
John C. Hill, *The Love Songs and Heroines of Robert Burns* (London, 1961); Hugh
MacDiarmid, (ed.), *Burns Love Songs* (London, 1962).
[3] Hugh MacDiarmid, *Burns Today and Tomorrow*, (Edinburgh, 1959), p. 33.
[4] James C. Dick, (ed.), *The Songs of Robert Burns*, (London, 1903), pp. 401–2.
Henceforth, *Dick*.
[5] Hans Hecht, (ed.), *Songs from David Herd's Manuscripts* (Edinburgh, 1905), pp. 238,
240, 326.
[6] Alexander Warrick, (ed.), *Chamber's Scots Dictionary* (Alabama, 1965), p. 368.
[7] Mairi Robinson, (ed.), *Concise Scots Dictionary* (Edinburgh, 1999), p. 425.
[8] *Lyrics by Oscar Hammerstein, II* (Milwaukee, 1985), p. 214.
[9] Carol McGuirk, (ed.), *Robert Burns Selected Poems*, (London & New York, 1993)
p. 247
[10] G. Ross Roy, (ed.), *The Letters of Robert Burns*, 2nd edn., 2 vols. (Oxford, 1985), I,
pp. 324, 464.
[11] James Mackay, *A Biography of Robert Burns* (Edinburgh, 1992), pp. 279, 353, 513–15.

BURNS 'THE OUTRÉ BEING' AND 'THE BEAUTIFUL NYMPH OF BALLOCHMYLE'

❧

RHONA BROWN & KIRSTEEN MCCUE

'The Bonny Lass of Ballochmyle' or 'Twas ev'n – the dewy fields were green' is one of the most beloved and popular of Burns's love songs. Known now, mostly, as a real crooner's love ballad often performed at family gatherings, Burns suppers and, of course, in legendary vocal recordings, it holds a special place in the hearts of many Burnsians and the wider public.[1] But the scholarly jury is still out on the artistic merit and the personal background of this particular song. Regarded by Andrew Noble and Patrick Scott Hogg as a product of Burns at 'his excessively sentimental worst',[2] it has been, like other Burns songs, dismissed precisely because of its popularity. Yet Thomas Crawford and James Kinsley have noted that it is in fact one of Burns's most impressive Augustan lyrics, directly reflecting works by Alexander Pope, Allan Ramsay, James Beattie and Oliver Goldsmith. In Crawford's opinion, this song, like 'Lass of Cessnock Banks', reads like a 'conducted tour of the Archetypes with a visit to Arcadia thrown in for good measure'.[3] So what is the story behind this song, and why do some make such 'snobbish judgements'[4] about Burns's undoubtedly popular sentimentality?

By working through Burns's letters and the three key editions of Burns songs – by James C. Dick in 1903, James Kinsley in the 1968 and Donald A. Low in 1993 – we can see the basic story emerging. Burns wrote this song in the spring of 1786 after seeing one Wilhelmina Alexander (1753–1843) walking in the woods of the Ballochmyle estate. She was the sister of Claud Alexander (1753–1809), who had retired from the East India company the previous year and had used his profits (one assumes) to buy the estate. All editors note that Burns's original choice of melody – as usually the tune came first in the writing of song lyrics for Burns – was 'Ettrick Banks'. This tune had appeared in William Thomson's *Orpheus Caledonius* in 1733 and had, as Dick catalogues, appeared in numerous other music publications which Burns knew well including fiddle collections by James Oswald and William McGibbon. Dick also claims that this tune had been associated with Allan Ramsay and that lyrics by him were included in the fourth volume of his *Tea Table Miscellany* (in its 1740 edition), another publication which greatly inspired Burns. Moreover the tune 'Ettrick Banks' appears with an unattributed set of lyrics in the first volume of James Johnson's *Scots Musical Museum* in 1787 (No. 81). Stenhouse's notes to this appearance describe the tune as 'another of those delightful old pastoral melodies, which has been a favourite during many generations',[5] and it is therefore found in virtually all of the important vocal music collections of the period. As is so often the case with his song writing, then, Burns isn't creating something wholly new. Kinsley provides more information about the manuscript of the song. He thinks that Burns sent Miss Alexander the song shortly after composing it along with a letter of 18 November in which he asks for her permission to include it in his new 'Edinburgh' edition of poems. But Kinsley also claims that, in the meantime, Burns had packaged it up with other songs which he sent to Mrs Stewart in September 1786, as part of the collection which came to be known as the Stair Manuscript.

What all three editors note, correctly, is that Miss Alexander failed to respond to the song and Burns's letter, and, still wanting permission, the song remained unpublished in the poet's lifetime. Dick lists the *The Polyhymnia: being a collection of poetry original and selected by a society of Gentlemen* (Glasgow 1799) as the first source. Interestingly James Kinsley and later editors make no mention of this volume, but a copy does exist in the Special Collections of the University of Glasgow and it does, indeed, feature Burns's song. The copy there is undated, but the first poem in the first issue of *The Polyhymnia*, entitled 'Fragment' is dated 1798, so presumably, unless Dick had seen a dated copy elsewhere, he was making a reasonable assumption that this was a very early, if not the first printing.[6] All other editors list James Currie's first edition of *The Works of Robert Burns* of 1800 as the

Etrick Banks.

81 { On Etrick banks, ae sum_mer's night, At gloaming

Andante

when the sheep came hame, I met my laf_sy bra' and tight, While

wandring through the mist her lane. My heart grew light, I,

ran, and flang my arms about her bon_ny neck; I kifs'd and

clap'd her there fu' lang, My words they were na' mony feck.

I faid, my laffie, will ye go
   To the highland hills the earfe to learn?
I'll baith gi'e thee a cow and ewe,
   When ye come to the Brig of Earn.
At Leith, auld meal comes in, ne'er fafh,
   And herrings at the Broomy-Law;
Chear up your heart, my bonny lafs,
   There's gear to win we never faw.

All day when we have wrought enough,
   When winter frofts, and fnaw begin,
Soon as the fun gaes weft the loch,
   At night when you fit down to fpin,

I'll fcrew my pipes, and play a fpring:
   And thus the weary night will end,
Till the tender kid and lambkin bring
   Our pleafant fummer back again.

Syne when the trees are in their bloom,
   And gowans glent o'er ilka field,
I'll meet my lafs among the broom,
   And lead you to my fummer fhield.
Then far frae a' their fcornfu' din,
   That make the kindly hearts their fport,
We'll laugh and kifs, and dance and fing,
   And gar the langeft day feem fhort.

Ettrick Banks score

first publication of the song. The first time it is published with music is in George Thomson's 1802 edition of Volume 3 of *A Select Collection of Original Scottish Airs*, where it appears as No. 8 with a musical setting by Joseph Haydn.

The story behind the publication of the song in James Currie's controversial edition of the poet's life and work in 1800 has not been told in its entirety. In fact the song does not appear under 'works', but as part of the life and correspondence which Currie worked so hard to compile for this first edition. He places the story of this song within a discussion of the 'purification of his [Burns's] taste' which Currie sees as preparation for the poet's introduction to the culture of the Edinburgh literati.[7] Amongst such 'preparations', for example, is the establishment of the Bachelor's Club in Tarbolton, a debating club which Burns founded with his brother Gilbert and some other friends in 1780. It's worth noting the background to Currie's project here before exploring the detailed context of 'The Bonny Lass of Ballochmyle', for this edition has received a great deal of bad press and is the focus of much misunderstanding. Recent work by scholars at the University of Glasgow on the fascinating archive of Currie's manuscript correspondence at Glasgow's Mitchell Library and else-where is allowing us finally to see the whole context of Currie's 'Life and works of Robert Burns' for the first time. Currie was approached by Burns's close friend, John Syme, shortly after the poet's death in 1796, and asked to compile the first edition of Burns's work for the benefit of his widow and children. Currie was aware of the project's magnitude and its revolutionary potential, in terms of the poet's place within national culture, and was initially uncomfortable about taking it on. The story goes that Currie was given all of Burns's existing papers and was left to make of them what he would. Currie's decision was to contact a large pool of Burns's friends and colleagues to ask for permission to use their own papers connected to the poet, and thus to be able to compile a fuller picture of Burns's personal and artistic lives. Some of them refused, regarding their own letters from Burns as prized private possessions which they did not wish to share more widely. Others were willing to subscribe to the volumes or to give their letters not for any personal gain, but because they were also aware of the dire financial straits of Jean Armour and the family.

One such individual was Burns's second song editor, the Edinburgh civil servant, musical impresario and publisher George Thomson (1757–1851), who noted in one of his letters to Currie, of 14 September 1798,[8] that, although he reckoned the public would see that his correspondence with Burns was not intended for publication, he hoped Currie would 'do me the justice to mention the motive on which I permit my letters to appear'. Thomson supplied his own correspondence with the poet, but also became an envoy for Currie, soliciting letters and documents from other associates of Burns for inclusion. Several of Thomson's letters to Currie describe the process of trying to convince individuals to provide their correspondence for Currie's edition. Sometimes Thomson persuades them, and on other occasions he's not so successful. On 26 July 1799 he notes that Robert Ainslie 'postively refuses to give up the original letters of Burns. He values them highly he says, and likes to show them occasionally to particular friends who relish that species of wit they contain'.[9] And indeed his letter of Sunday 8 September 1799 provides further information about Ainslie as one of the 'The Happy Trio' as Thomson calls the men who formed the drunken content of Burns's song 'O Willie Brew'd a peck o' maut'.[10]

Thomson is particularly delighted when he comes across 'in the possession of a friend, a copy of a Letter & Song written by Burns, which appeared to me well worthy of a place in his works'. In his letter of 14 September 1798 Thomson explains to Currie that he has identified the above song and letter as that of 'The Bonny Lass of Ballochmyle' and its accompanying letter from Burns to Wilhelmina Alexander. Thomson notes that she had apparently 'refused' permission for Burns to publish the song initially, but, inspired by the potential of a publishing 'coup', Thomson decides to write 'a letter ostensible to the Lady in which I solicited the favour so earnestly, as to have procured it'. Miss Alexander thus sends Thomson the original manuscript for copying and asks that the original be returned to her. Thomson duly sends said copy (with a copy of Burns's letter to her) to Currie, but not before suggesting a couple of emendations for Currie to take on board. These alterations appear to have been part of Thomson's bargaining process with Miss Alexander, for he notes to Currie: 'that I might the more readily obtain the ms, I told her that in printing the letter, I would recommend it to you to omit the last two lines, which you'll see I have scored out'. Thomson also makes suggested emendations to the lyric itself (given below in square brackets). A transcript of the letter and song Thomson enclosed is as follows:

Copy Letter from Robert Burns to Miss Wilhelmina Alexander, Ballochmyle (July 26th, 1799)

Madam,

Poets are such outré Beings, so much the children of wayward Fancy and capricious whim, that I believe the world generally allows them a larger lassitude in the rules of Propriety, than the sober Sons of judgment and Prudence. – I mention this as an apology all at once for the liberties which a nameless Stranger had taken with you in the inclosed; and which he begs leave to present you with. – Whether it has poetical merit any way worthy of the Theme, I am not the proper judge: but it is the best my abilities can produce; and what to a good heart will perhaps be a superior grace, it is equally sincere. –

The Scenery was nearly taken from real life; though I dare say, Madam, you don't recollect it: for I believe you scarcely noticed the poetic Reveur, as he wandered by you. – I had roved out as Chance directed, on the favourite haunts of my Muse, the banks of Ayr; to view Nature in all the gayety of the vernal year: – the Sun was flaming o'er the distant, western hills; not a breath stirred the crimson opening blossom, or the verdant spreading leaf. 'Twas a golden moment for a poetic heart. I listened to the feathered Warblers, pouring the harmony on every hand, with a congenial, kind regard; and frequently turned out of my path lest I should disturb their little songs, or frighten them to another station. – "Surely," said I to my self, "he must be a wretch indeed, who, regardless of your harmonious endeavours to please him, can eye your elusive flights, to discover your secret recesses, and rob you of all the property Nature gives you; your dearest comforts, your helpless, little Nestlings." – Even the hoary Hawthorn twig that shot across the way, what heart, at such a time, but must have been interested in its welfare; and wished it to be preserved from the rudely browsing Cattle, or the withering Eastern Blast.

Such was the scene, and such the hour, when in a corner of my prospect I spyed one of the finest pieces of Nature's workmanship that ever crowned a poetic Landskip; those visionary Bards excepted who hold commerce with the aerial Beings. Had Calumny and Villainy taken my walk, they had, at that moment, sworn eternal peace with such an Object. –

What an hour of inspiration for a Poet! It would have raised plain, dull, historic Prose to Metaphor and Measure.

The inclosed Song was the work of my return home: and perhaps but poorly answers what might have been expected from such a scene. ~~I am going to print a second Edition of my Poems, but cannot insert these verses without your Permission.~~

> I have the honor to be,
>   Madam,
> Your most obedient, humble serv^t,
>
> Robert Burns

Mossgiel, 18 Nov. 1786

A Song – Tune: Ettrick Banks

'Twas ev'n – the dewy fields were green,
    On ev'ry blade the pearls hang;
The zephyr wanton'd round the bean,
    And bore its fragrant sweets alang;
In ev'ry glen the Mavis sang,
    All Nature listening [list'ning] seem'd the while,
Except where green-wood echos rang,
    Amang the braes o' Ballochmyle.

With careless step I onward stray'd
    My heart rejoic'd in Nature's joy,
When, musing in a lowly [lonely] glade,
    A Maiden fair I chanc'd to spy:
Her look was like the Morning's eye,
    Her air like Nature's vernal smile;
The lilies' hue and roses' die
    Bespoke the Lass o' Ballochmyle.

Fair is a morn in flowery [flow'ry] May,
    And sweet a night [ev'n] in Autumn mild;
When roving through the gardens [garden] gay,

Or wand'ring in the lonely wild;
But Woman, Nature's darling child,
   There all her charms she does compile,
And all her other works are foil'd,
   By the bony Lass o' Ballochmyle.

O if she were a country Maid,
   And I the happy country Swain; [!]
Though shelter'd [shelt'red] in the lowest shed
   That ever rose on Scotia's plain:
Through weary Winter's wind and rain,
   With joy, with rapture, I would toil;
And nightly to my bosom strain
   The bony Lass o' Ballochmyle.

Then Pride might climb the slipp'ry steep
   Where Fame and Honors lofty shine:
And Thirst of gold might tempt the deep
   Or downward seek the Indian mine:
Give me the Cot below the pine,
   To tend the flocks or till the soil;
And ev'ry day has joys divine
   Wi' th' bony Lass o' Ballochmyle.

[In Thomson's hand] The letter and song compared with the original MS.
G.T.

The tone of Burns's letter has been described by Noble and Scott
Hogg as Burns the 'hyperman of feeling' at his 'excessively sentimental
worst', who willingly exposes his 'erotic credentials'.[11] But this letter
might easily be seen a different light, when it is examined in the
context of Currie's effusively sentimental introduction. Here Currie
prefigures Crawford's idea of Arcadian bliss with his description of the
river Ayr and Burns's almost illicit meeting with 'his Muse':

The whole course of the Ayr is fine; but the banks of that river, as it bends
to the eastward above Mauchline, are singularly beautiful, and they were
frequented, as may be imagined, by our poet in his solitary walks. Here the
Muse often visited him. In one of these wanderings, he met among the

woods a celebrated Beauty of the west of Scotland; a lady, of whom it is said, that the charms of her person correspond with the character of her mind.[12]

On nearly all occasions he dismisses Thomson's suggestions of elision and chooses to spell the words fully (e.g. 'listening' or even' rather than 'list'ning' and 'e'vn'.) The last two lines of the second verse are completely different: here Currie prints 'Perfection whispered passing by, /Behold the lass o' Ballochmyle.' But he does note that this is a variation on Thomson's version, and gives his two lines – 'The lilies' hue and roses' die/Bespoke the Lass o' Ballochmyle'- in a footnote on the same page. Interestingly Currie chooses to change 'Scotia' to 'Scotland' in the penultimate verse. This is a fascinating emendation because of the overtly classical content of the song, which celebrates female beauty in powerful pastoral imagery – where 'The Zephyrs wanton'd round the bean', where the 'green-wood echoes rang' and where the lass's air is compared to 'nature's vernal smile'. This narrator isn't lured by the search for gold and treasures in an Indian mine, but by the lonely local cot, the tending of flocks and the tilling of soil, for only here is he able to engage in 'joys divine' with his bonny lass of Ballochmyle. The finely balanced mix of 'high' Augustan sentiment and 'low' peasant activity is notable for its similarities to the best of Ramsay's pastoral lyrics in *The Gentle Shepherd*, as is Burns's choice of a tune also associated with Ramsay. In addition such powerful floral image, which is one of Burns's key signatures in his pastoral songs, links this song to a much older Scottish tradition harking back to William Dunbar's *Thrissil and the Rois*. Even the rhyme scheme here – especially notable for its chiming 'ang' sounds, which seem to elongate the lines in the opening verse – is reminiscent of the alliterative verse of medieval and renaissance Scottish poetry. And as other critics have commented the song also relies on that combination of Scots and English vocabulary, again common to many of Burns's finest love songs and to the Scottish pastoral tradition in general. Far from being the work of a whimsical 'outré Being' this is a finely constructed lyric clearly identifying Burns as an Augustan and more-over a pastoral lyricist of the highest calibre.

Thomas Crawford suggests that Burns's letters at this point in his life are 'those of a man trying to feel what he thinks he ought to feel,

The Braes o' Ballochmyle from *John Wilson's 'Land o' Burns'*

because a higher class has decreed that "refined" emotions are better than those experienced by the swinish multitude in their cottages and barns'.[13] This argument indeed sits comfortably with Currie's contextualisation of this song and the apparent purification process of Burns as he becomes a published poet and ultimately 'the heaventaught ploughman', but the song itself rather inverts such assumptions. In the lyric Burns is appealing to a beautiful yet aristocratic woman to share his swinish 'cot below the pine' and as Currie explains in his commentary, Burns doesn't see himself elevated to her level but 'presumed to reduce her to his own' and 'to strain this high-born beauty to his daring bosom'.[14] It is only too easy to guffaw at Currie's discomfort over Burns's 'straining' and he does go to some lengths to explain Miss Alexander's refusal to coerce. The lyric speaks rather more sincerely. Burns states in his final verse, following all the temptation that goes before, that pride, fame, honour and thirst for lucre are sinful attributes of the lady's class. He actively rejects them for the apparent purity and simplicity of his own kind which is presented as divine by comparison. That Miss Alexander refuses to acknowledge Burns's advances in real life, as it were, is something he finds difficult to accept gracefully, and in his own note beside the transcript of the letter in the famous Glenriddell Manuscript, the swinish imagery is this time connected to the bourgeois Alexander family: 'She was too fine a Lady *to notice* so plain a compliment. – As to her great brothers . . . Ye canna mak a silk-purse o' a sow's lug.'[15] Currie is unwilling to include this particular comment, merely stating that she 'wounded his self-love'[16] and, emphasising yet further the classical connections of the story, Currie gives a long and involved account of the possible reasons for her silence: 'Her modesty might prevent her from perceiving that the Muse of Tibullus breathed in this nameless poet, and that her beauty was awakening strains destined to immortality on the Banks of the Ayr'. And, Currie continues, Burns himself may have been inspired by 'freedoms among the poets of Greece and Rome'.[17]

Currie's belief that Miss Alexander had no knowledge of Burns, his poetry or newfound fame, is hard to accept, bearing in mind that Burns's first *Poems Chiefly in the Scotish Dialect* had appeared three months earlier with such a flourish of interest both locally and further afield. Finally Currie suggests that she is too modest and pure a lady to stoop to Burns's sexual advances. Unlike most other women who, as he states, 'have generally submitted to this sort of profanation with patience and even with good humour' his account gives the impression that the reader should forgive the bonny lass of this story and that she should be allowed to remain the 'beautiful nymph of Ballochmyle, whoever she may have been'.[18] Maintaining the lady's anonymity was crucial for Currie and for Thomson who had done the deal over the manuscript.

But later editors have been neither so kind nor understanding! In 1903 James Dick adds a little to the story of Miss Alexander's refusal – noting that 'Many years later, when the poet had become famous and she was a maiden past her prime, she had the song and the letter framed and hung them up in the hall'.[19] Now in circulation, editors and critics are able to run with this embellishment. Wilhelmina Alexander is heavily criticised for her refusal to let Burns print his song in the first place. In 1906 Robert Ford produced *The Heroines of Burns and their Celebrating Songs*. Ford also remembers the fashion for mounting such important items in glass cases, but he spins the story further, by explaining that the manuscript of the song and letter stayed with her until she died at the age of 88 and that her nephew erected a 'rustic seat on the spot where she is believed to have met Burns, and above it was hung a framed facsimile of the song and letter. Thus' he states 'amends were made, only the poet did not live to enjoy the right-about-face'.[20] The story doesn't stop here. The most recent edition of the poems and songs, *The Canongate Burns*, also provides a note stating that this song is 'a kind of preliminary caricature of Burns's relation-ships with upper class women which, in the course of his life, evolve from this near farce, to, with Maria Riddell, incipient tragedy'.[21] They suggest that Miss Alexander, who is already in her thirties by the time of the event with Burns, was clearly heading for spinsterhood and, in doing so, they assume that she was therefore no great catch in the first place. But everyone else disagrees on the basis of Burns's wonderful lyric, the muse for which is clearly Miss Alexander's beauty.

In the intervening years this song – one of a group of regularly performed Burns love songs, which also includes 'Ae fond kiss' and 'O my love's like the red, red rose' -gained huge popularity. And this clearly has something to do with the melody which has latterly become most closely associated with the lyric, but the nature of which is far from Burns's original choice of tune as discussed above. 'Ettrick Banks', Burns's first choice, is typical of many so-called traditional tunes of the time: the melody is highly repetitive, but in two halves with two sections in each half. The tune in Thomson's *Orpheus Caledonius* is the one also presented by Johnson in his *Museum* with one or two variants, and is in the minor key, quite jaunty, but with an air of sadness or melancholy about it. The tune George Thomson publishes with Burns's lyric, in the first musical appearance of 'The bonny lass of Ballochmyle' in 1802 is not totally different: it has the same structure, and is also in the minor key, but feels generally 'happier' than Burns's original choice. Thomson has never been forgiven by many Burns scholars for the frequency with which he brought tunes of his own choosing to sit alongside Burns's lyrics after the poet's death. It might be suggested that this was a practice Burns was well aware of and which he used himself when collecting songs and tunes for the *Museum* and providing choices of tunes in his letters to Thomson. Ironically, after all the stramash associated with Thomson, the tune which was to become synonymous with Burns's lyric is altogether different – a big broad Victorian ballad in the major key, which has a climactic note (usually performed with a long pause!) at the end, and which insists on the frequent repetition of the phrase 'the bonny lass'. This tune was created by William Jackson, who is believed to be buried in Doune Cemetery. That grave provides another coincidental connection with Burns, for the cemetery is part of the Stair Estate, and it's the Stair manuscript which includes a copy of this very song.

A broadside ballad produced in Dundee in c.1880 prints the Burns lyric, referring to its tune as 'original' (see pages 230/231), but with the repetitions required for the words to fit the Jackson melody.[22] So it's clear that by this period, and certainly by 1896, when the big centenary volume of Burns songs with arrangements by Kenyon Lees appears, that the tune was well established. The song has nearly always been recorded with this melody and has, to our knowledge, only one commercial recording with 'Ettrick Banks' – in Fred Freeman's new Linn *Complete Songs of Robert Burns* (volume 11) sung by Rod Paterson. This William Jackson is also most probably the composer of the popular Irish ballad 'The Dear Little Shamrock' which appears to have been widely circulated during the last decades of the nineteenth century. And the Irish connection with 'The Bonny Lass of Ballochmyle' is also not to be dismissed, for one of the first appearances of Burns's lyric in chapbook form was around 1800 in a Kilmarnock-produced pamphlet which also included the Irish song 'Paddy Carey'.[23]

'Twas ev'n &c.— Air, Johny's grey breeks

Andantino

'Twas ev'n the dewy fields were green On ev'ry blade the pearls hang The

Ze-phyr wanton'd round the bean And bore its fragrant sweets a-lang In

ev'-ry glen the ma-vis sang All nature list'ning seem'd the while Ex-

-cept where greenwood echoes rang A-mang the braes of Bal-loch-myle.

George Thomson score

What does emerge is that this song, which is created to emphasise and even to showcase Burns's skills as an Augustan pastoral lyricist, is able to be enjoyed without any special awareness of its classical context: that a lyric beginning its life as an excursion through Arcadia has become a populist love song. As the creation of the song shows, Burns's original choice of melody forges his connection with Ramsay and the genre of Scottish pastoral while his obvious allusion to Pope and Goldsmith states clearly his Augustan literary credentials. Such characteristics were much appreciated by the literati, to whom Burns was clearly appealing in 1786 as he planned his visit to Edinburgh. But even those of high literary standing were sniffy about this lyric from the start. While Burns's correspondence with Miss Alexander suggests that he would not go against the lady's wishes, he nonetheless sent a copy of this song, along with another very similar love song – 'Young Peggie blooms', written for Miss Peggy Kennedy – to his agents in Edinburgh in the hope of securing a place for them in his new edition. Henley and Henderson's note to the song states that this 'jury' threw both songs out on account of their being 'found defamatory libels against the fastidious powers of Poesy and Taste'.[24] Whether or not these judges were taking the personal circumstances into consideration is not clear. However, Henley and Henderson also mention the existence of a note in Burns's hand which explained that the song could not be published without 'the consent of a lady', thus un- doubtedly helping to deter them. While their editorial predecessors refused this song for publication, Thomson and Currie saw past these apparently 'snobbish judgements'[25] about its 'taste' and clearly saw something of quality both in the story and in the song itself. The pastoral setting and the sentiments of the lyric, in which love conquers all, were precisely what Thomson desired to present to his female clientele.

Although one could argue that William Jackson's setting of the song dilutes this somewhat bourgeois past and does indeed make it a piece fit for popular consumption, today's critics are hypocritical in their appreciation of the song. Dismissed by some as flippant mawkishness, the song is perhaps ironically rejected by academics because it has come to be a favourite almost in spite of its 'high brow' credentials. While critics are swift to pounce on any pretension to social 'im- provement' in Burns's works, they also reject his undeniably popular

THE BONNIE LASS O' BALLOCHMYLE.

Melody by Wm JACKSON.

Kenyon Lees score

rang, A - mang the braes o' Bal - loch - myle, A - mang the braes o' Bal - loch-
by, Be - hold the lass o' Bal - loch - myle, Be - hold the lass o' Bal - loch-

cres.

myle, A - mang the braes o' Bal - loch - myle.
myle, Be - hold the lass o' Bal - loch - myle.

The bon - nie lass! the

mf

mf

bon - nie, bon - nie lass! The bon - nie lass o' Bal - loch - myle!

rall.

Last time

f

rall.

mf

rall.

p

3.

Fair is the morn in flowery May,
   And sweet is night in Autumn mild,
When roving thro' the garden gay,
   Or wandering in a lonely wild:
But Woman, Nature's darling child!
   There all her charms she does compile;
Ev'n there her other works are foil'd
   By the bonnie lass o' Ballochmyle.
     The bonnie lass! &c.

4.

O, had she been a country maid,
   And I the happy country swain,
Tho' shelter'd in the lowest shed
   That ever rose on Scotland's plain!
Thro' weary winter's wind and rain,
   With joy, with rapture, I would toil;
And nightly to my bosom strain
   The bonnie lass o' Ballochmyle.
     The bonnie lass! &c.

appeal. Just as Jeremy Paxman dismisses Burns's output as mere 'sentimental doggerel' (*Glasgow Herald*, 14 August 2008), this lyric demonstrates the poet's depth and breadth – attractive to an upper-class audience in eighteenth-century Scotland, his appeal translates to Scots of the twenty-first century. Burns, in his letter to Wilhelmina Alexander, describes himself and his fellow poets as 'outré Beings'. But 'The Bonny Lass of Ballochmyle', in turn, demonstrates the often 'outré' response to Burns's work. Rather than examining the many facets of Burns's literary enterprise, critics often respond to posthumous constructions of his work. A close examination of this song's conception and long life demonstrates that Burns's sentimentality is enduringly attractive to the reading and listening public alike.

NOTES

1   See Thomas Keith, 'A Robert Burns Discography' in *Studies in Scottish Literature*, 2004 for a comprehensive listing of recordings of Burns's songs by a wide variety of performers.

2   *The Canongate Burns*, Andrew Noble and Patrick Scott Hogg, (eds) (Edinburgh: Canongate, 2001), pp. 600–2, this quote p. 601.

3   Thomas Crawford, *Burns: A study of the Poems and Songs*, (Edinburgh: James Thin, 1978), p. 7.

4   Ibid., p. 290. Crawford's remark is made of Henley and Henderson's comments on 'The Banks o' Doon' where they thought the third verse the worst because it was the most popular.

5   William Stenhouse, *Illustrations of the lyric Poetry and Music of Scotland*, (Edinburgh: Blackwood, 1853), p. 85.

6   *The Polyhymnia: Being a Collection of Poetry, Original and Selected. By a Society of Gentlemen*, (Glasgow: John Murdoch, n.d.). The volume was made up of a number of weekly issues which were then bound together in a volume when there were enough. They thus appeared separately in a kind of chapbook format. 'The Bonny Lass of Ballochmyle is the first song in No. 18, pp. 5–6 and sits alongside 'Song, by a Lady' and 'The Bonny Lass of Cree'. Burns's song is introduced as 'The Bonny Lass of Ballochmyle by Robert Burns', while the others are unattributed. This volume is in the Euing Collection at the University of Glasgow Library, Spec Coll BG60–k.4.

7   *The Works of Robert Burns with an Account of his Life, and A Criticism of his Writings. To which is prefixed some observations on the character and condition of the Scottish Peasantry. In Four Volumes*, (Liverpool: M'Creevy; London: Cadell; Edinburgh: Creech, 1800), Vol. 1, p. 120. The discussion of the song's context and copies of the letter and song connected are presented on pp. 120–8.

8   Mitchell Library Currie Correspondence, Envelope 16 No. 1 (1/6).

9   Ibid., No. 2 (2/6).

10 Ibid., No. 3 (3/6).

[11] *The Canongate Burns*, all quotes p. 601.

[12] Currie, p. 122.

[13] Crawford, p. 6.

[14] Currie, p. 127.

[15] See notes on the song in *The Poems and Songs of Robert Burns* James Kinsley, (ed.) (Oxford: Clarendon Press, 1968), vol. 3, p. 1170.

[16] Currie, p. 126.

[17] Both quotes, Currie, pp. 126–7.

[18] Currie, p. 127.

[19] *The Songs of Robert Burns*, James C. Dick, (ed.) (London etc.: Henry Frowde, 1903), p. 358.

[20] Robert Ford, *The Heroines of Burns and their celebrating songs* (Paisley: Alexander Gardner, 1906), p. 100.

[21] *The Canongate Burns*, p. 601.

[22] A copy of this broadside version is available to access through the National Library of Scotland broadsides website at: www.nls.uk/broadsides

[23] This Chapbook 'Paddy Carey. The roving bachelor. The lass of Ballochmyle', (Kilmarnock, [1800?] is available to access in *Eighteenth Century Collections Online*.

[24] *The Poetry of Robert Burns*, W.E. Henley & T.F. Henderson, (eds) (London: Jack, 1897), vol. IV, p. 87.

[25] Crawford, p. 7.

'THE GREAT ENCHANTER'

✌

Robert Burns in Ulster

CAROL BARANIUK

A few summers ago, in a conversation with a producer from the Irish television company TG4, I learned that Robert Burns had been a highly popular read among Irish language poets of the 1930s and 40s who perceived him in background and employment of language to be what they themselves aspired to be: a true poet of the people. Not being, personally, an Irish speaker, I have as yet been unable to explore the work of these poets in depth, but a further fascinating instance of Burns' capacity to excite admiration in many and varied quarters came when I chanced on an online article from a back issue of *An Phoblacht* (Republican News), the journalistic wing of Sinn Fein. The piece was expressed in Irish, but I could clearly see Burns' name included in the final paragraph and, fortunately, I was able to ask an Irish- speaking friend to supply a translation. The author of the article, Colm de Faoite, was discussing the Ulster-Scots vernacular writers of the eighteenth century, many of whom were Presbyterians, members of the Society of United Irishmen and active in the 1798 Rebellion, through which they hoped to establish an independent, democratic and inclusive Ireland. The concluding paragraph ran thus:

> The Scottish dialect and its literature should be put on the northern school curriculum. The main writers of the speech are Robbie Burns and Hugh MacDiarmid, committed nationalists and republicans. They would breathe a healthy wind through our schools.[1]

It can hardly be disputed that the Ulster school curriculum would be significantly enriched (as would that of its Irish counterpart) by engagement with the Scots language and literature that due to

Irish-Scottish cross-fertilisation over many centuries is part of the whole heritage of the island of Ireland. It is intriguing to observe, however, de Faoite's easy incorporation of Burns and MacDiarmid into the gallery of republican literary heroes, an act which lacks the humility of the Burns dictum that we should learn to 'see oursels as ithers see us', but smacks rather wishfully of imposing on others (who are unavailable for comment) our vision of ourselves.

To be fair, this is hardly a feature of the republican mindset alone. The same appropriation of Burns has in the past been effected in Ulster loyalist communities with some startling results, as Liam McIlvanney demonstrated in a recent essay when he included the following quotation from the early twentieth-century Ulster poet and novelist W.R. Rodgers:

> There would be a bonfire in our back street that night. It would light up the roses on the wall-paper of the return room. It would flicker on the picture of Robbie Burns. It would glimmer on the tallboy with its deep drawers full of treasures –. . . a copy of the Solemn League and Covenant, a Volunteer hat that looked like a cowboy's, a silver sovereign-case. The bonfire would redden it all . . .[2]

Here Burns is served with a garnish of Orange and illuminated by the flames of an 'eleventh night' bonfire.[3]

As has been well documented[4] Burns' poetry attained an unprecedented level of popularity in Ulster during the revolutionary decade of the 1790s. The largely Presbyterian United Irishmen of Belfast[5] frequently published his work in their newspaper the *Northern Star*, for in this period when Thomas Paine's *The Rights of Man* was inspiring democrats everywhere, pieces such as the radical anthem 'Is There for Honest Poverty' helped set the politically correct tone of egalitarianism. After the disaster of the failed United Irish Rebellion in 1798 the British Government sought to suppress further dissent through the 1801 Act of Union which dissolved the Dublin parliament and incorporated Ireland fully into the United Kingdom, as had happened in Scotland almost a century earlier. The Union was and has remained highly controversial in Ireland. The eighteenth-century Presbyterian patriot and poet William Drennan published three pamphlets protesting vehemently against it. In the twentieth century, Seamus Heaney in his poem 'Act of Union'[6] presented it uncompromisingly as a brutal

THOMAS PAINE .

Thomas Paine by John Kay

imperialist act of conquest. There is some evidence, however, that the contemporary British Government intended it as a measure to bring stability and prosperity to the nation and to deliver emancipation for the Catholic majority, though crucially that promise was not fulfilled.

In Belfast during the Union and post-Union eras Burns continued to be published regularly in *The Belfast News-letter*, which throughout the 1790s had favoured gradual and constitutional reform rather than revolution and independence. Unsurprisingly, in the wake of the rebellion and its aftermath, the poetry editor avoided potentially controversial works which appeared to express radical sentiments. Instead he opted for lyrical pieces such as 'Address to the Wood-Lark'[7] or 'By Allan Stream'.[8] Perhaps there was a desire among literary enthusiasts, or among those who wanted no further civil disorder, to promote a romantic Burns who would threaten no-one. There were certainly several readers ready to supply their own patriotic compositions in praise of the union of the kingdoms. The following is a typical example:

> Old England's fair Rose
> In fresh beauty shall blow
> And the thistle of Scotland
> More vigorously grow
> With Ireland's green Shamrock
> A stranger before
> On *one stem* engrafted
> To part now no more.[9]

In a recent publication Gerard Carruthers has clearly demonstrated that Burns was a 'synthesizer of disparate strands of Scottish culture', who recreated Jacobite song and extended human sympathy to the Highlander. In addition, though, he was 'Burns the 'British' poet. As much influenced in his imaginative landscape by the English poets John Milton, Alexander Pope and William Shenstone [. . .] as by the Scots language writers Allan Ramsay and Robert Fergusson'.[10] In fact, so varied is the multi-faceted persona of Burns that it has always been possible for partisans of vastly differing persuasions, whether political, literary or religious, to claim him as their own bard. David Goldie offered a striking example of this in a paper for the Eighteenth Burns International Conference at Glasgow's Mitchell Library[11] when he revealed that during World War I the popular press whipped up support for the war effort by conflating Burns' Scottish patriotism with jingoistic British nationalism.

If Burns' adroit shape-shifting has tempted Ulster readers of different political affiliations to re-create the Scots bard in their own preferred (and opposing) images, at least one Ulster writer has left a clear record of Burns as a breaker of barriers who enabled boundaries of class, religion and generation to be transcended. The writer, now almost forgotten, was Leslie Alexander Montgomery (1873–1961) who published under the pseudonym Lynn Doyle.

Doyle, a middle-class Protestant from a Scots Planter background, was both a popular playwright, associated with the Ulster Literary Theatre,[12] and an author of short stories during the early and mid-twentieth century. His stories are set in fictional Ballygullion, in reality a rural area of County Down that now borders on the Irish Republic. They employ the comic, eccentric characters and whimsical, sentimental tone that Scottish readers would instantly recognise as characteristic of the Kailyard school. His subjects include lonely, inarticulate farmers on the look-out for wives or land or both; man-hungry widows and spinsters; the havoc wrought by drink; family feuds; petty snobbery and pretension; rural cunning or naivety; and young love. Also in common with Kailyard literature, the rural characters speak in the vernacular, which here means English that has been heavily influenced in syntax and lexis by the Irish and Scots languages.

Doyle's period as a writer coincided with some of the most momentous events in Ireland's turbulent history: the Home Rule Crisis, the Easter Rising of 1916 and the partition of Ireland into Northern Ireland and the Irish Free State. His autobiography *An Ulster Childhood*[13] is in some respects an idealised, elegiac pastoral, set well back in the nineteenth century, but it is within this narrative that he pays homage to the works of Burns and to the individual who introduced him to Scotland's bard.

In the early chapters of his memoir Doyle makes the reader aware of his privileged position: he enjoys material security while being brought up by his childless aunt on her large farm. He is well shod, fed and dressed, and conscious of his social superiority over what seems to have been a small army of servants, labourers and their barefoot children. It soon becomes clear, however, that such superiority is a mixed blessing, since it prevents his full integration with the young Lenaghans, children of the second ploughman, whose diet of griddle-bread and praitie-oaten[14] tempt his palate, while their freedom from the rigours of study along with their detailed knowledge of the local wildlife 'and many other arcana of nature'[15] arouse his envy and admiration.

It is not long before Doyle refers to the two cultural traditions that co-existed on his Ulster farm: the Celtic Irish represented by the Lenaghans, and the Lowland Scottish tradition in which he himself was reared. The former tradition he associates with the romantic Gaelic Revival, and with the legends of Cuchullin, Conchobar and the Children of Lir. His own people, by comparison, he characterises as prosaic. They are 'not given to literature' and very suspicious of the mythical Gaelic heroes whom they suspect of 'having their origin not in Ireland, but somewhere among the Seven Hills'.[16] Doyle has given us the stereotypical view here, and quickly overturns it, for it was a Celtic Irishman who became his 'Gamaliel', and opened up for him the poetry of the vernacular Scottish tradition, represented by the works of Robert Burns.

Paddy Haggarty was a farm servant who slept in a small room off the stable. Doyle describes him as 'a quiet, modest little fellow, not dull, for he had a pawky mother-wit, but not much given to speech, and taking no part in the rough horse-play that passed for humour among his fellows'.[17] It was he who first reached out to Doyle, inviting him into his chamber, teaching him to smoke and take snuff, and finally reading to him all the familiar Burns favourites: 'The Twa Dogs', 'Address to a Mouse', 'Hallowe'en', 'The Death and Dying Words of Poor Mailie' and the rest. For Doyle this experience proved a genuine epiphany, and in his text he repeatedly employs the language of religion to describe it and his relationship to Paddy. He himself fulfilled 'the part of congregation at our worshippings'. He was Paddy's 'disciple'. In the end 'Tam o' Shanter' became his favourite poem and he vividly conveys the power of Paddy's delivery of the tale and the lasting impression it left:

I feel still the stirrings among my hair. It was many a year before I could hear the thunder after nightfall without a cautious glance round for His Majesty; and even now I am easier on a country walk by night when I have put a running stream between me and the powers of darkness.[18]

Paddy's teaching proved a deeply significant catalyst for Doyle in his study of poetry. His interest soon ranged wider, and began to include the works of Robert Bloomfield and Robert Fergusson. Paddy proved himself a true and unshakeable Burnsian, however. First he dismissed Bloomfield's language as too far removed from the talk of a genuine labouring man to be worth taking seriously. Then, when Doyle showed Paddy a copy of 'The Farmer's Ingle', suggesting it might perhaps be a greater work than 'The Cotter's Saturday Night', Paddy took the book from him and turned the leaves over discontentedly before announcing his considered verdict: 'The man has got most of his words from Rabbie'.[19]

Undoubtedly, it was Paddy Haggerty who, empowered by 'the great enchanter, Rabbie Burns',[20] crossed the traditional boundaries that divided him from young Lynn Doyle and thus enabled him to access the literature of the Scottish Lowland tradition into which he had been born. In contrast to many who have approached Burns in order to enlist him in their own causes, Haggerty and Doyle simply read, absorbed, admired and were enriched by the poetry and by the shared experience it afforded them. The Irish language poets were correct in their assessment of Burns: he is a true poet of the people – all the people.

NOTES

[1] *An Phoblacht*, 31 July 1997

[2] Quoted in Liam McIlvanney, 'Across the narrow sea: the language, literature and politics of Ulster Scots' in *Ireland and Scotland: culture and society, 1700–2000*, Liam McIlvanney and Ray Ryan, (eds) (Dublin, 2005), p. 223.

[3] The prelude to the Orange parades that mark July 12th in Ulster.

[4] Liam McIlvanney and others, including the Royal Irish Academy linguistic scholar, Linde Lunney, have written about Burns' popularity in eighteenth-century Ulster.

[5] The United Irishmen represented an attempt to establish an independent Ireland of equals, inclusive of Protestants (Anglicans), Catholics and Dissenters. Presbyterians were in the majority in the northern capital, Belfast. Catholic emancipation and the abolition of the tithe, paid by all to the minority Anglican church, were two of the main aims of the United Irishmen from their earliest days. The Society of United Irishmen was founded in Belfast in 1791.

[6] Seamus Heaney, *Selected Poems 1965–1975* (London, 1980), pp. 125–6.

[7] *Belfast News-letter*, 19 Sept. 1800.

[8] Ibid., 31 October 1800.

[9] 'A Song on the Union' by Carolan, Slieve Gullion, *Belfast News-letter*, 16 January 1801.

[10] Gerard Carruthers, *Robert Burns* (Tavistock, 2006), p. 2.

[11] 13 January, 2007.

[12] Supporters of this enterprise included many northern Protestant nationalists.

[13] Lynn Doyle, *An Ulster Childhood,* (London, 1921).

[14] Bread made from a mixture of oatmeal and potatoes.

[15] Lynn Doyle, *An Ulster Childhood,* (London, 1921), p. 12.

[16] Ibid., p. 19.

[17] Ibid., p. 20.

[18] Ibid., p. 23.

[19] Ibid., p. 27.

[20] Ibid., p. 28.

DID ROBERT BURNS WRITE 'THE TREE OF LIBERTY'?

಄

GERARD CARRUTHERS and NORMAN R. PATON

'The Tree of Liberty' is, perhaps, the most mysterious text associated with Robert Burns. Not untypical of the situation where many of Burns's poems and songs only came to published notice well into the nineteenth century, nonetheless the story of the text's retrieval leaves more unanswered questions regarding its provenance and transmission than any other work attributed to the poet. If scepticism as to Burns's authorship was sometimes justified, sometimes not well argued, something similar can be said in the case for Burns's authorship, in the sense that there are things to be said in favour of this attribution, though equally some commentators have been too quick to dismiss what look like clear impedimenta. What follows below is a survey of the historical situation regarding 'The Tree of Liberty', a discussion of some of the internal 'evidence' of the text and a tentative suggestion as to an alternative author. This is a text on which a great deal more work will have to be carried out for the recently announced, multi-volume edition of *The Collected Works of Robert Burns* commissioned by Oxford University Press.[1]

The first major historical event in which trees of liberty flourished as political symbols was the American War of Independence (1775–83) when the people planted poplars to signify their growing demands to obtain freedom from the yoke of British rule. The most famous reference to this came in Jefferson's renowned Tree of Liberty letter in which the great democrat stressed that the blood of patriots and martyrs would be necessary to supply the natural manure of the trees.[2] Six years after American independence had been secured, came the outbreak of revolution in France, and in 1790, the Jacobins, who were to furnish the world of politics with the expression 'leftwing', raised a Tree of Liberty in Paris which they adorned with tricoloured ribbons; circles to indicate unity; triangles to imply equality, with a red Cap of Liberty placed on its top. Rumours swept England that Thomas Paine, who had been forced into exile, would return in triumph and plant a Tree of Liberty on his native soil. In Scotland such trees were erected at Perth and Dundee in November 1792.[3] Later, the United Irishmen adopted the Tree of Liberty as a populist cultural emblem:

What is in your hand?
It is a branch.
Of what?
Of the tree of liberty.
Where did it first grow?
In America.
Where does it bloom?
In France.
Where did the seeds fall?
In Ireland.[4]

This brief background serves to introduce 'The Tree of Liberty' which first appeared in The Poetical Works of Robert Burns, edited by Robert Chambers in 1838. The two-line introduction to the poem, or song, stated that it had not previously been in print, and confirmed the source of the manuscript. It read as follows:

THE TREE OF LIBERTY

[Here printed for the first time, from a MS. in the possession of Mr James Duncan, Mosesfield, near Glasgow.][5]

The poem had no sooner made its appearance before the literary world than the controversy over its authorship began. Chambers's great rival as a Burns editor, Allan Cunningham, emphatically declared that: 'There are eleven stanzas in *The Tree of Liberty* of which the *best* compared with 'A man's a man for a' that' of Burns, sounds like a cracked pipkin, against the heroic clang of a Damascus blade'.[6] Based on, internal evidence, Cunningham had no hesitation in refusing the

poem entry into his criterion of the Burns canon! In 1843, however, a
Glasgow edition of Burns, edited by Alex Whitelaw, laid claim that the
MS. was, 'in the Poet's hand-writing.'[7] Robert Chambers, it should be
noted, offered no specific information as to whether the MS. he had
worked from was holograph, or merely transcribed in another hand.
To complicate matters, James Duncan died shortly after the publica-
tion of Chambers's edition; thus preventing any further enquiries
concerning the MS. and by what means he had acquired it. The verses
were also regarded as a song, being admitted into *Whistle Binkie – A
Collection of Songs for the Social Circle,* in which it was set to the air, 'Up an'
waur them a', Willie'. This songbook was first published in 1832, and
enjoyed many revised editions, its best known editor being David
Robertson (1795–1854), whose bookshop at 188, Trongate, Glasgow,
was a popular meeting place for the literary people of the day.
Robertson was decidedly sceptical about Burns's authorship of
'The Tree of Liberty' and it was listed as 'Anon.' in *Whistle Binkie:*

> This song is said to be a production of the Ayrshire Ploughman, and
> although it is not equal in concentrated power and vigour to some of his
> avowed poems, it must be admitted to be a piece of no ordinary merit, and
> a most successful imitation of his manner. We have submitted it to a
> gentleman of the highest respectability, to whose opinion Burns paid great
> deference, and to whom he was in the habit of showing his compositions,
> and he had never heard the Poet allude to 'The Tree of Liberty.' Burns too,
> who outlived the stormiest period of the French Revolution, would
> doubtless have qualified many of the expressions, had he given them,
> after having seen some of the effects of that dreadful political hurricane
> which deluged that unhappy country with blood.[8]

The similarity in metre and measure between, 'The Tree of Liberty'
and Burns's 'Ballad on the American War', no doubt prompted the
later idea of setting the verses of the former, to the airs, 'Gillicrankie'
(Killiecrankie), and also, 'M. freicedan' (The Black Watch). In the
massive 962 page edition of *The Songs of Robert Burns* (1993), the musical
copy-editor, David Johnson, acknowledges both airs for 'The Tree of
Liberty' with a preference for 'Gillicrankie'. Robert Burns had, in fact,
intended his 'Ballad on the American War', to be sung to this tune, and
only introduced the alternative air, 'M. freicedan' when he submitted
his song to *The Scots Musical Museum* in 1788, because 'Gillicrankie' had

already been used in that particular publication, and the editor, James Johnson, was anxious to avoid repeating a tune.[9]

In the course of time several prominent editors were to omit 'The Tree of Liberty' from their publications, notable among them, Robert A. Willmott (1856), Alexander Smith (1865), and William Scott Douglas (1877). The latter had, in fact, admitted the poem into his earlier edition of 1871, though with strong doubts about Burns's hand in its composition.[10] Henley and Henderson (1896) gave the poem in reference only, roundly condemning it as 'trash' which they were sure, 'Burns neither made . . . nor copied.'[11] In the same year William Wallace revised Robert Chambers's 1851, 4 volume set, with the publication of the popular Chambers-Wallace edition. Wallace, in general, followed Chambers's introductory note to the poem, but is more open to the possibility that Burns had a hand in 'The Tree of Liberty':

There is one piece which was probably written or at least freely touched up by Burns and which, but for the ultra-Jacobinical fashion in which it introduces the name of the unfortunate Louis XVI, might have been read by the poet's contemporaries without any pain, as expressing the feelings of a man who was too sanguine about the success of the popular cause of France.[12]

One edition which did attempt to defend 'The Tree of Liberty' as genuine Burns was the Philadelphia self-interpreting, 6 volume (1886–87), edited by Hunter and Gebbie, which was based on W. Scott Douglas's works of Burns:

The authorship of this poem has, we think, been very unreasonably called into question. Since first given to the world by Chambers in 1838, and although printed then direct from the undoubted MS. of the poet, some of the best editors have left it out of their editions . . . Especially taken in connection with the Ode to Liberty, and taken in the stride of events, we say there can be no doubt of the authorship . . . As regards the literary quality of 'The Tree of Liberty,' it is unfair to judge of verses that Burns certainly never intended for publication during his lifetime, having probably written them for the edification of his radical friends Syme and Maxwell . . . The original MS. was in 1876 in the possession of Mr. James Duncan, Mosesfield, Glasgow.[13]

Whatever else may be said concerning the views of Hunter and Gebbie, they had certainly called it completely wrong with regard to the existence of the MS. as late as 1876, by which time James Duncan

had been long since dead. The Centenary edition of Burns (edited by
Henley and Henderson) probably got it just about right in suggesting
that the MS. had never been traced after 1838. James Duncan was one
of the best known booksellers in Glasgow, of his time, with premises
in the Saltmarket and the Trongate, a descendant and namesake of the
man who had introduced type-making there in 1718. Duncan was born
in the Barony area in 1773, and, somewhat late in life, 1829, married
Mary Dalglish, in the same parish. He had purchased Mosesfield in
1824, but in 1838, had a new property built on the site whilst retaining
the original building. He died soon afterwards, and within a short time
of this his widow was subjected to a frightening experience in what
became known as, 'the great burglary at New Mosesfield by a large
gang of housebreakers.'[14] Showing immense courage Mary Duncan
took up a shotgun and managed to drive them out of her home;
however, many valuable items were already in the robbers' possession,
and, 'they managed to get away with a large haul.' Unnerved by this
traumatic event, and concerned for the safety of her young family,
Mary Duncan decided to leave Mosesfield – it was to remain vacant
for several years Mrs Duncan's movements thereafter are obscure, but
it has recently been established that she died at Benmore on the 29th
December 1875 – this breakthrough might allow for further research
on the missing manuscript to be done.

   This, of course, raises the question as to whether or not the valuable
manuscript of 'The Tree of Liberty' perished as a result of the robbery?
It seems reasonable to assume that the Duncans would have stored it
in a safe box with other treasured possessions, which would have
proved an obvious target for the organised gang, who, no doubt,
carried off as much as they could cope with in taking their hasty
departure from the scene. When convenient to assess their ill-gotten
gains it may be that not much consideration would have been given to
the manuscript of the poem, if it was now in their hands, and alas,
destruction would have proved its fate (alternatively, the thieves might
well have tried to sell an object valuable enough to be in a safe-box in
the first place). At any rate, no authentic source ever came forward,
after 1838, to verify having seen, or examined, James Duncan's copy of
the manuscript – nor has any other copy of the poem ever been found.

   Coming down closer to our own times it is worthwhile to consider
four further publications and their respective comments on 'The Tree
of Liberty'. Thomas Crawford's excellent book, *Burns: A Study of the*

Poems and Songs (1960), offers considerable scope on the subject. Although 'certain internal indications' present doubts for Mr Crawford, such as, 'many fewer Scots words than one would expect for a poem in the 'Gillicrankie' measure . . .' and, 'the writer speaks of 'England' when he appears to mean Britain, a fault which Burns rarely committed', nevertheless, he explains these 'blips' away to the extent of satisfying himself that, just possibly, Burns may have composed the poem.[15] James Kinsley, the most respected of modern Burns editors, reflected doubts over the manner of the poem being, 'less firmly and finally expressive and less richly vernacular than that of Burns when he is fully engaged'.[16] He therefore placed 'The Tree of Liberty' in the 'Dubia' section of his three-volume edition of 1968.[17] James Mackay, the editor of the bi-centenary souvenir edition of 1986, assumed that the MS. used by Chambers, in 1838, was, 'a holograph, apparently now lost', and, in his opinion, the verses seemed to blend with 'Burns's Jacobin sympathies in 1792–3'.[18] The most recent 'collected' edition, *The Canongate Burns* edited by Andrew Noble and Patrick Scott Hogg, carries an extensive footnote to 'The Tree of Liberty' which carries their answer that, having 'completed a thorough investigation', and having found 'no other appropriate candidate' the conclusion must be that Burns composed these radical verses![19]

Why then did so many previous Burns editors and so many highly respected Burns scholars, express doubt over the poet's involvement with this particular poem? This had very little to do with the political tone of the poem, and considerably more to do with the lack of literary merit shown in most of the eleven stanzas. This is, perhaps, best illustrated by the works of several writers who have projected a radical, even revolutionary Burns, and have done so without recourse to the poem. John S Clarke, in his chapbook, *Robert Burns and His Politics* (1925), declared: 'we can afford to kick 'The Tree of Liberty' . . . out of his book.[20] More than enough remains upon which we can form an estimate of the poet's revolutionary ardour.' Clarke regarded it as 'a rotten poem' anyway. In one of the finest pieces yet written on Burns's politics, *Poetry and Politics: Burns and Revolution*, W. J. Murray argued a convincing case for a radical and republican Burns without as much as a mention of 'The Tree of Liberty'; while, in a recent, full-length book, *Burns the Radical* (2002), Liam McIlvanney ignores the poem completely, though he does mention the Tree of Liberty from an article in the *Edinburgh Gazetteer*, 7 December, 1792, but with no connection whatever to Burns.[21]

The editors of, *The Canongate Burns* however, seem driven by the idea that rejection or denial of the poem by Burns scholars is motivated solely by the extreme political opinions expressed in its verses. Even the much respected James Kinsley is taken to task: 'Influenced unduly by (this) nineteenth century legacy and apparently mistaking political bias for literary expertise, Kinsley places *The Tree of Liberty* in his Dubia section.'[22] Most would surely regard this charge as being rather unreasonable! The lengthy footnote in *The Canongate Burns* is, in fact, flawed with several niggling errors. The editors seem unaware that they have confused Chambers's 1838 edition with the introductory note to the poem in his 1851 edition; the manuscript seen by Chambers has never been authentically described, therefore, their denials of it being a forgery are no more than meaningless speculation; their claimed proof that the MS. was extant in 1877, simply cannot be sustained by any definite evidence. It relies on comments made by Scott Douglas requesting that the MS. should be more closely examined – in which case, why did he not seek it out and inspect it, if he thought it was still available? Did nobody else act on his advice and attempt to trace the MS.? The answer to these questions is simple enough – the MS. had long since perished, a fact that had seemingly escaped the attention of the usually careful and competent William Scott Douglas! The 'purely speculative' emergence of James Duncan, in *The Canongate Burns* as possibly the son of Burns's correspondent, William Duncan, need not be commented on at any length – James Duncan was well enough known in his own right to provide some biographical detail on his career; his father's first name was, as it so happens, also James – not William! The criticism of Kinsley for suggesting that, 'The Tree of Liberty' is, 'less richly vernacular' than one would expect from Burns in this type of poem, is certainly questionable. Thomas Crawford, incidentally, also thought the verses had too few Scots words in them, and indeed, if an independent check is taken from the Chambers-Wallace edition of Burns, against those verses in a similar metre, 'Ballad on the American War', it is found that, in these nine stanzas, there are forty-seven words glossed in the page margins, as against thirty-one glossed in the eleven stanzas of 'The Tree of Liberty'.[23] It would appear that Kinsley and Crawford, in their respective comments, have made a valid point.

Noble and Hogg, by insisting that Burns is the undisputed author of 'The Tree of Liberty', have taken the pendulum through full tilt from the verdict given over a century ago, by Henley and Henderson, who were appalled at the very idea of this poem being attributed to Robert Burns. The extremes of forcing the issue to total acceptance, or absolute denial of Burns's authorship are equally affronts to the truth. What we must do is keep posing the question: did Burns write 'The Tree of Liberty'? Even if the *Mosesfield manuscript* was in his handwriting it is not sufficient proof that he actually composed the poem. Ironically, Chambers himself refused to acknowledge Burns as the author of 'Sketch' (Hail, Poesie! thou nymph reserv'd) though he knew a copy of this pastoral poem, in Burns's handwriting, had been found among the poet's papers. As Scott Douglas observed:

> Chambers in 1838 expressed his belief that it ('Sketch') might be the composition of Fergusson or Dr. Beattie; but he had 'scarcely a doubt that it is *not* by the Ayrshire bard.' That editor, however, at (the) same time admitted into his edition a very weak production, called 'The Tree of Liberty' which has scarcely a trace of Burns's manner in it.[24]

It also seems rather odd that neither Robert Chambers nor James Duncan ever made known the story behind 'The Tree of Liberty' MS., including, of course, the important issue of whether or not it was holograph. Scott Douglas certainly claimed that he had been assured it was, but he ventured no name as the source of this information, nor did it persuade him to include the poem in his 1877 Edinburgh edition of Burns's complete works. Several poor quality lines in the poem remains the most telling aspect of the scepticism in accepting Burns as the author. There is also the questionable feature that most of the past participle verbs in the text are given in full – it was Burns's common practice to place an apostrophe at the end of such words – 'water'd' (in stanza 4) is the only exception of nine past participle verbs in the poem. Careless copying would be an obvious explanation for this if the MS. was not in Burns's hand; however, if Chambers had worked from a holograph, it is likely that his editorial skills would have ensured a verbatim transcript. It was also so unlike Burns to be forced to a same word 'rhyme' as is the case with 'thrive' in stanza 5.

The problem of finding an alternative author if Burns is dismissed from association with the poem is not easily solved. Perhaps a clue lies in the reference to England in stanzas 8 and 11 – is it possible that the author was a Scottish poet, writing radical verse, living south of the

border? The oft cited interpretation that Scotland, being a good deal
more progressive politically than her southern neighbour, had inspired
the poem's author, (Burns or another), into chiding the English to
plant their Tree of Liberty, simply doesn't ring true in the light of the
oppressive measures of Dundas's regime post-1792. The poem, as can
be deduced from stanza 5, must have been written after King Louis's
execution, January 21, 1793 and is probably written, as Thomas
Crawford wisely speculates some time between this date and 1795.
Is there a case to be made that Scotland is more receptive to radicalism
in the period 1793–95? From the point of view of radical trials we have
on the Scottish side the cases of Thomas Muir and T. Fysshe Palmer
in 1793 and Adam Skirving in 1794. All of these individuals were
sentenced either to lengthy transportation or banishment. In 1794
Thomas Hardy and John Thelwall among others were found not guilty
of High Treason in London. In this period, then, Scotland might be
seen to be a place where reformers were dealt with much more harshly
than in England. On the basis of making the case for Burns's
authorship and explaining that Burns would be unlikely to use
'England' thoughtlessly and interchangeably with 'Britain' as the poem
seems to do, Thomas Crawford has argued that there is national
symbolism in the lines: 'Let Britain boast her hardy oak,/Her poplar,
and her pine, man!' He sees the oak as emblem of England and the
pine standing for Scotland (the author of the poem, then, is in control
of a finely nuanced meaning). This solution is worth a try, but,
ultimately, is strained (for one thing, Crawford has nothing to say
about what the poplar might stand for in this set of symbolism). A
simpler, more credible reading of the significance of the three trees is
that the oak stands for 'strength', the pine is chosen for its 'evergreen'
nature and the 'poplar' for 'ruggedness' and 'longevity'. In spite of the
seeming health of Britain, the writer is saying, this is an illusion: the
really healthy tree is the Tree of Liberty, a foreign (French) import.
The idea of startling French superiority in the sudden rise of democ-
racy is current, to some extent, in pro-radical poetry of the 1790s. It is
found for example in the following lines:

> 'Tis strange, 'tis passing strange! And, yet, 'tis plain,
>   Parisians quaff a purer draught then We!
> And the once sluggish, slow and soilly Seine,
>   Than Thames itself, flows freer to the sea![25]

LKAY 1793   125

Illustrious Martyr in the glorious cause
Of truth, of freedom, and of equal laws.

Thomas Muir by John Kay

This is the work of the radical poet who, during the 1790s, takes the Tree of Liberty as a recurrent theme. In his 'Secular Ode for the Year 1793', he writes:

> Green be thy leaf, thy branches shoot
> O'er earth, fair tree! Adorned with fruit;
> And shortly be the precious load
> On man's rejoicing race bestowed
>
> O give me, give me Sire Supreme!
> To see this plant thus nobly teem:
> Then, gladly, sated with the sight,
> I'll yield when fate direct my flight.
>
> Meantime, o let me from the tree
> The Gaul's chaste Freedom, rear to thee,
> Hang my loved harp, of voice benign,
> Though e'en the lowliest bough be mine.[26]

One thing that is interesting here is the religious frame of reference, something that is also found in Burnsian 'The Tree of Liberty.' For instance, in stanza 7 we have the reference to 'the new born race', a trope found quite widely around this time suggesting that the new democratic ideals would undo original sin and the suffering attendant upon it. One of the things that always has to be borne in mind with the revolutionary politics of the 1790s is frequent association with dissenting Christianity (and a new Protestant visionary sensibility found, most prominently, in William Blake), which alarmed the establishment very deeply. We should not be surprised that the Tree of Liberty itself has a strong religious connotation, both with the tree of knowledge and, more prominently, in the 1790s with the cross of Christ. This is found most explicitly in an interesting pamphlet published in Edinburgh in 1796, 'The Cross of Christ: the Tree of Liberty' by David Gelletly.[27] Burns criticism has been slow to pick up on this element of religious rhetoric in 'The Tree of Liberty'

The author of 'Ode for the Year 1793' also writes 'Ode to the German Despots, on their burning the Tree of Liberty' dating from either 1793 or 94. There are two manuscript versions of this poem (it was probably never published, although a version from the newspapers of the day may yet turn up. Stanza 6 of 'The Tree of Liberty' is interesting in its idea of 'beagles hunting game'. 'Ode to the German Despots on their Burning the Tree of Liberty' urges the other governments of Europe not to aid the anti-revolutionary cause, exhorting, 'call in your hounds of blood.'[28] We see at least a familiar imagery among the poems (which, if nothing else, shows, probably, that 'The Tree of Liberty' must date from the 1790s – it is not a forgery written much later in the nineteenth century). The author of 'Ode to the German Despots' also writes a poem that takes this metaphor and uses it *in extenso* – in his 'The Northern Hunt, or Brunswick's Beagles' (1801) protesting about what he saw as a growing police state in Britain.[29] These are simply a few hints from the political and poetic vocabulary of this poet that makes him, currently, the most credible alternative author of 'The Tree of Liberty.' He is a Scot moving between London and Scotland in the 1790s, and he is the most prolific Scottish Foxite and pro-French revolution poet publishing in the British radical press during the 1790s. He is also, since this might seem to be a necessary part, a frequent writer of songs in Scots with a political slant, such as a the forceful anti-Dundas piece, 'Wha wants me', a new song to the tune of 'He's Lowdown in the Broom' published in the *Historical Register* in May 1792; and the anti-Pittite 'New Favourite Scotch Song: Up and war them a' Willie'. These are pieces in the Bursian idiom, but tend to be less densely Scots in vocabulary.

So who is this individual? He is Alexander Geddes (1737–1802), poet, path-breaking Biblical scholar, and student of the Scots language whose legacy in the latter two spheres resound down to the present day. Geddes is a Roman Catholic priest at some periods during the 1780s and 90s saying mass for the Glasgow Catholic community in the Saltmarket (as far as can be worked out around 100 yards from where James Duncan had his printing and publishing premises – there is something here to follow up). Surprising to some, given Geddes's denomination, will be his association with Protestant dissenting ideas (the point is that Catholics by the 1790s could quite easily find themselves in broad anti-establishment alliance with dissenting Protestants – one need look no further that Burns's friend Dr William Maxwell to see a similar pattern). Recent Romantic scholarship has shown Geddes as a highly pertinent figure during the Romantic period, particularly influencing Blake and Coleridge, among others;

5 Kay 1798

THE MODERN CAIN'S LAMENT

O Harrie whether shall I fly: I am this day, A Murderer of thousands, Every one that finds me will count me his Enemy and Slay me. ———

256

Pitt & Dundas by John Kay

and yet, for various cultural reasons, Geddes whose poem *Carmen Seculare* was read to the French Assembly of Deputies to assure them of international, intellectual support, has been persistently overlooked in accounts of Scottish literature and history. In promoting Burns's authorship of 'The Tree of Liberty', Geddes is a figure who must be properly eliminated from enquiries that have only just begun.

NOTES

[1] *The Collected Works of Robert Burns*. General Editor, Gerard Carruthers. Oxford University Press. Work on the first three of a dozen volumes in this series began in 2008.

[2] See Thomas Jefferson's letter to W. S. Smith of 13th November 1787.

[3] See Thomas Crawford, *Burns: A Study of the Poems and Songs* (Oliver & Boyd: Edinburgh & London, 1965; 2nd edn; first edn, 1960), p. 247.

[4] From the 'United Irish Catechism', Cork, December 1797; see Kevin Whelan, *The Tree of Liberty: Radicalism, Catholicism and the Construction of Irish Identity 1760–1830* (Cork University Press in association with Field Day: Cork, 1996)), p. 57.

[5] Robert Chambers (ed.), *The Poetical Works of Robert Burns* (Edinburgh: William and Robert Chambers, 1838), pp. 129–130.

[6] Allan Cunningham (ed.), *The Works of Burns* (London: George Virtue:? 1842), preface, p. i.

[7] Alexander Whitelaw (ed.), *The Works of Robert Burns* (Glasgow: Blackie & Son, 1846), pp. 129–30;

[8] David Robertson (ed.), *Whistle Binkie, or The Piper of the Party* (Glasgow: Oliver & Boyd etc, 1878), p. 294.

[9] Donald Low (ed.), *The Songs of Robert Burns* (London: Routledge, 1993), pp. 916–19.

[10] Robert Aris Willmott (ed.), *The Poetical Works of Robert Burns* (London: Routledge, 1856); Alexander Smith (ed.), *Life and Works of Robert Burns*, 2 vols (London & Cambridge: Macmillan & Co., 1865); William Scott Douglas (ed.), *The Works of Robert Burns* (Edinburgh: Nimmo, 1877).

[11] W. E. Henley & T. F. Henderson (eds), *The Poetry of Robert Burns* vol. IV (Edinburgh: T. C. & E. C. Jack, 1897), p. 107.

[12] William Wallace (ed.), *The Life and Works of Robert Burns* [edited originally by Robert Chambers] vol. IV (W. & R. Chambers, 1896), p. 133.

[13] J. Hunter & G. Gebbie (eds), *The Complete Works of Robert Burns* [Self-interpreting] (Philadelphia: no publisher, 1886–7) 6 vols, vol. VI, p. 76.

[14] See the *Glasgow Evening Times* (19th November 1904) for information on the Duncans and the robbery.

[15] Crawford, *Burns*, p. 247.

[16] James Kinsley (ed.), *The Poems and Songs of Robert Burns* (Oxford: Clarendon Press: 1968), Vol. III, p. 1528.

[17] Kinsley (ed.), *The Poems and Songs of Robert Burns*, II, No. 625.

[18] James Mackay (ed.), *Robert Burns: The Complete Poetical Works* (Alloway Publishing: Darvel, 1993), p. 478.

[19] Andrew Noble & Patrick Scott Hogg (eds), *The Canongate Burns: The Complete Poems and Songs of Robert Burns* (Edinburgh: Canongate, 2001), p. 851.

[20] John S. Clarke, *Robert Burns and His Politics* (Glasgow: J. B. Payne, 1925), p. 11.

[21] W. J. Murray, 'Poetry and Politics: Burns and Revolution' *Revolution, Burns Chronicle* 1990, pp. 52–66; Liam McIlvanney, *Burns the Radical: Poetry and Politics in Late Eighteenth-Century Scotland* (East Linton: Tuckwell, 2002), p. 204.

[22] Andrew Noble & Patrick Scott Hogg (eds.), *The Canongate Burns*, p. 848.

[23] Ibid., p. 850.

[24] William Scott Douglas (ed.), *The Complete Poetical Works of Robert Burns* Vol II, pp. 404.

[25] See Alexander Geddes, *Carmen Saeculare* (London: Joseph Johnston, 1792), p. 6.

[26] See manuscript copy in Essex County Records (Chelmsford) D/DP Z.57.

[27] David Gellatly, *The Cross of Christ, The Tree of Liberty* (Edinburgh: No Publisher, 1796).

[28] See manuscript copy in Essex County Records (Chelmsford) D/DP Z.57.

[29] Ibid.

'THE DEIL'S AWA' WI' THE EXCISEMAN'

๛

Robert Burns the Giver of Guns to Revolutionary France?

JENNIFER ORR and GERARD CARRUTHERS

Jim Smyth writes that 'For conspiracy theorists, the 1790s were a golden age' where radical plots, reformist societies and a revolution in France were just some of the terrors that William Pitt's government saw underlying the tense atmosphere in Britain during the last decade of the Eighteenth century.[1] The colourful figure of Robert Burns has often been appropriated as a radical icon, representing the currents of contemporary counter culture, giving a voice to the people and reformist values. It is well known that the poet entertained sympathy for the cause of the French revolution and Burns 'the radical' is a figure debated widely in current scholarship. A previously large part of Burns's radical curriculum vitae so far as apprehension of this developed in the nineteenth century is that of Burns the would-be donator of large pieces of artillery to the Jacobins of post-revolutionary France, but the circumstances surrounding this episode and indeed how credible it can be taken to be, has been little discussed in recent years.

In a highly-detailed article published in 1935, Franklyn Bliss Snyder refuted claims that Burns purchased and sent carronades to France in 1792 on the basis that 'evidence on the matter is entirely lacking'.[2] This conclusion in defence of his 1932 biography of Burns had developed out of several years of controversy surrounding new discoveries of material that suggested that Burns the excise man might have seized guns from an impounded smuggling ship, subsequently purchased these at public auction and sent them to the revolutionary French Convention in February 1792. Snyder's book was designed to be a break with the tradition of reckless biography of Burns that had gone before. A review of this *Life of Burns* described Snyder's efforts positively: 'Professor Snyder, it may be said at once, has carried through his task without succumbing to its characteristic dangers'. These were the words of W.A Neilson, referring to the tendency of Burnsian biography to become clouded in a particularly Scottish patriotism where Burns's personal heroism was a lofty feature. Quite properly, Burns's political songs and reformist expression have played a part in making Burns a national icon but, as Neilson opined, '[t]he biographer of Burns today enters the field with his life in his hands.' Snyder himself was clearly taken aback by the outraged vehemence with which his honest assessment on the guns to France episode was eventually received.[3]

The incident of the smuggling vessel, *Rosamond* does not appear in James Currie's path-breaking 1800 biography of Burns accompanying the first collected works of the poet, but rather, for the first time, in J.G Lockhart's biography, his *Life of Robert Burns* in 1828, 32 years after the death of the poet. Lockhart seemed determined to put some new material into the public domain about the Ayrshire poet and his rounding out of the *Rosamond* episode is the most striking exemplar of this innovation. He tells the story of the smuggling ship, *Rosamond*, setting the scene of Burns, having been promoted within the Dumfries Excise Division, being employed to intercept contraband traffic along the coasts of Galloway and Ayrshire:

> On the 27th of February, a suspicious-looking brig was discovered in the Solway Frith and Burns was one of those the superintendent conducted to watch her motions. She got into shallow water the day afterwards, and the officers were enabled to discover that her crew were numerous, armed, and not likely to yield without a struggle. Lewars, a brother exciseman, an intimate friend of our poet, was accordingly sent to Dumfries for a guard of dragoons; the superintendent, Mr. Crawford, proceeded himself on a similar errand to Eccelefechan and Burns was left with some men under his orders, to watch the brig.[4]

It is here that Lockhart alleges that Burns chanted to himself the now well-known song, *The Deil's awa' wi' the Exciseman* while walking along the beach, one of two different stories of its spontaneous composition both of which perhaps are of dubious veracity (is Lockhart's version of the composition in keeping with his depiction of a somewhat irresponsible Burns as argued in what follows?).[5] Once Lewars arrived with the dragoons, the crew submitted and the vessel was condemned and impounded. Lockhart asserts that subsequently her effects were sold at auction the next day at which point Burns is supposed to have purchased four carronades, seemingly by way of trophy. Lockhart continues:

> But his glee went a step farther; – he sent the guns, with a letter, to the French Convention, requesting that body to accept of them as a mark of his admiration and respect. The present, and its accompaniment were intercepted at the custom-house at Dover; and here, there appears little room to doubt, was the principle circumstance that drew on Burns the notice of his jealous superiors.[6]

The story is compelling and fits in with the romantic concept of Burns the radical but, like most myths, is certainly in some of its detail, a mixture of truth embroiled by imagination. Six years after Lockhart's biography, Allan Cunningham wrote his own account of Burns's life but claimed, 'I have never heard it added that he purchased [the *Rosamond's*] guns and sent them to the [French] Directory',[7] and it is true that thus far the sources of Lockhart's version of the *Rosamond* episode had been entirely shrouded in mystery until Robert Chambers in 1853 published his own biography of the poet. Chambers cited Joseph Train, Supervisor of Excise in Castle Douglas from 1825, who claimed that he had seen three sources of evidence: 1) a journal by Crawford, the superintendent Excise Officer narrating the capture of the brig; 2) 'an account of the seizure and sale of the vessel by Burns himself'; 3) an account by Burns's companion on that day, John Lewars, narrating the purchase of the guns, and Burns's subsequent sending of them to 'the French Convention'.[8] Train was said to have passed these to Sir Walter Scott and Chambers apparently saw none of these documents first hand. It would seem that the contemporary paucity of extant documentary evidence led Snyder in his 1932 biography to conclude that '. . . no more picturesque legend was ever invented by the ingenious brain of a romantic biographer . . . the whole thing would do justice to Gilbert and Sullivan . . . The brig *Rosamond* affair should be absolutely deleted from any account of Burns's life.'[9]

Two years later, Snyder found his dismissive conclusion called into question. The librarian of the National Library, Dr Henry Meikle, discovered two of the manuscripts surrounding the Rosamond in-

cident, these two items of the three at least, which Walter Scott as well
as Joseph Train had claimed to have seen. The Walter Scott Centenary
[of the novelist's death] had occasioned an examination of Sir Walter's
library at *Abbotsford*, and here the actual journal of the Excise officer,
Walter Crawford, came to light, as did two sheets of Burns's own
handwriting setting forth the expenses of condemning the vessel and a
summary of the amounts received at auction. As a result, Snyder was
branded a 'sceptical dogmatist' both in the *Burns Chronicle* and the
Glasgow Herald newspaper.[10] Responding in his 1935 article Snyder laid
out the evidence held against him in great detail. The summary of
Crawford's journal is that the *Rosamond* of Plymouth was indeed
captured and that Robert Burns was present, leading his party of
men. Robert Burns's pieces of handwriting lay down the cost of
repairs and an account of the damage done to the vessel by her crew as
well as a clue to the date that the schooner was lifted off the sand: 9th
March. There is no hint as to what her contraband cargo might have
been, but listed on the inventory were:

> Four four pounders Carronade Guns mounted on Carriages with tackle
> and furniture compleat. Round, Case, doubleheaded & Grape shot, &c.
> &c. &c

The newfound documents provide crucial evidence as to the basic
facts of Burns's professional involvement in the *Rosamond* episode.
However, what was lacking was the one piece of evidence impacting
upon the supposedly wider political significance for Burns's biogra-
phy. This was the third, and crucial, jigsaw piece that Train claimed to
have included in the bundle of documents he had put together for
Walter Scott, which has never come to light. This was a document
supposedly 'detailing the circumstances of Burns having purchased the
four carronades at the sale.'[11] So, as Snyder was at pains to point out,
in the light of this not altogether compelling new evidence, there was
not in verifiable existence even a suggestion of Burns's having
purchased carronades and absolutely no evidence of his sending them
to France. Why had two of the documents survived without the third
from Train's bundle? What we do know is that the guns were sold at
auction and brought £4–2–6 but the name of the purchaser is not
given. Lockhart's original assertion that Burns bought the carronades
for £3, then, was clearly not taken from Joseph Train's record nor, in

turn, we must logically say, from the evidence left in Sir Walter Scott's collection of material that found its way somehow in unexplained circumstances into the National Library of Scotland.

Catherine Carswell makes a brief mention of Burns purchasing the four carronades in her biography in 1930, but makes no attempt to offer any evidence or even any annotation for her narrative. She merely justifies his alleged actions, stating that '[Burns] was merely expressing in concrete poet's fashion what thousands of his country-men felt, irrespective of station, and at first perhaps irrespective of party.'[12] Here we might begin to suggest both an interesting change and a continuation in the received biography of Burns. For Carswell, Burns is very much in tune with the revolutionary zeitgeist. For Lockhart, it is quite clear that Burns, although something of a genius, was lacking in the full demeanour that he expected of the gentlemanly Romantic artist of the period (of which Lockhart's father-in-law, Walter Scott, was exemplary). Burns more humble origin and forma-tions, his politics as Hugh Blair expressed it, 'smelling of the smithy', led him, so far as Lockhart was concerned sometimes into rash and wild behaviour.[13] It may well be that Lockhart's promulgation of the story of Burns's sending the carronades to France, was an instance of the biographer fleshing out his diagnosis of the unwise and imprudent peasant poet. Was the story, in fact, entirely his invention? Asking this question, necessarily poses a couple of others that have not, seemingly, been posed previously. Did Train ever actually have a document proving the truth of the story? Might he even have invented the story of the third document, or indeed, might Chambers have done so, one or both merely parroting, actually, and supplementing the original myth as spawned by Lockhart?

Dismissing the tale of Burns and the carronades in the balance of evidence should not be mistaken for disparagement of Burns's radical sentiments. There is no disputing that Burns entertained sympathy for the reformist cause and possibly even radical politics, but the question remains as to whether or not, not only on the balance of the evidence but on the balance of probability, he really did go so far as to send four carronades all the way to France with the risk to his career that was likely to ensue. It is true that Britain was not at war with France in 1792 and so such an action was certainly not treasonable. However, if Lockhart is to be believed (and on this much of the professionally

written history might suggest that he can be trusted), the climate of
Britain was very much gearing up in its hostility towards France, and
conflict if not inevitable was reasonably to be expected. It seems
unlikely in these circumstances that such an act of bravado on the part
of a member of His Majesty's Excise, as Burns was supposed to have
practised, would have gone unnoticed.[14] From what we do know of
Burns in the revolutionary period, not only was he one of the original
members of the loyalist Dumfries Volunteers,[15] but he was also not a
member of any organised radical association, though he did subscribe
to the reformist newspaper, the Edinburgh Gazetteer.[16] The mood in
Scotland, generally, seems to have been rather cautious as no organised
reformist body such as the Friends of the People yet existed in
Scotland at the time of the *Rosamond* incident and when such con-
vention was finally called and attended at the end of 1792, the Scottish
Friends of the People refused to join their English and Irish counter-
parts in sending congratulatory addresses to the French National
Convention.[17] Was Burns, then, a maverick revolutionary sympathiser
who took matters into his own hand in early 1792, before going on to
cover the tracks of his political sentiments? Or, alternatively, is it not
more likely that Burns surrounded by noticeable Scottish reticence for
the cause of reform in the early 1790s would be unlikely to blaze such a
trail by himself? An outspoken poet he may have been, but he was also
a crown employee. Such an act on the part of Burns would have been
singular, uncoordinated and downright conspicuous.

Despite Walter Scott's failure to trace the port records (his search one
might well infer prompted by Scott's suspicions as to the veracity of
his son-in-law's version of the story), later biographers of Burns have
alleged the carronades were seized at Dover.[18] Subsequently lost
documents aside, if a letter from Burns had been attached, the poet,
as a government employee surely would have fallen immediately under
censure to some degree. It is not logical to argue, as Lockhart does,
that the government was simply uncharacteristically lenient towards
Burns, Pitt being too fond of Burns's poetry to act against him.[19]
There is no reason to believe that Burns's career was in any way
harmed after the *Rosamond* incident. Letters written on his behalf by
Robert Graham of Fintry to the Excise board maintained Burns's
reputation as a man both of professional talent and of impeccable
honour so far as officialdom was to be concerned.[20] Somewhat

William Pitt by John Kay

curiously given his championing of the guns to France story, Lockhart quotes Alexander Findlater, Burns's supervisor at Dumfries, who asserted that he did not believe 'that [Burns's] promotion was thereby [owing to any substantial suspicions of the poet's politics] affected, as has been stated. That, had he lived, [he] would have gone on in the usual routine [which is to say, enjoying a decent career as Britain's continental relations became increasingly fraught and complex].'[21] Lockhart also accurately points to Burns's promotion to Acting Supervisor two years before he died.[22] The account by Findlater seemingly corroborated by Burns's upward career trajectory in 1794 is in marked contrast to the insinuations of several of Burns's biographers, that disappointment in the excise was part of a bundle of cares that led the poet to an early grave. In any case it has long been credibly hypothesised that Burns most likely died from endocarditis a disease of the heart membrane contracted, probably, as a boy.

Beyond the material evidence, such as it is both in what is in existence and in the glaring gaps, the practical considerations and consequences might be taken to be fairly compelling evidence in itself against the likelihood of the carronades to France episode ever taking place. Burns was only recently promoted to the Dumfries Third Port Division in February 1792, just weeks before the *Rosamond* incident, and luxuriated in his salary in a letter to Maria Riddell:

> Cash paid, Seventy pounds a year, and this I hold until I am appointed Supervisor . . . So rejoice with them that do Rejoice.[23]

It would seem most irresponsible of a man who had just reached an all-time salary high of £70 per year, who also had eight mouths to feed at home, to then spend a substantial portion of that income on carronades, and further, to send them to France entailing the risk of losing a respectable salary and livelihood. At £3 for the purchase, as according to Lockhart, this would represent over two weeks salary; at over £4, as according to the auction inventory, the lion's share of a months salary. Not only this, however, Burns supposedly paid for the transportation via Dover of the guns to France. The sum involved then would rise substantially over the purchase price (most probably doubling, at least). Burns going to such expense, then, becomes even less credible. We might also ask did they not have guns for purchase in France? Would anyone wishing to support the French Jacobins not much more sensibly and economically 'order' guns in France, or even send the Jacobins a monetary donation, not least given the likely danger of 'interception' (and probable seizure) as Lockhart suggests turned out to be the case at Dover?

With a lack of substantial proof and also concrete motivation, the balance of evidence does not support the claim that Burns was a sender of guns to France in the aftermath of the French Revolution. The recklessness of character attributed to the poet by his biographers whether it is Currie's insinuation that Burns's was led to death by alcoholic indulgence, or Carswell's careless assertion (following but adapting Lockhart) that Burns's passions led him to risk his livelihood in the name of a morally righteous politics, is an interesting staple in Burnsian biography. Most often, however, this recklessness seems to support fiction rather than fact. It is perhaps the case that a more accurately prudent Burns has been somewhat absent in the numerous biographies written about 'the Bard'. It is most probably to be argued on the balance of things that Burns's attempts to send large and heavy guns to France did not happen and, rather paradoxically, is the invention of a snobbish Tory biographer, Lockhart, who unwittingly contributed to the later mythography of Burns in the hands of others of very different political predilections intent upon Burns's superhuman amplitude as an apostle of radical political behaviour. Certainly, more historical work might be carried out in the case of the *Rosamond* incident, and it is to be hoped that this will occur, but it needs also to proceed with more rational and logical insight than has sometimes accompanied past attempts to elucidate it.

NOTES

[1] Smyth in Dickson, Keogh & Whelan, *The United Irishmen: Republicanism, radicalism and rebellion*, Dublin: Liliput, 1993, p. 167.

[2] Snyder, 'Burns and the Smuggler Rosamund', PMLA, Vol. 50, no. 2 (June 1935), p. 521

[3] Neilson, W.A, Review of *The Life of Robert Burns* by Franklyn Bliss Snyder, *Modern Language Notes*, vol. 49, no. 2 (Feb. 1934), p. 127

[4] J.G Lockhart, *The Life of Robert Burns* (Edinburgh: 1828), p. 218f.

[5] William Scott Douglas in his revised edition of Lockhart's *Life of Burns* (London and New York, 1892), p. 229n; Maurice Lindsay, *Robert Burns: The Man, the Work, the Legend* (London: MacGibbon and Kee, 1954), p. 229.

6 Ibid., Lockhart.

7 See Allan Cunningham, *The Works of Robert Burns; with his life* (London, 1834), I, p. 284 for the claim that the piece was composed at an excise dinner, for which there is a little more credible evidence than Lockhart's version.

8 Robert Chambers (ed.), *The Life and Works of Robert Burns*, revised by William Wallace (4 vols. Edinburgh, 1896), III, p. 317n.

9 F. B. Snyder, *The Life of Robert Burns* (New York, 1932), p. 395–7

10 *Glasgow Herald*, Nov 11, 1932. Meikle, *Burns Chronicle* 1934, p. 47.

11 Lockhart, *Life of Robert Burns* (London and New York, 1892), p. 230n.

12 Catherine Carswell, *The Life of Robert Burns* (Edinburgh: Canongate, 1990), p. 336. Originally published Chatto & Windus, 1930.

13 For further discussion of Lockhart's motivation and methods, see Gerard Carruthers, 'Remaking Romantic Scotland: Lockhart's Biographies of Burns and Scott' in Arthur Bradley and Alan Rawes (eds), *Romantic Biography* (Aldershot: Ashgate, 2003), pp. 93–108.

14 J. Lockhart, *The Life of Robert Burns* (Edinburgh 1828), p. 309: 'We were not, it is true, at war with France; but every one knew and felt that we were to be so ere long; and nobody can pretend that Burns was not guilty, on this occasion, of a most absurd and presumptious breach of decorum.'

15 Lockhart, *Life*, p. 319.

16 J. C. Ewing and Andrew McCallum, 'Robert Graham of Fintry', *Burns Chronicle*, 1931, p. 53.

17 John Brims in Dickson, Keogh & Whelan (eds), *The United Irishmen* (Dublin: 1993), p. 154.

18 This claim by Joseph Train is quoted in Lindsay, *Robert Burns*, p. 229.

19 Lockhart, *Life*, p. 322–3.

20 Lockart (ed.) William Wallace, p. 85.

21 Findlater quoted in Lockhart, *Life*, p. 318

22 Lockhart (ed.) William Wallace, p. 89.

23 *The Letters of Robert Burns* Vol. II [1790–1796] J. De Lancey Ferguson (ed.) 2nd edn, G. Ross Roy (ed.) (Oxford: Clarendon Press, 1985), p. 135.

BURNS AND IRELAND

☙

OWEN DUDLEY EDWARDS

There are two things in which, all men are manifestly and unmistakably equal. They are not equally clever or equally muscular or equally fat, as the sages of the modern reaction (with piercing insight) perceive. But this is a spiritual certainty; that all men are tragic. And, this, again, is an equally sublime spiritual certainty, that all men are comic. . . . Every man is important if he loses his Life; and every man is funny if he loses his hat and has to run after it. And the universal test everywhere of whether a thing is popular, of the people, is whether it employs vigorously these extremes of the tragic and the comic. . . . For the tragic and the comic you must go, say, to Burns, a poor man.

– G. K. Chesterton (1874–1936) *Charles Dickens* (1906)[1]

I.

Ireland is not a familiar theme in Burns's life or works. If he noted the advent of Irish migrants across his native Ayrshire, as, say, the Minister does in John Galt's *Annals of the Parish*,[2] he remarked on them less or, if more, it has not come down to us. He did not cast Ireland as best prospect for a revolution, as Shelley did, or deplore the desirable Irish conflict when it happened and desperately seek to evade its infection, as Coleridge did, He did not give himself a congenial Irish Boswell, as Tom Moore enabled Byron to do, nor did he salute an Irish tutor, as Maria Edgeworth was acknowledged by Scott. He was professionally interested in Ireland – and in certain respects he was more of a professional than any of the above save perhaps for Scott – for in his mastery as folklorist, collector, conservator and creator he would want to know whether a song or verse had Irish parallels, antecedents, variations or derivations, as he mused to George Thomson in mid-August 1793:[3]

> By the way, I have met with a musical Highlander in Breadalbane's Fencibles which are quartered here, who assures me that he well remembers his mother's singing Gaelic Songs to both, Robin Adair and Gramachree [love of my heart]. They certainly have more of the Scotch than Irish taste in them. – The man comes from the vicinity of Inverness; so it could not be any Intercourse with Ireland that could bring them – except, what I shrewdly suspect to be the case, the wandering Minstrels, Harpers, or Pipers, used. to go frequently errant through the wilds both of Scotland & Ireland & so some favourite airs might be common to both. – Case in point. – They have lately in Ireland, with great pomp, published an Irish air, as they say, called Caun de deish [Song of the Right?]: – the fact is, in a publication of Corri's, a great while ago, you find the same sir, called a Highland one, with a Gaelic song set to it, – its name there, I think, is, 'Oran Gaoil' [Gaelic song?] – & a fine air it is, – Do, ask honest [David] Allan, or the Reverend Gaelic Parson [Joseph Robertson Macgregor] about these matters.

Let us suppose ourselves in a late twentieth-century Scottish Studies seminar, we would find nothing in this to suggest the speaker is our senior by some two centuries, apart from his bibliographical references, we would want some elucidation as to what he meant by 'Scotch' and 'Irish taste', but in most late twentieth-century seminars we would probably need (rather than want) similar elucidation as to what any contemporary users meant by such terms. Do we mean Highland Scotch or Lowland Scotch? Do we mean Protestant Irish or Catholic Irish? Admittedly Scotch or Irish 'taste' would carry more alcoholic implication, in our youth than in Burns's.

That Burns is wrong about 'Robin Adair' is irrelevant.[4] Good scientist that he was, he promptly recorded his impression, scrutinised it empirically, subjected that to rational extension of argument noting its recoil against him, forcefully acknowledged the blow comparative bibliographical evidence dealt to his thesis, and sought opinions of appropriate authorities. What better example could we give our students?

Burns's superiority to ostensibly professional scholars in our lifetime is indeed painfully evident at times. Professor Karl Miller, himself a fine if somewhat less exact scholar, reviews a posthumous compilation of Hugh Trevor-Roper supposedly on Scotland, in the current *Scottish Review of Books*.[5]

> The romantic Cavalier Montrose, a poet and a political ally of the Anglo-Scottish poet William Drummond of Hawthornden, belonged, he claimed to an 'exquisite generation' which 'contrived to produce a poet even in Scotland – the last poet ever to arise in that prosaic peninsula'.

We may set aside the reader's bewilderment as to who is this 'last poet' – Montrose or Drummond? Trevor-Roper – and indeed Professor Miller – must at least have some inkling that we have here two poets for the price of one, however deficient their grasp of statistics. But we may leave the living and the dead to extricate themselves (apart from noting that Professor Miller's insistence that the deceased was 'a good writer' devalues goodness by robbing it of lucidity). Professor Miller continues:

> He claimed, moreover, that it was natural that eighteenth-century Scots 'seeking compensation for the end of their Independent history and politics, should turn to discover and appreciate their native literature. Unfortunately, when they looked, for it, they could not find it. There was none.'

Professor Miller, summing up rather than endorsing (we may charitably assume) adds:

> The cupboard was bare. Scotland had never had a literature, and it was not about to have a poetry.

In the book for which Trevor-Roper originally wrote of the 'Invention' of Scottish tradition[6] (apparently looted by Trevor-Roper's resurrectionists for the present volume), he informed his readers that Irish Gaelic poetry was superior to Scots Gaelic poetry and that Scots Gaelic poets were deported from Ireland. He thought he was making this point about the year 1700 although his source, John Toland, was speaking of the sixth century.[7] Most of his audience in British and Irish academic circles would have been fairly sure Trevor-Roper knew not one line of the Gaelic poetry of Ireland, or Scotland, but enough readers unacquainted with his limitations may have existed to constitute his activity here as fraud, quite apart from its stupidity.

Professor Miller presumably recognises this as nonsense if his indulgence in its discussion refrains from the direct charges of fraud which Trevor-Roper himself would have hurled in similar cases. But, innocently, it leaves one fearing a tinge of racism about this. Indulgence towards Trevor-Roper from Scots becomes dangerously akin to 'God help the poor English, what else can one expect of them?' And this really is not fair. The English produce many excellent scholars. Because some fool of a historian suffers from acute sado-masochism and wants to be assaulted for pig-ignorance on Burns's value – and some TV journalist uses his own even greater ignorance (if possible) to introduce a Scottish publisher's dictionary – should their fellow-countrymen be declared unfit for intellectual use? The village may vote that the earth is flat, but that does not prove that the country believes it. They may, many of them, show comparable scholarly standards to Burns however few of them approach him in poetry.

II.

Ireland may not have interested Burns,[8] apart from scholarly attention on a scientific level, but Burns won enormous attention from Ireland. We may take an obvious example the Irish cigarette. Tobacco was initially an Irish industry where the Irish industrial revolution had taken place, in the Lagan valley but after partition in 1922 the Free State wished to manufacture its own cigarettes and Messrs P. J.Carroll of Dundalk produced its famous brand, 'Sweet Afton' bearing the classic portrait of Burns in miniature and beneath it a watered landscape (perhaps more skin to Dundalk's county of Louth than to Ayrshire), and beneath that:[9]

> Flow gently, sweet Afton, among thy green braes,
> Flow gently, I'll sing thee a song in thy praise.

And how many of the purchasers who read it could supply the next two lines?

> My Mary's asleep by thy murmuring stream,
> Flow gently, sweet Afton, disturb not her dream,

Of course we cannot say, that the answer is surely in thousands. In the Irish 1920s the song would have been as familiar as today's chart-leaders. The cigarette-buying public would have heard it in parish halls, at local dances, at drawing-room parties, at pub sing-songs, at crossroads gatherings, and in more intimate moments of privacy appropriate to the poet. That the manufacturers selected Burns's song, with emphasis on Burns himself, makes it very clear. There was certainly a local association; Burns's sister Agnes, junior to himself but eldest of his sisters, married well after his death to William Galt and having moved with him to Stephenstown near Dundalk, died there in 1834. She had gone to work as a farm labourer when a girl of eighteen, and so was the man she had married in 1804 but he became a land steward in Ireland. They probably remained Presbyterian, but the laws of Ireland forced their burial in Protestant episcopalian grounds, the Church, of Ireland having been kept in that faith. By public subscription in 1859, Burns's centenary, a pillar stone was erected to their memory near the entrance gate of St Nicholas's churchyard, but it would take more than an old stone in a Protestant cemetery to provide a brand-name likely to win the pence of the Irish Catholic majority in quest of a smoke.[10] Women might respond to the tender sentiment (the music sheets used that adjective) but men could identify with the handsome face. Was his Scottishness a barrier? Not in the least. He would have been known to them primarily as a ploughman, as his poems best known to Irish school-children – 'To a Mouse' and 'To a Mountain Daisy' – proclaimed. That is to say, he was one of ourselves.

Benedict Kiely (1919–2006), Irish novelist, critic, social historian, short-story writer, lecturer, talker, journalist, literary editor, institution, began a socio-anthropological inquest on Irish writing:[11]

> My first Irish writers were Andy McLoughlin, Alice Milligan, Peadar O'Donnell, Robert Burns. Patrick McGill and Dean Swift. Andy McLoughlin was never, except to a select circle, as well known as the others. Chauvinistic Scotsmen may be surprised, if you could surprise them, at finding the Bard of Ayr sandwiched between two Donegal men. . . . Andy McLoughlin . . . was the last bellringer and town crier in Omagh, Co. Tyrone, and a sort of laureate too, for he commented, something in the fashion of Dryden, on passing events. He claimed a

'poetic license' (much as if he had bought it like a dog license or, more aptly, a gun license) to call everybody names . . . He had . . . but little recognition and died sometime in the 1930s in the poorhouse. But on one occasion, he said, and with a gravity not to be laughed at: 'Burns was the best of us'.

Burns is on my list because Burns was, at least before Dunkirk and television, a folklore figure in rural Ulster . . . Most of the folklore about him indicated that he was a dacent fellow, but dirty. When my mother was primer to a country schoolhouse, the teacher, a Master Reid presented her with a volume of Burns with heavy black lines pencilled through the poems she was not to read. Then there was a Popular Underground Burns unknown, as far as I know, even to David Daiches and the scholars in Underground Burns. There was the couplet he spoke to Lord Byron when the Saxon milord walked through a byre that Bobby was sweeping and haughtily ordered the Scottish groom to lift the broom and let Lord Byron by. What was Byron doing in that there byre? Or, for that matter, Burns? There was the quatrain he spoke for a bet when one of a group of drinking companions, a man from Leith, had had as much as his gut could hold and spewed over the table. Leith, I may tell you, rhymes with teeth. There was the quatrain he spoke quick as a shot when he had the girl against the gate and looked over his shoulder and saw a wee fellow watching him and eating a bun. The subject of the quatrain was the wander of the works of nature. Full quotation is not advisable, but you do from my adroit hints get one popular Irish picture, or image, of the poet.

Kiely compared, the Ulster folklore Burns to the folklore Daniel O'Connell (1775–1847), radiated similarly across the nineteenth century, both of them with clear appropriations of the trickster, or Ulysses, *motif*, in which the form of words traps the opponent (usually a physically or materially superior would-be oppressor), with a slight hint of magical powers (with which Gaelic tradition invested the poet, probably through vague conflation with the poet's fellow-professionals, the Druids, or their successors the priests).

Ulster can be closer to Scotland than to O'Connell's native Kerry, and migrant labour between Donegal and the Scottish west kept that Scottishness lively. To apply Burns's own scepticism on Irish identity with the Scottish north, the Burns-Byron association may seem absurd. Burns, almost thirty years older than Byron (1788–1824),was dead when

Byron inherited his title, and Byron 'born half a Scot and bred a whole one' was frequently poorer than Burns in his Aberdeen childhood. But there is a faintly potential northeastern link through Byron's Gordon mother from Gicht, Aberdeen, or her ancestors, and Burns's father, who did not leave the Mearns until 1748. Probably there was no such encounter between Burns and Byron, forebears, but if Byron's own conduct to a servant is unlikely to have been condescended, his mother's might, and presumably her parents' might. I heard the folktale Kiely cites when in Aberdeen myself in the late 1960s. Its popularity arose from its personalization of anti-landlord folklore. The juxtaposition of Burns and Byron in itself was sound: Scott, who greatly admired them both (while deploring their radical politics) saw exceptional similarities.[12]

Burns might be an Ulster folk-hero, with some migration of spurious anecdotage to the rest of Ireland, but Burns in poem and song dominated the entire island. Dundalk, though in Leinster, is a frontier town with southeastern Ulster – the Church of Ireland graveyard where Burns's sister lies is under the jurisdiction of the Bishop of Clogher whose seat is in Kiely's native Tyrone – but Burns's conquest of the popular mind embraced the entirety to which Dundalk's Carroll wanted to sell his cigarettes, and Irish capitalists readily exploit sentiment in the purchaser without much danger of infection themselves. Burns was on the packet because Burns would sell, Ireland's answer to the English naval chauvinism exploited by Player with its heroic, or else Royal sailor.[13] In song, Burns was the most famous Bard available to the rural Irish and any peculiarities in Scots was no more alien than Ulster speech. My north Cork grandfather would entrance his audience with his rendition of 'Highland Mary' or perhaps 'Sweet Afton'(or the pseudo-Burns 'Bonnie Mary of Argyle'); at all events, it was a song commemorating one of Burns's actual or pseudonymous Marys because Grandfather would take care to utter a malediction on his personal Mary at the conclusion to ward off any suspicion, by the company that he was guilty of sentimental allusion to his own wife. He would have been horrified at any thought of looking at anyone else's wife – wasn't one wife enough trouble? – but he at least resembled Burns in deploring the shackles of monogamy for the same reasons as Tam o' Shanter. He was not literate.

III.

Burns had four more years to live when in, 1792 J. Jones, of 111 Grafton Street, Dublin, published

POEMS
OF
ESSAYS, LYRIC, ELEGIAC, &c.
BY
THOMAS DERMODY

Written between the 13th and 16th Year of his Age.

Dermody was a Clare boy, born in Ennis in 1775, son of an alcoholic schoolmaster who taught him Latin and Greek from the age of four, had him teaching at age nine, more or less weaned him on alcohol, but for whatever reason, caused the boy to flee to Dublin at age ten. He was dead at 27, in Sydenham, Kent, having attracted and then repelled a succession of patrons.[14] Dublin knew its Burns well by 1792 William Gilbert had published Poems Chiefly in the Scottish Dialect there in 1787, as had James Magee in Belfast; Gilbert published it again, with portrait, in 1789 and 1790.[15] Dermody therefore had already an assured interest on which to rely when including in his own *Poems* 'TAM to RAB. An ODAIC EPISTLE':[16]

> HAIL brither RAB, thou genuine Bard,
> May laurels be thy grand reward!
> Laurels, with gold, and siller hard,
>   To fill the purse,
> For else, they are not worth a card,
>   Or Beldame's curse.

> ARCADES AMBO! both are ready,
> T'invoke, and woo, each.tunefu' Lady,
> But thou, sweet friend, hast got a trade, I
>   Ken no such thing,
> Thou can'st e'en drive the ploughshare steady;
>   I can but sing.

Yet, would I glad, gang out with the,
To strew my barley on the lea;
Wow! We would gloriously agree,
      Poetics gabbling,
Ne, ever, o'er the dram, would we,
      Be squabbling.

Keen as thy wit, the scythe we'd wield,
Culling, each flow'r, the wild woods yield,
Together, urge our team afield;
      Together rhime,
And mark the Sun yon mountain gild,
      Till supper time.

ALLAN's bra' lilts we would rehearse,
And laugh, and weep, and talk in verse,
While grey-ey'd Judgment, sapient nurse,
      Our thoughts would prune,
And Fancy, roseate bands disperse,
      Our brow to crown.

Yes, RAB, I love thee in my heart,
Thy simple notes, uncurb'd by art;
That bid the tear of passion start,
      And, sure I am,
Ere from this wicked world we part,
      You'll jostle TAM.

And if you do, by PETER'S KEYS,
We'll quaff stout whiskey, at our ease,
Drive fools, before our verse, like geese,
      And clink the can,
Till we shall rise, by twelve degrees,
      'Bove reptile Man.

Now, as Wilde said of Gide, it is not enough to say 'I! I!' to enter the Kingdom of Art. Yet that is surely the greatness of the poem. Whatever its merits, its author's claim of equality with Burns is self-destruct on the same scale as he would later bring alcoholically

on himself. The denial that his aspirant dream of drinking with Burns
could involve 'squabbling' (a good word to which he gave unusual
poetic lodging) is deliberately disingenuous, Dermody's infant classical
training ensured that whatever work he might produce, it must always
contrive. His tribute to Burns, condescending as it might sound, was in
fact acknowledgment of what divided them:

> Thy simple notes, uncurb' d by art

could not be applied, to himself, ever. Education, like its accom-
paniment of alcohol, killed his youth early. The intrusive Virgilian
quotation, opening his second stanza symbolised it, but also opened
up the unspoken theme. The phrase amounted to a cliche by this time,
end of the Latinate eighteenth century, but Dermody would have seen
it in context instinctively:[17]

> *Ambo florentes aetatibus, Arcades ambo,*
> *Et cantare pares et respondare parati.*

Dryden (whose translation Dermody probably knew, to judge by his
derivations from the great Jacobite poet) rendered it:

> Both young Arcadians, both alike inspired
> To sing, and answer as the song required.

In context, the quotation is in contest. Virgil's Seventh Eclogue
describes a poetic duel between Corydon and Thyrsis, with Corydon as
clear victor. Dermody is therefore claiming equality with Burns, and in
code concedes Burns superiority, but the code is essential if Dermody
is to maintain his chutzpah. We may doubt if Burns ever saw it. Gilbert
of Dublin is unlikely to have felt bound by Scottish copyrights,
especially in the blissful era of Irish (nominal) parliamentary inde-
pendence, so if Dermody sent his poem, with or without its fellows, to
Burns's Dublin, publisher it probably stayed there, lest Burns discover
that he had a Dublin, publisher. Pre-literate post-Gaelic Ireland made
Burns an Irish poet by folk learning and transmission, literate Ireland
would have done so by piracy. (Magee was republishing Burns in
Belfast by 1803, Edwards in Cork by 1804, each of them adding Robert
Heron's deplorable memoir which made Burns a drunkard on a

Dermody scale: Gilbert included it in his printing in 1803). Heron, curiously, described his own reaction to Burns's poems at first encounter in the last line of the Seventh Eclogue

> *Ex ille Corydon, Corydon est tempore nobis!*[18]

whence Dryden

> Since when, 'tis Corydon. among the swains;
> Young Corydon without a rival reigns.

But Heron, although victim of an elegant shaft from Burns for failing to deliver him a letter,[19] had no known pretensions to be a rival poet. Dermody's use of Corydon to describe Burns may hold another clue. Corydon is the unsuccessful homosexual lover of Alexis in the Second Eclogue, hilariously mock-rebuked by Byron in *Don Juan*:[20]

> *But Virgil's songs are pure, except that horrid one*
> *Beginning with Formosum pastor Corydon.*

If there was a homosexual element in Dermody's yearning for a better class of drinking-bout with Burns, it might help explain the self-destructive urge, and Burns in our own day has a gay iconic status (with appropriate Burns suppers, toasts to 'The Laddies' &c). But whether the impulse be sexual or spiritual – or spirituous – the poem has this demand on posterity. For all of its contrivance and *chutzpah* it remains a grand celebration of Burns's appeal. Many readers have fallen in love (in any sense) with the work of great writers: Dermody, with all his imperfections, brings the fantasy within literary bounds.[21] It is also valuable because despite its classical ostentation, it is actually a voice from below Burns in class terms. Many allusions to 'the ploughman poet' meant a compliment unrelieved by condescension (myself, I like to borrow Raymond Chandler's view of Dashiell Hammett's services to the detective story and say Burns took poetry out of the drawing-room and dropped it into the ploughfield where it belonged[22]). But, socially, Dermody ranks Burns as his superior, *because he is a ploughman*. Ploughmen paid schoolmasters and thus were their superiors, although Dermody sensibly recognises in the ploughman's expertise a professionalism of his own. His Clare background had

evidently shown him personally or by observation how difficult a
ploughman's task may be (even without making detours to avoid mice
and mountain daisies).

Dermody's first language was probably not English which is to say it
would have been Gaelic, beating English, Latin and Greek by a short
head. His fellow-Clareman, Brian Merriman (?1747–1805), wrote the
great eighteenth-century Irish-Gaelic epic *Cuirt an Meadhon Oidche* (*The
Midnight Court*). (Frank O'Connor, possibly Ireland's greatest short
writer, concluded it was influenced by Burns.) The varieties of English
in which Dermody composed were all faintly artificial, and as much so
as the Scots he assumed in order to address Burns ('Munster Scots' as
Liam McIlvanney has so happily termed it).[23] That Burns himself had a
vital relationship with Scots Gaelic is clear enough, we have seen it in
musicological action. With respect to all forms of Gaelic he was the
obvious supplanter, in verse and in song. The decline of Gaelic,
principally in Ireland and chiefly on economic grounds, required a
new vernacular especially in imaginative pastoral. Scots presented no
greater problems for post-Gaelic assimilation than did English and
probably appeared as a more rational version than English. The ground
into which Burns's poetry and song would move had been well
prepared for him by Irish-Gaelic pacts of comparable life-style, fore-
most among them the Kerryman Eoghan Ruadh O'Suilleabhain (1748–
84) whose works include an elaborate lullaby of bribery promising the
most exotic plunder from Greek, Roman, Hebrew and Gaelic mythol-
ogy to his illegitimate child, if it will only stop howling. The litany in
'Tam o' Shanter' describing the articles on the table when the Devil held
court in Kirk Alloway is terrifying, but has its own kinship with that of
the bribes, and the invasion of ordinary if sinful life with the super-
natural distinguishes both. Both poets were, formally, Jacobite poets,
neither of them allowing that poetic convention to obstruct their careers
in the service of the deplorable but remunerative Hanoverian state. Fifty
years before them Gaelic Jacobite poetry was highly pragmatic, from
war-cry to news report. For O'Suilleabhain as well as Burns it was now
only a convention which conserved tradition, phrased more urgently in
Burns, more rococo in O'Suilleabhain. But however archaic the dream-
visions in O'Suilleabhain's voluptuous verse, they prepared their lis-
teners not for the nominal Jacobite Royal return but for the advent of a
more useful Scotsman.

IV.

Burns's poetic obituaries came more naturally from the part of Ireland closest to his verse in its own speech, and of these the most memorable came from the most famous 'rhyming weaver', James Orr (1770–1816) rescued with his fellows from oblivion, by a poet, critic and cultural visionary of our own time, John Hewitt (1907– 87). Here is Orr:[24]

ELEGY

On the death of Mr Robert Burns, the Ayrshire Poet

A great man, solely of God Almighty's making such.
HERON

The lift begud a storm to brew,
The cloudy sun was vext, and dark;
A forket flash cam sklentin' thro'
Before a hawk, that chas'd a lark;
Then as I ran to reach a booth,
I met a swain an' ax't 'what news?'
When thus he mourned the far-famed youth
Wha fills the dark, an' narrow house.

Sad news! He's gane, who baith amus'd
The man o' taste, an' taught the rude;
Whase warks hae been mair read an' roos'd
Than onie, save the word o' Gude:
Him genius foster'd on her lap,
An' for his fa' fand fancy mourns;
Dumfries might weel steek ev'ry shap,
An' sen' her tribes to bury Burns.

Oh Burns! oh Burns! the wale o' swains,
Wi' thee the Scottish music fell;
Till nature change, thy artless strains
Shall last, an' seem her second sel':
Was pain thy theme: or pastime daft?
Thou rais'dst the roar-, or mov'dst the tear;
Thy 'woodnotes wild' were sweet, an' saft,
As grace divine to sauls sincere.

Oh Scotia! Bards of note you've reared,!
E'en kings were counted i' their train;
But lo! a barefoot moorlun' herd
Frae a' their pipes the praise has ta'en:
Wha e'er before sae finely felt?
Sae 'strongly mark'd' your rustic rings?
What mopin' min' unapt to melt,
cauldrife when he swept the strings?

Nae mair wi' rash, repentant share,
He'll breeze the *Daisies* modest breast;
Nor thro' the fur claut here-and-there
The poor wee *Mousie's* motley nest;
Nae mair, at right, frae toll releas'd,
In 'social key' *Scotch Drink* he swiggs;
Nor on a palpitating breast
Is blest amang the *Barley Rigs*.

Nae mair in kirk he stands tip-tae,
To see Rooks *ordain* the Raven;
Nor hears his *Cotter* read an' pray,
An' tell the weans the way to heav'n;
But till, unsen't by ear an' e'e,
Auld memry's types ilk image tine,
Wi' a' I hear, an' a' I see,
Instinctive thought shall BURNS combine.

Death, wha delay'd, and doff'd his shaft,
An' leugh langsine, to hear his strain,
Has pent him in the cell, which aft
He wiss'd to close him in frae pain;
An' now the *aerial Wreath* he wears,
Adjudg'd him by the *Phantom Fair*,
An' comes wi' shadowy compeers
To warble on the *Brigs o' Ayr*.

But while the poet we applaud,
We manna less approve the man;
A heart to beauty ay he had,
An' to the brave a frienly han';

Nane felt the love of country mair,
Nor wiss't the BRETHREN'S peace an' health;
For Independence, firm, an' fair,
He strave as much as fools for wealth.

An' maun his fam'lie i' the slough
O' dreary poortith, pining, lye?
The want a' him is hard enough,
Without the want o' ought forbye:
Monie fine chiels hae set their hearts,
Like him, owre much on wine an' mirth;
The *failin*'s o' a man o' parts
Are nobler than a numscull's *worth*.

In times to come, tho' now obscure,
His line may flourish for his sake;
An' sons o' sang frae monie a shore
Cleave reliques frae his plough or braik:
Sublime, yet simple; wild, yet wise;
He ne'er was match'd wham Scotia mourns –
A noble peal convuls'd the skies,
'Twas nature's sel' respectin BURNS.

Burns was a bridge between Jacobite and Jacobin, between religious conviction, and enlightenment scepticism, between country and city, between Europe and America, between Gaelic and English, between new learning and old tradition, between books and memory, between Highland and Lowland, between medieval and modern, between tragedy and comedy. James Orr resembled him, and doubtless followed him, in much though certainly not in all of that, but nowhere more so than in bridging tragedy and comedy. Burns was a master of the hilarious epitaph, not simply the well-turned curses such as Byron oft pronounced on Castlereagh but winning applause for the joke rather than for the stroke. Orr's epitaph is in that tradition, where we can reconvene our initial sentiments for the uprooting of the mountain daisy and the eviction of the mouse, while enjoying the parody of old-fashioned laments where the beneficiaries of the deceased's activities are now bereft. The new immunity of daisies and mice is funny, and yet renews sympathy with what it affectionately mocks. It deliberately walks ground sacred to Burns, and in one glorious moment actually reaches the level of 'A man's a man for a' that', meriting an additional cheer to those demanded by its memory:

> The failin's o' a man o' pairts
> Are nobler than a numscull's *worth*.

Elijah's mantle has fallen on the right shoulders here.

And this was not simply the disciple's tribute in the days of bereavement. Heron's malice had come to haunt Orr, though his epigraph made the best of it, and the poem entered apposite defence, In fact it yielded gold from Heron's grudging. Heron's line, (some memory of aborted theological studies?) used by Orr for epigraph – banal in itself, since to believe in God the creator is presumably to believe He made all men – inspired a sublime analogy. Quoting Milton's rhapsody on Shakespeare in *L'Allegro*, Orr reached Miltonic heights in comparing Burns's poetry to the impact of grace on genuine people. Equally, at the close Orr turns an old convention of pathetic fallacy to new purpose. His poem is highly conscious of tradition, including Gaelic tradition – notably in the poet's discovery of his theme by a meeting with an informant – and the use of Nature in support of poetic sentiments was commonplace in use, though often not in execution. But here pathetic fallacy comes into play because Burns as Nature's interpreter and mediator prompts Nature's personal grief at his death. And unlike its illustrious predecessors, very often, the device is managed with economy, as punch-line however fore-warned in the beginning.

Orr's *Elegy* for Burns has a magisterial undertone despite the deftness and lightness of touch demanded by the subject of the poem and, Chesterton would insist, the economies of the poet. For this there was good reason. Dr Liam McIlvanney has vigorously, indeed explosively, described and celebrated Burns's days of glory among Ulster Radicals in the early 1790s, and its dark sequel when many of his minor poetic admirers took Burns's hostility to possible French invasion as apostacy from his former gospels.[25] Orr, whose literary claims star higher than most, if not all, of his Ulster fellow-poets, does not seem evident in the chorus against Burns, but he put his own principles to the test of participation in the 1798 rebellion in the battle of Antrim, after which he was jailed and exiled to America whence he returned to his own village of Ballycarry, early in the next century. Heron's biography is unlikely to have reached him before his return. His *Elegy* is, I think, a conscious settlement of accounts with Burns with the dust settled down on the last ten years, Heron to be assessed with the rest. The result is a courageous reflective statement, not the ecstacy of a Dermody – one cannot say a more sober account since Orr, too, became a heavy drinker – but the mature judgment of a poet of stature if not grandeur capable of seeing the place of his former idol in the service of posterity. What may have saved Orr collapse into the indignation of his lesser fellow-radicals in Ulster Protestantism, was probably his sense of humour, one of his strongest bands with Burns, and one of Burns's great calls across Ireland's geographical, religious and political divides.

V.

Burns naturally travelled as oral or written text with greatest ease to Ulster, where the language of Protestant settlers varied in minor particulars from his own, although his own was more adaptable to English. Both forms of speech reflected their neighbourhood to Gaelic, Burns's with its maker's scientific interests, the Ulster Protestants variously from irritation at unwanted infection, through indifference, to interested and even affectionate welcome, according to personal preference. Thomas Dermody had shown how Burns lay almost within the reach of an extremely talented southern Irish versifier, talented in linguistic understanding, whatever the value of his verse. And Dermody could pass for standard English literature when required, even to hints of Anglicised Burns, reminiscent at least in chutzpah. Dermody's 'An Ode to Myself' began:[26]

> Thrice hail, thou prince of jovial fellows
> Turning so blithe thy lyric bellows,
> Of no one's brighter genius jealous;
> Whose little span
> Is spent 'twixt poetry and alehouse,
> 'Twixt quill and can!

It offered linguistic reassurance to patrons, while honestly (at least in this case) warning them of his darker side. This would be all very

well for such patrons as the Countess of Moira, until his honesty made
further mutual respect impossible. But how would Burns fare among
gentility of more creative powers, all the more after he himself had
gone beyond the bounds of earthly patronage? The supreme Irish
professional in this regard. – so Irish that much of her life was spent in
England – was Maria Edgeworth, who put Irish dialect on its fictional
feet as far as the polite world was concerned, and whose Irish dialect in
Castle Rackrent (1800) and *The Absentee* (1812) convinced Walter Scott
that the source-material daily in his ears from lower-class Scots had the
making of great novels. Edgeworth's family estate lay in Longford,
within long walking distance from Ulster Scots speakers, but with its
own farsightedness firmly directed to Dublin and London. Her
magnificent modern editors warn us helpfully of her 'ambivalent
attitude' to the 'small number of working-class and comparatively
uneducated poets' of her time who had 'achieved a degree of fame and
critical success with their work', Burns among them: they cite Edge-
worth's disapproval of Ann Yearsley's 'ingratitude to her benefac-
tress',[27] and no doubt Edgeworth would have found sufficiently
stronger language to cover the case of Dermody. But however
prevalent such potential criticism might be, Burns's relations with
female patrons were (given their intimacy) matters beyond Maria
Edgeworth's reach, and be lived for her among the relatively immune
dead. Her first known allusion to him in print opens up a startling if
apposite field, and one indeed which he would continue to occupy in
Ireland – a suitable example for children. Her insight was impec-
cable:[28]

> Simplicity is a source of the sublime peculiarly suited to children; accuracy
> of observation and distinctness of perception are essential to this species
> of the sublime. In [Bishop] Percy's collection of ancient ballads, and in the
> modern poems of Ayrshire ploughman we may see many Instances of the
> effect of simplicity. To preserve our pupil's taste from a false love of
> ornament, he must avoid, either in books or in conversation, all verbose
> and turgid descriptions, the use of words end epithets which only fill up
> the measure of a line.

This indeed was salutation of Burns as a professional and while
clearly hailing him as craftsman, with the best of all tributes, that
children, should read him, its context acknowledged his expertise with

popular and traditional folklore sources. Citation alongside Thomas Percy (1729–1811) editor of the famous *Reliques of English Poetry* (1765) makes the latter very clear. That Percy is given his bare surname (which is all informal scholarly acknowledgment requires for the famous) while Burns is introduced by his other occupation, is noteworthy. Percy was still Bishop of Dromore (had been since 1782) but his Bishopric was wag irrelevant and hence allusions to it would be mere 'ornament'. He was in theory a prince of Edgeworth's Church, his see to her north-east, but his expertise was English. Bishops had to be content with what deference Edgeworths accorded them, which in this case was what his work, not his status, merited. Burns's ploughmanship told her readers what was his first credential in observation and simplicity. Burns would have been gratified to have been found as edifying as a Bishop.

Thus Edgeworth in her *Practical Education* (1798). Her *Moral Tales for Young People* advanced Burns further, when she made clear that to have read him – or Virgil – was a mark of refinement, especially for those themselves engaged in pastoral work. (She exhibited golf as the interest of the Philistine who ignores such writers.[29]) Ultimately (in her last novel, *Helen* (1834), Burns served her as upper-class coding device:[30]

> . . . her attention now attracted by the song which Lady Castleford seemed to be practising: the words were distinctly pronounced, uncommonly distinctly, so as to be plainly heard –
>> 'Had we never loved so kindly,
>> Had we never loved so blindly,
>> Never met, or never parted,
>> We had ne'er been broken-hearted,'
> . . . Cecilia could not help suspecting that Louisa had intended her song for other ears than those of her dear cousin, and that the superb negligence of her dress not unstudied, but that well-prepared, well-according sentimental air, changed instantly on seeing – not the person expected, and with a start, she exclaimed, 'Cecilia Clarendon!'

Burns had conquered the Irish drawing-room, a trusty weapon in the hands of its most formidable manipulator. He had, in fact, been adopted. Thomas Moore (1779–1852) bard of the drawing-room thanks to Gaelic and other lower-class sources, generously acknowledged how much better Burns would have performed his task:[31]

MᴿᴱOBRIEN the IRISH GIANT the TALLEST MAN IN the KNOWN WORLD BEING NEAR NINE FEET I

Byrne, the Irish giant by John Kay

If Burns had been an Irishman (and I would willingly give up all our claims upon Ossian for him,) his heart would have been proud of such music, and his genius would have made it immortal.

But if Moore measured himself as falling far short of Burns, these was a candidate for Burns *Hibernicus*. Speaking of his protégé William Carleton (1794–1869)s the Revd Caesar Otway (1780–1842) told his readers:[32]

Carleton has been in the poetry of his prose to Ireland what Burns has been to Scotland in the poetry of his verse. There is in both the exhibition of the better feelings of the people – the same heart-touches of the scenes of the happy fireside – the same satire on the follies and faults of the people, if it be right to use the term satire to descriptions in which, no feeling of unkindness mingles. The faults and the follies are there. But they are all coloured by the glow of the virtues that are ever portrayed on the same canvas.

It is impossible, indeed, not to feel the strong and singular analogy between much of the history as well as the genius of Burns and Carleton. Both were born in the humbler walks of life – both won for themselves fame and distinction by efforts that made them known at once – both knew well the people among whom their youth was passed – both had known the difficulties and sorrows which were the inheritance of genius upon earth – both have their faults originating perhaps, in circumstances nearly similar. The time perhaps, is not yet come, when the parallel can be completely traced out – both must rest in their grave before both can be spoken of with equal freedom.

And the first objection to Otway's thesis is that Burns never found a patron as devoted and provident as Caesar Otway. Otway acknowledges the pull of certain punches: he is in fact telling us that the Burns of 'The Cotter's Saturday Night' is echoed in Carleton's 'The Poor Scholar', and that the author of neither is as brutal a critic of religious practices as he could be. Otway had hired Carleton to write anti-Catholic diatribes; Carleton did, but also wrote with slightly sentimental sympathy for Catholic priests in 'Poor Scholar' whose literary merits Otway evidently valued too highly to regret Carleton's generosity to the faith of his fathers.

But while Otway might spell out that analogy he left it to well-

informed readers (and clearly he expected his Dublin audience to
know their Burns) to see in 'Holy Willie's Prayer' the counterpart to
Carleton's denunciation of false religion in the very first piece he did at
Otway's request, 'The Lough Derg Pilgrim'. Neither work is as genial
as Otway implies in acquitting Burns and Carleton of unkindness. His
own propaganda was where he broke from the Irish anti-Catholic
tradition among the Protestant clergy by loving the people who
worshipped in the Catholicism he hated, whence he did not want
to admit that Carleton's propaganda called forth by himself could be
any more unkind than what he thought permissible. And perhaps he
was right to see an element of subordinated and repressed affection for
the hypocritical religious targets for the Carleton-Burns satire: even
Holy Willie is made too intimately known to us to be purely a figure
prompting hatred. Besides, both Carleton's superstitious and simo-
niacal Catholics and Burns's Holy Wlllie can never be fully repre-
hended as alien to their audience: we have something of Holy Willie in
us, all of us, and Burns knows it, just as Carleton knew from the
marrow of his own bones why Caesar Otway's mission would fail.
Nobody may have directly pointed it out, but Holy Willie must
definitely have been a kenspeckle figure in Ireland as well as Scotland,
in Catholicism as well as Protestantism, and Burns's apparent address
to Ireland from its own nature won him automatic Irish status.

Otway's identification of Burns with Carleton would be followed by
others, notably by the Young Ireland nationalist journalists Thomas
Osborne Davis (1814–45) and Charles Gavan Duffy (1816–1903), and
by their latter-day ideological catechumen W. B. Yeats (1865–1939).
The basis was simple enough. No other writers brought more to life
the ordinary people of Scotland and Ireland respectively, for their own
times at least. What Edgeworth and Scott put under their literary
microscopes from their contemporaries were invaluable to the histor-
ian, but they necessarily lacked the breadth of Burns and Carleton. We
are dealing with floating evidence – Edgeworth drew supposed
contemporaries in part from long dead protagonists, Scott exploited
contemporary observation for some of what he presented as historical
– but the insights of Burns's verse, and the range of Carleton's prose,
were unrivalled. Another quality forcing itself on our great compara-
tists is the astonishing ability of Burns and Carleton to assume and
discard styles with the speed of an actor – 'Tam o' Shanter' even

changes languages in its course, and Carleton's 'The Party Fight and Funeral' moves between styles as it changes its narrator's class. In fact both writers adopted styles so convincingly that their satirical intent has not always been evident. So too was the question of narrator credulity; is 'Tam o' Shanter merely a joke? No, it comes too near tragedy when speaking of the grandmother making the cutty sark in which Nannie dances before the Devil. Did it happen? Who knows? I don't, you don't, does Burns? Carleton's fairy-stories are more obvious fiction, but 'Neal Malone' as anticipation of *'The Incredible Shrinking Man'* (book and movie-script by Richard Matheson, 1957) reminds us that what one generation called magic another termed science, and the same is true for fairy-story and science-fiction, something the kaleido-scopic moods of 'Tam o' Shanter' similarly proclaim.

VI.

Davis and Gavan Duffy in their triumphantly successful nationalist weekly *The Nation* (founded 1842) were nothing if not pedagogic, and Burns was heavily pressed into service, discovering *en route* qualities of edification beyond even Edgeworthian lengths. Gavan Duffy's *The Ballad Poetry of Ireland* (1845) asserted:[33]

> Every household in Scotland, from peasant-farmer's upwards, as [John Gibson] Lockhart['s *The Life of Robert Burns* (1828)] proudly assures us, has its copy of Burns lying side by side with the family Bible. The young men, nurtured upon this strong food, go forth to contend with the world; and in every kingdom of the earth they are to be found filling posts of trust and honour trustfully and honourably.

He concluded by anticipating for Ireland that after nurture on the ballad-poems he was editing therewith, the Irish Burns might emerge in full versification, no longer limited simply to Carleton's prose:[34]

> a great Peasant-Poet may sooner or later be expected to arise who will give voice and form to sentiments and aspirations which are the common property of entire people.

Davis, inevitably reviewing the book for their *Nation* felt (as is customary among sufficiently interested parties) that Duffy's compilation, filled a long-needed want, though the Scottish tenants of the place into which Duffy's book was to move might have resented the opprobrium into which their hitherto valued services were now dismissed:[35]

> Worse than meeting unclean beds, or drenching mists, or Cockney opinions, was it to have to take the mountains with a book of Scottish ballads. They were glorious, to be sure, but they were not ours – they had not the brown of the climate on their cheek, they spoke of places afar, and ways which are not our country's ways, and hopes which were not Ireland's, and their tongue was not that we first made sport and love with. Yet how mountaineer without ballads, any more than without a shillelagh? No; we took the Scots ballads, and felt our souls rubbing away with envy and alienage amid their attractions; but now, Brighid be praised! we can have all Irish thoughts on Irish hills, true to them in the music, or the wind, or the sky.

Davis's endless enthusiasm for Hiberniana made for vigorous journalism, and if it sounds like nothing so much as an Englishman heartily going native, it had its superiorities over the depressing colonist provincialism gorging itself on very stale regurgitations of London fashions. The pathetic attempts at local dialect by timid raids on a Gaelic largely unknown to him are more derisive in the eyes of historians who have lived through the results than they were to eager Young Ireland: Brendan Behan accurately described 'shillelagh' as the English for 'blackthorn', the former term so boldly flourished by Davis having been long ago annexed by stage-Irishry across the British Empire (past and present), while Brighid was presumably the Gaelic goddess of song rather than the formidable early Christian virgin. The demand for 'all Irish thoughts on Irish hills' is a sinister origin of *1984* the totalitarianism on which all ideologies fattened once their votaries had tasted power. In addition it identified Ireland with something too close to xenophobia, ultimately to develop into early twentieth-century *Sinn Fein*, ('we ourselves') valorising immunity from everyone and everywhere. Daniel O'Connell, Young Ireland's official leader but in fact too pacifist and too pragmatic – for Young Ireland had set the example of universalist reform, identification with antislavery &c, but as Young Ireland aged any visible attitudes to slavery it exhibited were favourable. And for all of Davis's torrid, embrace of Ireland's ballads, (more specifically of Duffy's book) Burns radiated authenticity and universality. Davis responded with artificiality (however sincere) and parochialism (however profound). Yet Davis could show an awareness of what made Burns's products succeed, even if at the end he took refuge in a chauvinistic tautology which boded ill for the nationalism he was spinning in Ireland:[36]

> The Scotch songs evidently are full of heart and reality. They are not written for the stage. They were the slower growth of intense passion, simple taste, and a heroic state of society. Love, mirth, patriotism, are not the ornaments, but the inspiration of these songs. They are full of personal narrative, streaming hopes and fears, bounding joy in music, absolute disregard for prettiness, and, then, they are thoroughly Scotch.

Yeats, coming to terms with this a half-century later, found that Davis's heirs rejected his admiration, for the ex-Catholic William Carleton and wrote bitterly on 3 January 1890 to the *Nation* (now under T.D. Sullivan (1827–1914), soon to be one of Parnell's harshest opponents over his part in the O'Shea divorce):[37]

> your good critic has no word for [Carleton] but 'renegade'; no other mention of his genius than to call it 'envenomed'. Scotland left Burns in the Excise; the world has mocked her for it. The coming century would find it a strange thing to look back on, if we, many years after our great prose Burns had been rotting in his grave, and when all other reading folk had learned to honour him, if we in his own country should find nothing more for his memory than what your critic is pleased to call 'the Literary Pillory'. It would think us wholly given over to never-lifting night and ignorance.

This was to assert themes which dominated so much of Yeats's life, the struggle against *crescendo* from Catholic Puritanism ultimately to consolidate its power by establishment of book censorship (chiefly of the work of Irish authors) in the Irish Free State whose midwives (ironically) would include Yeats himself. Beyond that was the deeper challenge of his place as Protestant nationalist in a land seized by its formerly dispossessed Catholics. Burns as populist poet humiliated by his own people was a good vantage point whence Yeats might rebuke the cultural lynch-mobs howling against the equally representative but equally victimised Carleton, and, by implication, against Yeats himself if they would think him important enough to merit ostracism.

Some nine years later Yeats was identifying Burns with himself, not simply as victim or as hero, but as poet:[38]

> The school of poetry which I admire believes that the subjects of poetry are ideal, and so far above 'the normal human consciousness' that they are invisible and imperceptible to it, and that the poet can only express them, or rather bring the 'normal human consciousness' into their presence by combining the images and things he has seen with his mind's eye or his body's eye, into an ideal harmony. He combines images and things into patterns, and chants a melancholy or resolute music, which affects the minds of his readers much as the ceremonial dance and the ceremonial music in the forest affected the ancient priests and priestesses. . . . The most beautiful lines that Burns ever wrote are
>
> > 'The white moon is setting behind the white wave,
> > And Time is setting with me Oh.'
>
> And these lines are a perfect example of a symbol. The whiteness of the moon falling among the whiteness of the sea and Time falling into an unknown deep, and the wavering rhythm of the words and the last inarticulate cry, evoke an ideal passion which cannot be defined, because it is not in the same world as the faculty that defines.

This marks the apogee of Burns in Ireland in pure aesthetics; national poet responds to national poet. Yet if this was identification with Burns, two years later saw his public doubts that he or anyone else could be Ireland's Burns:[39]

> I believe that Ireland cannot have a Burns . . . because the mass of the people cease to understand any poetry when they cease to understand the Irish language, which is the language of their imagination . . .

Yet he would shortly complain that Burns could have a simplistic, not to say a dumbing-down, effect on his correspondent in that letter, D. P. Moran .(1869–1936) of the *Leader*:[40]

> Such men – I have met a few – commonly judge all poetry by Burns because they see his effect on Scots men & because he is easy to understand . . .

this last, however involuntarily, being a remarkable tribute to Burns as Irish literary fare, and seems to assume his affinity to Irish speech, presumably Ulster varieties preferred. He instanced Moran's reply to conversationalists defending Yeats:[41] 'why did I not write like Burns etc etc' to meet the rejoinder:

'could he change the shape of his nose by trying'

which ought to have been conclusive.

And in Summer 1903 he told an American correspondent that if he were to be offered a wish by an Irish fairy hero[42]

I would say 'I do not ask even a fiftieth part of the popularity Burns has for his own people, but I would like enough to help the imagination [s] that were most keen and subtle to think of Ireland as a, sacred land'.

In different ways Yeats's great contemporaries gave their form of concurrence with his turn to Burns as national poet. Oscar Wilde (1854–1900) in prison (1895–97) asked for Burns's poems.[43] George Bernard Shaw (1856–1950) in 1903 proclaimed the superiority of Burns to his class superiors:[44]

The aristocracy . . . had its mind undertrained by silly schoolmasters and governesses, its character corrupted by gratuitous luxury, its self-respect adulterated to complete spuriousness by flattery and flunkeyism. It is no better today and never will be any better: our very peasants have something morally hardier in them that culminates occasionally in a [John] Bunyan [(162.88)], a Burns, a [Thomas] Carlyle [(1795–1881)].

Yeats's *protégé* John Millington Synge. (1871–1909) who sought to climb the mountain of Art from recording peasant speech in southern Ireland, prefaced his *Poems and Translations* ([1909] 1912) by asserting:[45]

The poetry of exaltation will always be the highest; but when men lose their poetic feeling for ordinary life, and cannot write poetry of ordinary things, their exalted poetry is likely to lose its strength of exaltation, in the way men cease to build beautiful churches when they have lost happiness in building shops.

Many of the older poets, such as [Francois] Villon [(1431–?)] and [Robert] Herrick [(1591–1674)] and Burns ['Burns and Shakespeare and Villon' in draft], used the whole of their personal Life as their material, and the verse written in this way was read by strong men, and thieves, and deacons, not by little cliques only.

VII

Yeats's manifesto in 1892 'To Ireland in the Coming Times' firmly stated his own Hibernian affiliations:[46]

> Nor may I less be counted one
> With Davis, Mangan, Ferguson,
> Because, to him who ponders well,
> My rhymes more than their rhyming tell
> Of things discovered in the deep,
> Where only body's laid asleep.

Davis's verse – and indeed prose – derived heavily from Burns, directly or indirectly. Mangan (1803–49) in one of the last poems of his life, 'The Nameless One', identified his own self-destruction with 'what he saw as Burns's:[47]

> And he fell far through that pit abysmal,
> The gulf and grave of Maginn and Burns,
> And pawned his soul for the Devil's dismal
> Stock of returns- –

Samuel Ferguson (1810–1865) was Ireland's Burnsian supreme among its Makars. We have reflected on Burns, and on James Orr, as bridges. Ferguson is a bridge too, but on foundation-stones not always level enough for endurance. Orr and the other Ulster versifiers in Ulster-Scots valued their cultural and racial common ground with Burns, but Ferguson's great reach into antiquity simultaneously made him a Scottish and an Irish patriot, sharply honed by Protestantism. His great essay on Burns (Dublin University Magazine, January, March 1845) deplorably ignored in anthologies of Burns criticism) began by defensive warfare against traducers of Burns and of Scotland:[48]

contempt and hatred for Scotland and the Scottish people . . . just before
the generation of Burns, flowed in a torrent of obloquy from so many of
the ablest pens of the age – and out of which , under God, it was Robert
Burns' sincere and generous eloquence, speaking in melodious strains of
love, and hope, and courage, that first raised his developing country, and
in the proud position which she has ever since maintained, still crowns her
with the freshest, and perhaps the most enduring, of all the intellectual
wreaths yet won for her by her children.

This was fervent enough to warn the brighter members of his
largely Unionist audience (whose primary loyalties would be either
English or Irish rather than Scots, in any case) that his symptoms
suggested infection from Davis's endless defensiveness over things
Irish in the *Nation*. Adversarially, if attractively, this in his second
paragraph, sharply reacted against the thesis of his first:

> Literary censors have long taken a distempered pleasure in trying to terrify
> our intellectual youth from the pursuit of poetry . . . among the multitude
> of examples for ever in their mouths, of penury pursuing the foot steps,
> and disappointment corroding the minds of men of genius, there is no
> name oftener dragged up, with all its dreadful accompaniments of want,
> drunkenness, and self-torture, than that of Robert Burns.

Burns had saved Scotland's reputation, yet his own lay chiefly in
reproach. This critical schizophrenia is valuable to the historian
(whatever its value to the critic). Ferguson's paternal ancestors settled
in Ulster two centuries before this essay, but his own career in poetry
had begun at age 21 when 'The Forging of the Anchor' was published
in *Blackwood's Edinburgh Magazine*, whose 'Christopher North' (John
Wilson 1785–1854) he would imitate for Dublin audiences, and whose
John Gibson Lockhart (1794–1854), son-in-law and biographer of
Scott (1771–1832) had partly rescued Burns biographically from
Heron's thin but long hold. Carlyle had completed Burns's vindication
for London by hailing him in his lecture 'The Hero as Man of Letters'
on 19 May 1840, published as part of *On Heroes, Hero-Worship and the
Heroic in History* (1841). Dublin's digestion of this would have been
more belated than London's, and thus Ferguson was justly, if para-
doxically, celebrating Burns still on a cusp.
   And he kept him on it. Ferguson's Protestant evangelical soul, in

harmonic company with many of his fellow-contributors and readers, worried about Burns, at moments hinting at Calvinist predestination more than evangelical salvation. If Burns was damned, however, he had saved Scotland, and here once again Ireland – predestined if not predictable – could take comfort:[49]

> We who, in Ireland, occasionally smart under the petulance of our small metropolitan wits, so powerless in comparison with the satirists of the reigns of Anne and of the First and Second Georges, ought to draw a lesson of patience and courageous hope from the example. Our Poet has not yet arisen.

What followed was virtually a summons to Yeats, twenty years before his birth:

> God, to the contemplative man, gives few more signal encouragements to virtue, than the power with which he has invested the words of the poet, speaking the sincere utterances of the soul, in allaying the splenetic heats of faction, and even in composing the bitter objurgations of theology. Where almost an angel from heaven would be disregarded, by the obloquy and clamour of party or sectarian warfare, if a true poet arise, and speak according to his mission, he will undoubtedly be heard – even, as in old times, the bard could put an end to the battles of the Gauls, by shaking his chain of silence between the hosts. That such a man will some day arise among us, as Burns, sixty years ago, arose among the Scotch . . . it is as reasonable, as it is consolatory and cheering, to expect . . .

This is the whole spirit of the agenda of the young Yeats, and indeed an ironic foreshadow of the disappointments haunting the old. Hence he was 'one' to rhyme in all senses with Ferguson: hence also an additional bitterness for 'Meditations in time of Civil War' and 'The Man and the Echo'. Even Yeats's iconisation in 'The Fisherman' for all of its passionate austerity is akin to Ferguson's celebration of the ploughman:[50]

> From the kings and sovereigns of the world, to the beggar by the way-side, all who pray for their daily bread, depend, under God, on the ploughman; and the occupation which in former times exercised the hands of Ulysses and Cincinnatus, still exists unchanged as the basis of all national and

individual prosperity. All the pursuits of agriculture are in this sense heroic, being still the same with those practised in heroic times by the chiefs and sages of the early world . . .

. . . Our nobility and gentry, ashamed to be seen between the stilts of a plough, or digging with the spade, purchase a fatigue not half so sweet or so natural from their costly field sports.

Ferguson as critic was far from fundamentalist in Burns-worship, or rather he found it somewhat at variance with what was fundamental to him.

. . . Burns had used a reprehensible freedom in espousing the quarrel of his friend, bringing religion itself into contempt in his exposition of 'Holy Willie', 'Daddy Auld', and the rest of the bitter promoters of that charge . . .

– which brought Ferguson to see 'The Cotter's Saturday Night' as a self-vindication, though, he added, an artificial one.[51]

. . . the 'Saturday Night' was a piece which might always be safely praised; and many who have felt, but dare not acknowledge, their obligation to Burns for his bold vindication of common sense and humanity elsewhere have discharged their consciences by bestowing an excessive and strained admiration on this beautiful but, we think, over-rated poem.

That seems certainly a report from Protestant Ireland- rather than Scotland or England, and evangelical Dublin as well as pious Ulster. As evidence it is first-class, on Irish precautions on reading Burns. Ferguson also used the Carleton parallel, but with the same scholarly exactness we might expect from so great an authority on ancient Irish MSS. He thought for instance that Burns's father's 'habitation' probably resembled that of Carleton's father, more than that of the 'Saturday night' Cotter. He had been one of the earliest critical celebrants of Carleton.[52]

In his second essay on Burns Ferguson reversed the usual perception. Burns was not just a reporter, but a creator, and in the linguistic complexity between English, Ulster and other Scots, Irish and Scots-Gaelic (all well known to Ferguson) creation had close but productive breeding, with an unexpected touch from so conscious a middle-class voice:[53]

> Thus it is that the poet is, to use the phrase of the economic school, a true and meritorious producer, a right operative, and one of the real working class. The man who makes two blades of wheat to grow where one blade grew before, says the economist, is a benefactor to his kind. So say we; the man who makes two true, tender, pious, or lovely thoughts to grow up in a mind, or blossom in a heart where there but one before, is a benefactor to his kind; a producer also, and a maker of wealth more essential to happiness of mankind, than any other production, of land or sea, after the needful daily bread, clothing and shelter, without which life itself could not exist, to be the *nidus* for virtue.
>
> When therefore, the young ploughman of Mossgiel began to sing songs which took his brother farmers, and the sons and daughters of his brother farmers, by the heart, and shook up, as it were, in all their souls, that host of new notions of nature, of humanity, and of social relations, of which the song of every true poet is as fruitful in unsophisticated bosoms, as the plough is of a teeming crop in virgin soil; it was as if a new sense had been revealed to the whole people of Kyle, and the course and tender, the generous and the sordid, almost simultaneously and unanimously accepted these gifts of his genius as positive boons, and things of practical value, singing them, repeating them, and out of them learning to convey sentiments to one another, till that time inexpressible and unknown.

This might not have been an exact replica of post-poetic conditions in Kyle, but it was a shrewd guess as to the impact of poetry on primeval man, and T. B. Macauley (1850–59) in the *Edinburgh Review* sixteen years before, had declared the best poetry the product of primitive society:[54]

> The few great works of imagination which appear in a critical age, are, almost without exception, the works of uneducated men. Thus, at a time when persons of quality translated French romances, and when the Universities celebrated royal deaths in verses about Tritons and Fauns, a preaching tinker produced the Pilgrim's Progress. And thus a ploughman startled a generation which had thought Hayley and Beattie great poets, with the adventures of Tam o' Shanter.

To conform with this Ferguson had to juggle with the dates of the Scottish Enlightenment, but he managed:[55]

He lived at a time when the mass of lowland Scottish people had got over the sordidness of feudal slavery and ignorance, but before they had acquired the fastidiousness and delicacy of taste that great mental cultivation has since caused, even among them, to so morbid an extent.

But however distorted this historical lens, Ferguson knew where he was with 'Tam o' Shanter' itself:[56]

. . . we must allow Tam the rare merit of combining, with a sustained interest and uninterrupted progress, a marvellous variety of picturesque detail, and humourous characteristics. It comes home to the feelings of husbands and wives, of rakes and decent people, of the bold and the timid, the lovers of humour and the lovers of fun, rolling out a swift-evolving panorama of scenery and situation, that flashes past the eye in successive bursts of fire-light, and lightening glare, and corpse candle illumination, with darkness like pitch, and thunder bellowing 'loud, deep and lang' between, while the floods of Doon resound through the woods, and the scream of the infernal bagpipes tirls the slates over the goblin dancers in the haunted ruins; a series of scenes as of characters all in contrast and all in keeping – undoubtedly a rare and admirable piece of its kind, and one which we can well imagine to have given Burns extraordinary enjoyment in producing.

Ferguson succeeded here, as critic, by himself becoming artist as the author of 'The Burial of King Cormac' shows from time to time he can be. The essential lay in piling on the litanies in conscious homage to the original. Probably no Irish critic of Burns was so successful in appreciation of 'Tam o' Shanter' until it was parodied, looted and homaged by James Joyce (1882–1941) at the close of the 'Circe' chapter in *Ulysses*.[57]

VII.

Joyce (who would be livid to hear it said) wrote as a Catholic, the clearest illustration of Burns crossing the Irish divide. And I trust we have now done enough to show Burns's impact on Ireland, north or south, Protestant or Catholic, was limitless. But the sense of duty to show discipular status to Burns remained at its height among the Ulster Protestants, ecumenical or otherwise. Ferguson was required in 1859 to speak on 'the character and genius' of Burns at the Mansion House, Dublin as suitable centenary fare after dinner. He rightly singled out as unavoidable but unpredictable the Burns cult amongst the Scots, the defining cult among the people. (And what other people defines its identity by a poet?):[58]

> A nation, eager and eminently successful in the pursuit of practical objects, proverbially prudent, habituated to rigorous self-control, selects for the object of its reverence – not a man like [Jeremy] Bentham [(1748–1832)] or like Benjamin Franklin [(1706–90)] – not a divine, a philosopher, or an economist, but a child of impulse and of passion, a proud, an improvident, an unworldly man.

For all of Ferguson's readiness to identify himself as Scots despite 'Six generations and more' of his people in Antrim, eating dinners in the deceased's honour and the Lord Mayor's residence was a highly Dublin homage. In Ferguson's native Ulster, and in Britain, a competition sought the more uncertain tribute of restringing the bardic instrument. The results were in some cases startling. Thomas Henry of Belfast took first prize in the Belfast Competition, presumably not for the satirical implications of his second verse, showing Nature's effect on Burns:[59]

> She bared the human bosom to his vision,
> Till its mysterious scrolls were all unfurled,
> And rolled his thoughts in melodies elysian
> That sound for ever o'er and o'er the world.

'Excelsior' of Belfast even compared his Genius to the Sleeping Beauty[60]

> Like the princess who, for ages,
> In a death-like slumber lay,
> Till a touch of life aroused her –
> As the fairly legends say –

Other poems, however indifferent, carried a common message with dignity: that Burns had been lionised by the rich but, living or dead, remained the poet of the poor. Robert Wilson of Enniskillen, co. Fermanagh ('Highly Commended by the Belfast Committee') sounded a class-war note inviting respect:[61]

> In *his* day how patronage ran
>   'Mong the high-born, wealthy, and wise;
> God made him a orator, poet, and MAN –
>   They made him a hound of the Excise!

That crackle of anger is real, and the Belfast Committee itself reflected some spirit of Burns in that commendation (though the poem's more successful rivals do not seem to have bettered it). But the sound of Burns, whatever about the spirit, is missing in the printed competitors. Perhaps there was an echo of Burns at his most Edinburgh social; there is none with the voice Jimmy Orr and some of the other 'Rhyming Weavers' echoed from Ulster at the turn of the eighteenth century.

Yet Ulster poetry has had the latest words on the sound of Burns, in a rich essay by Seamus Heaney (born 1939):[62]

> . . . Burns knew that his 'sound of sense' originated in the undersong of the spoken tongue, in a speech-world where people cracked rather than conversed and where they wrought at rhymes rather than composed poetry. So that part of Burns speaks to a part of me that would prefer to crack than to lecture, a part which has survived out of that older rhyme world which was still vestigially present when I was growing up in rural Ulster half a century ago.

Ferguson had reflected:[63]

> Nothing more pathetic in this peculiar combination of tenderness and wit has ever been written, than the Address to the Mouse. . . . The painful contemplations suggested . . . are indirect, associative, in perceiving which the consciousness of the congruity delights the sense of wit, at the same moment that the touching associations, so excited, stir the sense of the pathetic, . . . we experience a tender moral pity, and a keen intellectual

enjoyment together, the latter not amounting to humour . . . but to a development of the same faculty . . . This it is which prevents the Address to the Mouse from being mournful, and makes the reader rise with pleasant emotions in the midst of all his sighs from its perusal. . . . such a sweetener of whatever is sour is this ingredient of the wit.

Heaney, after extraordinary realisation of the impact of Burns's use of sound in ears 'from somewhere north of a line between Berwick and Bundoran', clearly agreed with Ferguson that[64]

this is not mere skilful verbal simulation of the behaviour of a frightened mouse but an involuntary outrush of fellow feeling.

But Heaney turns away from the poem with little sign of Ferguson's pleasant emotions on rising;

. . . the identification becomes more intense, the plough of the living voice gets set deeper and deeper in the psychic ground, dives more and more purposefully into the subsoil of the intuitions until finally it breaks open a nest inside the poet's own head and leaves him exposed to his own profoundest forebodings. . . . The sturdy, caring figure who overshadowed and oversaw the panic of the mouse in the beginning has been revealed to himself as someone less perfectly firm, less strong and robust than he or the reader would ever have suspected

I do not set up Heaney against Ferguson in any modern spirit, much less with a bright Whig conviction of human progress. (And as we have seen Macauley the classical Whig, essentially thought poetry worse with material human progress.[65]) Ferguson himself found 'To a Mountain Daisy' 'hardly so happy' in effect as those to the Mouse. What brings the difference is that Ferguson's nineteenth century demanded the use of aesthetic distance as trading counter in poetic appreciation. Ferguson was happy enough to parade the bicentenary of his own ancestors' arrival in Ulster, but his own rise in status – like most of his contemporaries' similar rises – inhibited the admission of Burns's ability to get inside his own irrational mind, instead of merely affecting sentiments whose public labels were comforting. Were it not for the wit of 'To a Mouse', thought Ferguson, it would be 'downright distressing' – but the distress is still for something at a distance.

Heaney as a product of the twentieth century knows that Burns gets inside us, now more than ever. He is Irish. He is us – all of us.[66]

Postscript

Burns ultimately received the supreme accolade from the island of saints and scholars, a poem by the Archbishop of Armagh and Primate of All Ireland, William Alexander (1824–1911), whose wife, Cecil Frances (1823–95) was the author of the carol 'Once in Royal David's City' and 'All Things Bright and Beautiful' almost the converse of Burns's 'A Man's a Man for A' That' ('The rich man in his castle,/ The poor man at his gate,/ God made them high or lowly,/ And order'd their estate', probably the most perverse interpretation ever of Jesus's parable of the rich man and Lazarus the beggar). Her husband's 'Robert Burns' ran:

All Scottish legends did his fancy fashion,
    All airs that richly flow,
Laughing with frolic, tremulous with passion,
    Broken with love-lorn woe;

Ballads whose beauties years have long been stealing
    And left few links of gold,
Under his quaint and subtle touch of healing
    Grew fairer, not less old.

Grey Cluden, and the vestals choral cadence,
    His spell awoke therewith;
Till boatmen hug their oars to hear the maidens
    Upon the banks of Nith.

His, too, the strains of battle nobly coming
    From Bruce, or Wallace wight,
Such as the Highlander shall oft be humming
    Before some famous fight.

Not only these – for him the hawthorn hoary
    Was with new wreaths enwrought,
The 'crimson-tipped daisy' wore fresh glory,
    Born of poetic thought.

From the 'wee cow'ring beastie' he could borrow
A moral strain sublime,
A noble tenderness of human sorrow,
In wondrous wealth of rhyme.

Oh, but the mountain breeze must have been pleasant
Upon the sunburnt brow
Of that poetic and triumphant peasant
Driving his laurell'd plough!

NOTES

[1] (London, [1906] 1926), 175. He is contrasting Burns with Shelley, an aristocrat, and wisely avoiding Byron.

[2] 1821. Galt (1779–1839) was recording the later eighteenth century.

[3] Burns to George Thomson, [September 1794], James A. Mackay, *The Complete Letters of Robert Burns* (1987), pp. 655–6.

[4] It is 'Eileen Aroon', originally a Gaelic song attributed to Cearball O Dalaigh, of a great family of Irish poets,

[5] *Scottish Review of Books* vol. 4, no. 3 2008.

[6] Eric Hobsbawm and Terence Ranger, (eds) *The Invention of Tradition* Trevor-Roper's contribution was 'The Invention of Highland Tradition'.

[7] Toland (1670–1722), *Pieces of Irish History*. The piece in question was a history of Druidism,

[8] Liam McIlvanney, *Burns the Radical* (2002), chapter 9, ' "On Irish Ground" Burns and the Ulster-Scots Radical Poets' is a discussion' of Burns's links with Ulster poets and I am deeply grateful for it. But the poem 'The Dagger' on which he relies (210–12) is authoritatively denied to be Burns's, as I am informed by Dr Gerard Carruthers, for which my thanks. It is an attack on Edmund Burke, I have ignored it.

[9] Robert Burns, *Poems and Songs* ([1969] 1971), p. 366–67, for the full text. It is assigned to 1789.

[10] H. G. Tempest *Gossiping Guide to Dundalk* (4th edn, 1983), p. 35. Maureen Wilson et al. *Dundalk: images and impressions* (1989), p. 44. Harold O'Sullivan, *Dundalk and North Louth* (1997), 28. Christine Casey and Alistair Rowan, *North Leinster* (1993), p. 262–4, Norman R. Paton, *Thou Lingering Star: the legend or Highland Mary* (1994), pp. 22–3,

[11] Kiely, 'The Whores on the Half-Doors or An Image of the Irish Writer', in Owen Dudley Edwards (ed.), *Conor Cruise O'Brian Introduces Ireland* (1969) pp. 148–9. A good example of Kiely's use of the Burns theme may be found in his short story 'A Great God's Angel Standing', in his *Ball of Malt and Madame Butterfly* (1973), pp. 7–28, which implies that a much earlier, more straightforward, and cruder story utilising Burns was published by Kiely in an extremely obscure journal in his youth.

[12] For Scott on Burns, and Byron on Burns, see Donald A. Low (ed.), *Robert Burns – The Critical Heritage* (1974), pp. 259, 260, 176–7, 257–8, 326.

[13] Ian Fleming, *Thunderball* (1962) has a somewhat embarrassing discussion on the attractions of the Player cigarette packet to the girl Domino. The notion, that it was based on George V may be true but is officially apocryphal, naturally.

[14] For Dermody see initially Robert Hogan (ed.) *Dictionary of Irish Literature* (revised & expanded edn 1996), II. pp. 343–6. Thomas Burke, author of some effective horror stories, wrote a novel of some authenticity. *Vagabond Minstrel, The adventures of Thomas Dermody* (1936).

[15] Mary Helen Thuente, *The Harp Re-strung: the United Irishmen and the Rise of Irish literary nationalism* (1994) notices Belfast editions also in 1789, 1790 and 1793 but misses Dublin 1787 (British Library Cataloguer; while she notes 'Tam o' Shanter' in *Anthologia Hibernica* (July 1793), Ibid. pp. 62, 76, 104, 136–7, 143.

[16] Dermody. *Poems* (1792), pp. 53–4, This and other verse here perfectly authentic. His very earliest work may include some input from his father.

[17] P. Vergilius Maro, Eclogues VII, pp. 4–5.

[18] Ibid.

[19] H[eron] 'A Memoir of the Life of the Late Robert Burns', *Monthly Magazine* (June 1797); reprinted Low (ed.), *Burns – Critical Heritage*, p. 123. James Mackay, *Robert Burns – a Biography* (1992) pp. 652–3.

[20] Canto I, p. 42, lines 7–8. At this point in the epic the narrator is supposedly a starchy (and repressed?) Spanish bachelor, but Byron forgot about him and fairly quickly took over the role as himself.

[21] The obvious antecedent is Dante's use of Virgil in his *Inferno* and *Purgatorio*, and there is a visible analogy for the place of Dermody's imaginary Burns in his life.

[22] Chandler, 'The Simple Art of Murder', *Atlantic Monthly* (December 1944), reprinted Howard Haycraft (ed.), *The Art of the Mystery Story* (1946), p. 234; 'Hammett took murder out of the Venetian dropped it into the alley'. Admittedly a Venetian vase isn't too far from a Maltese falcon, and Burns took himself into quite a few drawing-rooms.

[23] O'Connor [i.e. Michael o'Donovan], *Leinster Munster and Connaught*, [n.d.], pp. 225–6. O'Connor had translated Merriman's epic into English, in which language it was banned as was every other translation. The original Irish was safe being in a language in which officialdom apparently believed obscenity was impossible,' Liam McIlvanney, 'Across the narrow sea; the language, literature and politics of Ulster Scots', Liam McIlvanney and Ray Ryan,eds., *Ireland and Scotland; culture and society; 1700–2000* ([2005]), p. 215. Douglas Hyde, *A Literary History of Ireland* (1899, 1967), pp. 533–4; 'Of this old Gaelic prosody there appears to be a distinct reminiscence in Burns.' An example is given 'which the poet evidently pronounced exactly as an old Irish bard would have done'.

[24] Orr. 'Elegy', *Poems On Various Subjects* (1804), 9–12.

[25] *Burns the Radical*, pp. 238–40.

[26] Quoted Hogan (ed.), *Dictionary of Irish Literature*, I, p. 344.

[27] Elizabeth Eger, Cliona O Gallchoir and Marilyn Butler (eds) *The Novels and Selected Works of Maria Edgeworth* (2003), vol. 12, p. 261n.

[28] Susan Manly (ed.), Ibid., vol. 11, p. 346 (Edgeworth, *Practical Education*).

[29] Elizabeth Eger and Cliona O Gallchoir (eds), ibid., vol. 10, xv–xvii, p. 204. Forester, the relevant moral tale depicts the eponymous hero finding that 'The gardener's son, though his name was Colin, had no Arcadian simplicity nothing which could please the classic taste of Forester, or which could recall to his mind the Eclogues of Virgil . . . or the Ayreshire ploughman.' The allusion is to the self-styled, Colin Clout, a shepherd pseudonimity employed by Edmund Spenser (1552?-99) , for his *Colin Clouts Come Home Againe* (1595). The implication that Forester wanted to see Colin as an Eclogue shepherd is a little startling, but surely Maria Edgeworth would not have intended ribaldry, surely not.

[30] Susan Manly and Cliona O Gallchoir (eds), ibid., vol. 9, p. 290.

[31] Moore to Sir John Stevensons February 1807, Wilfred S. Dowden (ed.), *The Letters of Thomas Moore* (1964), I, 1793–1818 (1964), U6–17. 'James Macpherson's *Ossian*, allegedly based on a Gaelic text, was disputed by many English as a hoax, by many Irish as a plagiarism, since the Irish held that the subject of the poem Fingal, was really Fionn Mac Cumhaill, and not Scots as the poem indicated, but Irish. Had Ossian really existed (and maybe he did, in some form) he would not have known the difference between Scots and Irish).

[32] *Dublin University Magazine* (January 1841), reprinted Gordon Brand (ed.), *William Carleton – the Authentic Voice* (2006), p. 19.

[33] Charles Gavan Duffy (ed.), *The Ballad, Poetry of Ireland* ([1845] 1866), p. xxxii

[34] Ibid., p. xxxiii.

[35] Thomas Davis [presumably (ed.), Charles Gavan Duffy], *Literary and Historical Essays 1846* (1998), pp. 230–1. T. W. Rolleston ed., *Thomas Davis: Selections from his Prose and Poetry* (1915), p. 216. No satisfactory texts of Davis's writings exist, and the originals in the *Nation* might well suffer from at least some of the misprints disfiguring later book publication, Davis himself having died before he could assemble versions acceptable to him. The first source cited here puts Brighid in the accusative case, surely correctly, but the second offers 'attractions' where the first, less sensibly has 'attentions'. Thuente, *Harp Re-strung* p. 222n Davis's verse 'in imitation of Burns'.

[36] *Thomas Davis Essays and Poems*, foreword by Eamon de Valera (1945), p. 96.

[37] Yeats to the Editor, *Nation*, 3 January 1890, John Kelly et al. (eds), *Collected Letters of W.B. Yeats* (1986), I, p. 206. The *Nation*'s anonymous reviewer of Yeats edn, *Stories from Carleton* had praised Yeats's introduction before bitter sectarian denunciation of Carleton, ending;

> We thought we had passed the day when his envenomed caricature
> would be accepted as portraiture. But it seems not. But till
> that day passes the slanderous Carleton should be kept by Irish
> critics in the literary pillory.

[38] Ibid., p. 205n

[39] Yeats to the Editor, [Dublin] *Daily Express*. 8 November 1898, Ibid., II, pp. 296–7 and see ibid., p. 297n for correction pointing out Burns had actually written;

> The wan moon behind the white wave

[40] Yeats to the Editor, *Leader*, 26 August 1900, Ibid., II, p. 564.

[41] Yeats to Augusta Lady Gregory, 23 January 1901, Ibid., p. 19.

[42] W. Yeats to John Quinn, 28 June 1903, III, p. 389.

[43] Rupert Hart-Davis ed., *The Letters of Oscar Wilde* (1962) p. 416n.

[44] Shaw, Epistle Dedicatory to Arthur Bingham Walkley [i.e. Preface to *Man and Superman* (1903)], Dan H. Laurence (ed.), *The Bodley Head Bernard Shaw Collected Plays and their Prefaces* (1971), II, p. 513.

[45] Synge, preface [unpaginated], *Poems and Translations* ([1909] 1912). Synge, draft, Notebook 47, 1908. *Collected Works II Prose* Alan Price (ed.) ([1966] 1982), p. 347.

[46] Yeats, 'To Ireland in the Coming Times', *The Countess Kathleen and Various Legends* (1892), reprinted Yeats, *Collected Works*, Augustine Martin (ed.) (1990), p. 46.

[47] Jacques Chuto et al., Collected *Works of James Clarence Mangan: Poems* [1996], IV, p. 223.

[48] *Dublin University Magazine* (January 1845), p. 66.

[49] Ibid.

[50] Ibid., p. 66–67 70.

[51] Ibid., p. 72–73.

[52] Ibid., p. 73

[53] Ibid., (March 1845), p. 290.

[54] *Edinburgh Review* (January 1828). Macaulay did not reprint the essay in his lifetime but his friend Thomas Flower Ellis did so after his death, among his 'Miscellaneous Writings' under the title 'Dryden'.

[55] *Dublin University Magazine* (March 1845), p. 290.

[56] Ibid., p. 302.

[57] 'Laughing witches in red cutty sarks ride through the air on broomsticks' (Joyce, *Ulysses* ([1922] 1969), p. 695. 'The poem with its 'Walpurgis Night' elements – a witches' dance, abused altar, etc. – has much in common with this episode of Ulysses' (Weldon Thornton, *Allusions in Ulysses*. ([1961] 1968), p. 425.

[58] Ferguson, speech, in Mary Catherine Lady Ferguson, *Sir Samuel Ferguson in the Ireland of his Day* (1896), II.

[59] George Anderson and John-Finlay (eds), *The Burns Centenary Poems a Collection of Fifty of the Best out of the many Hundreds written on Occasion of the Centenary Celebration including the Six Recommended for Publication by the Judges at the Crystal Palace Competition, Many of the Highly Commended, and Several Prize Poems* (1859), p. 44.

[60] Ibid., p. 250.

[61] Ibid., p. 114. Wilson (1820?-1875) also wrote as Barney Maglone, served under Gavan Duffy in the *Nation* and died of alcohol-related causes while attending the O'Connell centenary. His pseudonyms also included 'Young Ireland' and 'Jonathan Allman' (David James O'Donoghue, *The Poets of Ireland* (1892–3), p. 85.

[62] Heaney, 'Burns's Art Speech' in Robert Crawford, *Robert Burns and Cultural Authority* (1997), p. 216. Any quotation from this must be inadequate: it is in its entirety a masterpiece in art and science.

[63] *Dublin University Magazine* (March 1845), p. 300–1.

[64] Heaney, 'Burns's Art Speech', p. 219.

[65] Ibid., p. 219–20. On Macaulay I am here (though not always elsewhere following G. K. Chesterton, *The Victorian Age in Literature* (1913), p. 32. For Chesterton's

views of Burns, see his Foreword to A. A. Thomson, *The Burns We love* (19   ), p. 5–
10. Chesterton was not Irish (although he was one Englishman who would have
been complimented to have been mistaken for one) but most Irish Catholics
between the world wars would have agreed with him, often regardless of their
anti-clericalism or ex-Catholicism.

[66] My thanks as always are due to the National Library of Scotland, for its eternal
providence, and for the endless kindness and wisdom of its staff. I must also
thank the Edinburgh Central Library in George IV Bridge, and Edinburgh
University Library. I am most grateful to Professor Declan Kiberd of the
Department of English Literature, University College Dublin, for aiding me with
problems of Burns's comparability to contemporary authors in the Irish Gaelic
language. I thank innumerable Burns Supper organisers and consumers. And I
thank my beloved friend Neil MacCormick who has inspired and encouraged me
to the end.

NOTES ON THE CONTRIBUTORS

࿔

Johnny Rodger has published several works of fiction, including The Auricle, g haun(s) Q, and redundant (all pub. Dualchas): he writes criticism for numerous magazines, journals and newspapers; and has also authored several full length critical works including Contemporary Glasgow (pub. Rutland Press), Edinburgh: A guide to Recent Architecture (Ellipsis/Batsford) and the monograph Gillespie, Kidd & Coia 1956–87 (RIAS). He is editor of The Drouth.

Gerard Carruthers is Reader and Head of Department in Scottish Literature at the University of Glasgow, and also Director of the Centre for Robert Burns Studies. He is General Editor of the new Oxford University Press edition of the collected works of Robert Burns, and his publications include Robert Burns (2006), as editor, The Devil to Stage: Five Plays by James Bridie (2007), Burns: Poems (2007) and as co-editor, English Romanticism and the Celtic World (2003). he has written many essays on Robert Burns and on other Scottish literary topics

Tim Burke is Research Fellow in Labouring-Class Poetry at Nottingham Trent University. He is a member of the editorial team that produced Eighteenth-Century English Labouring-Class Poets for Pickering and Chatto, and the author of numerous articles on Romantic-period culture and the relationship between work and writing.

Sheila Szatkowsksi is a writer and historian based in Edinburgh. Her particular research interests are eighteenth and nineteenth century Scotland and John Kay (1742–1826), the Edinburgh-based barber, miniaturist and social commentator. She is a Fellow of the Society of Antiquaries of Scotland

Alistair Braidwood is a PhD Research student in the Department of Scottish Literature at Glasgow University . His main areas of research are in Contemporary Scottish Fiction, Philosophy of Literature and Scottish Film. He has recently been working on a Filmography of Robert Burns which forms the basis of his article.

Ken Simpson was Founding Director of the Centre for Scottish Cultural Studies at the University of Strathclyde and organiser of the annual Burns International Conference. He has twice been Neag Distinguished Visiting Professor of British Literature at the University of Connecticut and W. Ormiston Roy Fellow in Scottish Poetry at the University of S. Carolina. Currently he is Honorary Professor in Burns Studies in the Centre for Robert Burns Studies, Glasgow University. His publications include, The Protean Scot (1988), Burns Now (1994), Love and Liberty: Robert Burns – A Bicentenary Celebration (1997), and Robert Burns (2005).

Ralph McLean is a PhD student at the University of Glasgow in the departments of History and Scottish Literature, where he is researching the development of literary criticism in the Scottish Enlightenment. He has previously published on the relationship between Burns and the enlightenment critic Hugh Blair.

Murray Pittock is Bradley Professor of English Literature at the University of Glasgow, and previously held chairs at the universities of Manchester and Strathclyde. His most recent books include Scottish and Irish Romanticism (2008) and The Road to Independence? Scotland Since the Sixties (2008). In 2002, he gave the British Academy's Chatterton prize lecture on Robert Burns and British Poetry, and he is currently the director of the AHRC-supported Global Burns Network'

Pauline Anne Gray is currently completing her PhD at the Department of Scottish Literature, University of Glasgow. She is very interested in Robert Burns's controversial literature, and so her research pays particular attention to Burns's songs included in The Merry Muses of Caledonia. Pauline has worked on a number of academic projects, including the James Currie project based at the University of Glasgow, and is Research Assistant to the Global Burns Network.

Nigel Leask is Regius Professor of English Language and Literature at the University of Glasgow. He has taught at many other universities, including Cambridge, Bologna and UNAM (Mexico City). He has published widely on Romantic period literature and culture, and has a special interest in travel writing, empire, and 18th century Scotland. He is currently completing a study of Robert Burns entitled 'Scottish Pastoral'.

Mitchell Miller is a writer, editor and filmmaker currently completing a book and documentary film on Scottish Show Travellers. Miller is a programmer for the Glasgow Film Theatre and regular contributor to Art Review, Varoom, Scottish Left Review, The Map and the British Film Institute's Screenonline. He teaches at Glasgow University and Edinburgh College of Art, and is editor of The Drouth

Graham Fagen is an artist based in Glasgow. He has exhibited at the Venice Biennale, the Busan Biennale and the Art and Industry Biennial, New Zealand. In the UK he has exhibited at Tate Britain and the V&A Museum and was the Imperial War Museum's artist commissioned to Kosovo during the conflict. He is represented in Scotland by Doggerfisher Gallery, Edinburgh. www.doggerfisher.com

Thomas Keith is an editor as well as the art director at New Directions Publishing in New York. He has written for Studies in Scottish Literature, Burns in America, and Burns Chronicle, and was the 2004 Roy Fellow of Scottish Studies at the University of South Carolina. Keith has edited several Tennessee Williams plays, most recently A House Not Meant to Stand, for which he also wrote the introduction.

Rhona Brown is a lecturer in the department of Scottish Literature at the University of Glasgow. She specialises in eighteenth-century Scottish literature, focusing on the works of Robert Fergusson and Robert Burns. She is currently writing a monograph on Fergusson's works and has published articles on James Currie, James Hogg, Thomas Chatterton, Laurence Sterne, James Tytler and Robert Burns.

Kirsteen McCue is lecturer in Scottish Literature and Associate Director of the Centre for Robert Burns Studies at the University of Glasgow. She is currently editing two volumes of James Hogg's songs for the Stirling/South Carolina Collected Works of James Hogg and will be editing Robert Burns's songs for George Thomson for the forthcoming new Oxford edition of Burns.

Carol Baraniuk was for three years a Project Officer with the Ulster-Scots Curriculum Development Unit at Stranmillis University College, Belfast. She has researched and published widely on Ulster poetry in the Scottish tradition, and is currently preparing to defend her thesis at the University of Glasgow.

Norrie Paton was born at Johnstone in the year 1937. He grew up and was educated in the shipbuilding town of Port-Glasgow, where, upon leaving school in 1952, he was employed in a local shipyard, eventually serving a five year apprenticeship as a draughtsman. His interest in Burns emerged around the time of the bicentenary of the poet's birth and has remained with him throughout his life. He is particularly fascinated by the controversy over the dubious pieces attributed to Burns, especially the revolutionary song, The Tree of Liberty

Jennifer Orr is a graduate of the University of Oxford. She is working on her doctoral thesis at the Department of Scottish Literature, University of Glasgow. Her research interests lie in the literature and history of the 'long' Eighteenth Century, particularly Irish radical poetry and the Scottish vernacular tradition.

Owen Dudley Edwards is Hon. Fellow of the School of History, Classics and Archaeology, University of Edinburgh, having taught history at Edinburgh since 1968. He and his wife Bonnie came to Scotland in 1966 when he became Assistant Lecturer in History, University of Aberdeen. He was born in Dublin in 1938 and he has written extensively about the Irish at home, abroad and in literature, including studies of Burke, Hare, and Eamon de Valera.

INDEX

❧